China Mishkid

My Life as a Missionary Kid
in China (1938–1955)

A. Donald MacLeod

To Diane
Don MacLeod

 FriesenPress

Suite 300 - 990 Fort St
Victoria, BC, V8V 3K2
Canada

www.friesenpress.com

Copyright © 2018 by A. Donald MacLeod
First Edition — 2018

All rights reserved.

ISBN
978-1-5255-3215-3 (Hardcover)
978-1-5255-3216-0 (Paperback)
978-1-5255-3217-7 (eBook)

1. BIOGRAPHY & AUTOBIOGRAPHY, PERSONAL MEMOIRS

Distributed to the trade by The Ingram Book Company

Cover Image

Exiled from China, the land of his birth,
My father is met by Mother and me, age 11,
At Kowloon Wharf, Kowloon, Hong Kong
27 September 1949

这是毛大龙教授的自述。毛教授的父亲曾於1933至1949间在位於山东藤县的华北神学院任教。他父亲毛克礼为中国浙江内地会宣教士的儿子。日战爆发前的二十年间，华北神学院为中国基督教研究院中最大的神学院，忠於圣经教导及福音派教义。因此多年後仍广泛地影嚮著中国教会的发展。毛大龙在加拿大多伦多一神学院担任教会历史研究教授，著作甚丰。毛教授在此写出了作为宣教士子女在战乱并革命中成长所面对的挑战，甚至在自己家庭和当时所属的自由基督教差会中经历的许多苦难和误解。这是一个讲述神如何在中国栽植教会的故事，在分离和家庭迁移下见證神信实的记录。详情可参阅《历史光影中的华北神学院》（香港：中国国际文化出版社, 2015年第三版）

This is the account by Professor A. Donald MacLeod (毛大龍), son of one of the teachers at North China Theological Seminary in Tengzhou (then Tenghsien, Shandong. His father, Alexander N. MacLeod (毛克禮), son of China Inland Missionaries in Zhejiang, taught there from 1933 to 1949. In the two decades before the Japanese war the seminary was the largest post-graduate Protestant theological institution in China. It was committed to biblical integrity and evangelical doctrine. As such it had a wide influence on the Chinese church in the years that followed. A. Donald MacLeod (毛大龍) is a theological college research professor of church history in Toronto, Canada. He has written many books and papers. He writes from the perspective of a missionary child who faced challenges growing up during war and revolution. He saw much suffering and misunderstanding even within his own family and the liberal Protestant mission board with which they were associated. It is a story of how God planted the church in China, a testimony to the faithfulness of God through separation and family dislocation. For further information consult 历史光影中的华北神学院》（香港：中国国际文化出版, the third edition of which was published in 2015.

TABLE OF CONTENTS

ABBREVIATIONS

CCC   Church of Christ in China

CIM   China Inland Mission (before 1950)

IBPFM   Independent Board for Presbyterian
Foreign Missions

KG-5   King George V School, Kowloon, Hong Kong

MMI   Mateer Memorial Institute, Tenghsien (now
Tengzhou), Shandong

NCTS   North China Theological Seminary

OMF   Overseas Missionary Fellowship (after 1950)

PCC   Presbyterian Church in Canada

PCT   Presbyterian Church in Taiwan (Formosa)

PC (US)   "Southern" Presbyterian Church

PC (USA)   "Northern" Presbyterian Church

PMH   Presbyterian Mission Home, 11A Carnarvon Road,
Kowloon, Hong Kong

PTS   Princeton Theological Seminary

SAS   Shanghai American School

SBS   Stony Brook School (for Boys until 1974)

UPCNA   United Presbyterian Church in North America (1858-1958)

WTS   Westminster Theological Seminary, Philadelphia

ACKNOWLEDGEMENTS

In writing this book I am greatly indebted to many:

Firstly to my parents, who kept voluminous records and letters of their China years. My father's daily diary entries date only from 1946 as earlier ones, I assume were lost during the war. Kept meticulously until his death in 1994 they provide a daily record of his activities and letters posted. Mother's weekly letters to her sister Marjorie Campbell were carefully filed and returned to her before her death. I have made generous use of this correspondence, noted by quotation marks rather than actual cumbersome citations. All correspondence is now in the special collections of the Princeton Theological Seminary.

As an only child, my parents preserved an astonishing amount of material from my childhood. Several of my contemporaries have come to my rescue as well; Stuart Braga of Sydney Australia and Cousins Frances Braga, Cool, California and her younger brother Joey (Joseph Peter) Braga also of Sydney. King George V School (KG-5) in Kowloon now has an Archivist, Yasmeen Ashraf, with whom I have corresponded. Lisa Jacobson, David Koch, Charlene Peacock, and Nancy Taylor staff at the Presbyterian Historical Society, Philadelphia, have always responded promptly to my requests for information. My friend of a lifetime, Rev. Dr. Carl Scovel of Jamaica Plain, MA, has been a constant encourager. Cousins Carleton Campbell, Pittsburgh; Robert Miles, Harrisonburg,

VA; and James Duncan Ingles, Ardmore, PA, helped in refreshing family memories. I was particularly grateful for Chinese friends, Jihe Song now of Edinburgh, Scotland and 曰北 敬上 of Tengzhou, Shandong. And the B62 Stamp Club of Toronto are enthusiastic supporters. I have tended to retain most of the Wade Giles transliterations and pre-Revolutionary place names I knew growing up to be authentic.

In recreating my Swiss summer of 1953, I thank Bernard and Monique Dunant, Chêne Bourgand and Jean-Jacques and Georgette Dunant, Chêne Bougeries, Switzerland as well as Suzanne Brown-Dunant and Peter Brown, Saint-Jérôme, Québec and Rev. George A. Malcolm, Pickering, Ontario, formerly of Taiwan, and a past General Secretary of the Canadian Presbyterian Board of World Mission. My cousin Christina MacDonald of Habost, Lochs, Isle of Lewis, helped with the Scottish details. Above all, I want to express gratitude to my wife Judy along with sons Rev. Alex and tech guru Kenneth. My daughter-in-law Judith's late father was David Michell, a child internee at Weihsien whose *Boys War* is a classic description of wartime China and his friendship with Eric Liddell.

Writing this book has put me in touch with many other China Mishkids with whom I had lost contact. It is my hope that it will encourage them to tell their stories and perhaps, in the process, give thanks to Almighty God (as it has for me) for His protection and love.

A. Donald MacLeod
7 October, 2017, Fiftieth Anniversary of Our Marriage

To the memory of China Mishkid

Catherine Margaret MacLeod Ruby,
My "Aunt Cathie" (1905-1957)
And her husband Paul Hart Ruby,
my "Uncle Paul" (1901-1963)

After great pain a formal feeling comes -
The nerves sit ceremonious like tombs;
The stiff Heart questions – was it He that bore?
And yesterday – or centuries before?

Emily Dickinson

A MOTHER LOOKS BACK

Dear son, and did I fail you then
A "Mother tense", whose ministration
Perhaps superfluous and when
With deep and tender aspiration,
With price and hope a flood,
I blew upon an opening bud
Of visions too alert to bide
The time, wanting but to guide.
Was this a fault? Or did the prayer
For wisdom, some times bring a rare
And helpful insight, not my own,
To watch and see the flower full-blown?
I need not know; for God's all wise
And over-ruling love and power
Will take both fault and insight, prize
The purpose deep; and bring the flower
To fullest beauty; using all
For blessing: letting nothing fall.

Found in my mother's papers on her death in 1994

INTRODUCTION

"*Ask the children, Look at what they grew up to be. We can only speak of the things we carried with us and the things we took away.*"[1]

The fictional daughters of Baptist missionary to the Congo Rev. Nathan Price in *The Poisonwood Bible* could speak for many of us mish-kids. Too often we are the forgotten so-called by-products, or possibly collateral damage, of the great global expansion of western Protestant Christianity in the nineteenth and twentieth centuries. Too often we were ignored or overlooked amid thrilling stories of missionary heroism and sacrifice. Dismissed with many names such as "MK s" (a derivative of "PKs", or "preacher's kid") and more recently (and insightfully) "TCK's" or "third-culture-kids", we were kept in the background, sent away to boarding school, left to grow up on our own.

With the coming of a new millennium and as suspicion of religious fanaticism grew, the lustre of foreign missionary service dulled in the popular mind. So inevitably this reflected on their children. Once heroic recipients of the prayers and charity of homeland piety and congregational concern, increasingly we became known for rebellion, anger, and

---

1   Kingsolver, Barbara. *The Poisonwood Bible*. New York: Harper Flamingo, 1998, 10.

rejection of everything that our parents stood for, and the faith that had sent them overseas.

So I tell my own story: not only as a China mishkid but also as the son of one. I grew up in the oldest civilization in the world, then convulsed in turmoil and war, and today a rising superpower and an economic powerhouse. I was privileged to be a spectator of a great people whose life and culture became part of me. Third-culture-kid that I was, I developed a deep love for the adopted country my parents had sought to serve and that so enriched my life.

Indeed, "ask the children. I can only speak of the things I carried with me and what I took away."

ENING GAZETTE, TUESDAY, AUGUST 16

RETURNING TO CHINA   1948

Rev. Dr. Alexander N. MacLeod, his wife, the former Dorothy Miles of Holden, and their son, Alistair Donald MacLeod, three months, who next month will return to China for foreign mission work.

Mission Worker Hopes China Will Win War

Rev. Dr. A. N. MacLeod and Family to Leave Holden for Orient Next Month

Most persons are leaving China as fast as means of transportation will afford, but in Holden Rev. Dr. Alexander N. MacLeod, his wife, the former Dorothy Miles, and their three-months-old son, Alistair Donald MacLeod, are preparing to return after an absence of

prehension for their safety, the North China Theological Seminary, anghsien, Shantung, China. He says he and his family were well out of the trouble area when fighting started, and the conflict has gone on from the vicinity of his post. In a few months he will be behind the Japanese lines, taking up the burden of aiding wounded and refugees. Latest dispatches from his friends say that five thousand refugees are living on the mission school campus.

Wants China to Win

An ordained Presbyterian minister, Rev. Dr. MacLeod will speak Sunday at Second Advent Christian Church. He said he will disclose some of the reports he has had from friends which confirm newspaper accounts of the bestiality of the Japanese soldiery. He expressed the hope that the present campaign in China would mark the end of the Japanese military party, which he said may have bitten off more than it can chew. He said he was pro-Chinese as far as the war was concerned because of the debasement of the Chinese population by the Japanese invaders.

Rev. Dr. MacLeod is a graduate of Wheaton College in Illinois, where he met his wife. He later studied at Princeton, where he received his master's degree and took up theology. Preparation for his doctorate was at Harvard, the University of Berlin and University of Edinburgh where the degree was conferred last June. During his academic career, Rev. Dr. MacLeod was an instructor at Stony Brook School for Boys, Long Island, and an assistant professor of history at Wheaton. He has completed one year term at the North China ogical Seminary.

'auds U. S. Standards

the University ange vi

CHAPTER 1:
China Bound, 1938

"Most people are leaving China as fast as means of transportation will afford, but in Holden [Massachusetts] Rev. Dr. Alexander N. MacLeod, his wife, the former Dorothy Miles, and their three-months-old son, Alistair Donald MacLeod, are preparing to return after an absence of two years and moreover remain for seven."

The news item in the 21 August 1938 Worcester Massachusetts *Evening Gazette* was accompanied with a picture of my father and my mother clutching me as I gaze out seemingly unfazed by all the publicity. It continued "Rev Dr MacLeod feels no apprehension for their safety," announcing that our departure from San Francisco was scheduled for 23 September. He should have. The Sino-Japanese War had entered its second year, the Japanese had occupied all of Shandong and the battle of Xuzhou, immediately south of our town, had been decisively won by them. Their brutality, as evidenced at the beginning of the year in the so-called Rape of Nanjing, made them an object of anxiety and dread. Into this carnage my father was now determined to take his wife and infant son.

What was worse, the headline clearly identified my father with the Chinese side in the conflict then raging in China. The bold headline said it all: "Mission Worker Hopes China Will Win War." The Japanese Embassy in Washington, as we now know, employed a newspaper clipping service that provided for them details of any comments made about Japan in the American press. Dad would later attribute the four and half years he spent as a Japanese prisoner-of-war (when others were repatriated) to this indiscretion, compounded by a further quote about "the bestiality of the Japanese soldiery," illustrating two family traits: a propensity for indiscreet outspokenness and a child-like (if endearing) naiveté.

At the time, however, it was heady stuff for a local girl. Worcester, where my mother was born, had not smiled on her father. The son of a respected contractor who had built schools, libraries, and government buildings in the area, he had failed in the family business soon after inheriting the company. He tried to get rich quick, speculating in the mid-1920s in Florida real estate, laying out a subdivision in North Miami that went bankrupt. The collapse of the family fortune and the rather tepid religious interest of my grandfather and her brothers shattered any sense of religious cohesion in her family and was a continuing and ongoing sorrow for my mother as the oldest sibling and the older identical twin.

Mother's mother, Rhobe Blanchard, was barely in her twenties when the twins were born. She was a pretty stenographer who married the boss' twenty-five year old only son. Twins represented twice as much work and she left much of their upkeep and their spiritual nurture, to her mother-in-law. Ella Boyden Miles was a devout Christian ("first day") Adventist and hymn-writer. Though she died at 59 when they were only thirteen, Ella left a lifelong impression on Dorothy, my mother, and her twin, Marjorie, that would impact them for all of their ninety-plus years. Her facility and fascination with language was passed on to the next generation. Her many hymns, which she started writing at 15, were not. We no longer sing "Now Is the Day," "He Cares For Me," "The Way," "The Invitation," "What Stands Between?," "A Present Help," or "Take It All To Jesus." Few today would feel comfortable with either the language or the sentimentality but Ella Miles was my mother's early example of an intense and introspective piety and she was profoundly impacted.

In its several references to the "Rev. Dr. Alexander N. MacLeod" (at the insistence of a family member, I assume) the article was drawing attention to his recently acquired status as the holder of a Ph. D. from the University of Edinburgh. Nobody in my mother's non-academic and basically anti-intellectual family knew what to make of my father. My grandmother called him disparagingly in my presence as a child a "bookworm" and there was even less understanding of his Reformed theology. This inverse snobbery also reflected social aspirations for their daughter. At Wheaton College my mother administered a generous personal family bank account for herself and Sisters Marjorie and Priscilla. Ironically, just at the time of the bankruptcy Marjorie married a Brooklyn doctor, son of a successful physician. Marjorie had attached herself to money and for the rest of the family, and particularly Mother as her friendly rival, she had married "up" while the rest of her siblings had married "down" or at best even.

My father, an impoverished "Missionary Kid" (MK) student, was the college janitor and summers worked on his mother's family farm in Indiana. My mother had her share of suitors: she was engaged at one time to Bruce Hunt, a Korea MK who later made a name for himself in Orthodox Presbyterian circles. It took my father seven years to persuade her to marry him after many rebuffs and only after she considered going to China on her own but on reflection thought it best to be accompanied by a partner. When she was well into her 80's a former suitor called her in her Toronto retirement home from Texas. They conversed for half an hour and he died several hours later. My mother refused ever to divulge what they said.

They were married on 26 June 1929 in the garden of my mother's home in Holden (now a Worcester suburb). After a summer my father spent supplying the pulpit of First Presbyterian Church, Gettysburg, my parents set sail for Scotland to pursue studies at the University of Edinburgh on a Gelston-Winthrop Fellowship from Princeton Seminary. It was a cultural challenge for my mother, coming from a small New

England town. She committed the usual expatriate American *faux-pas* but my father's Scottish family (whom he was really meeting for the first time) was embracing and accepting in spite of many gaffes. The cultural challenges escalated when they arrived in China. After a year of intense language study in Peiping (as Beijing was known then) and a short posting in Ichow, Shandong, they moved in 1932 to the North China Theological Seminary in Tenghsien. The school, known as the Princeton Seminary of China, the largest in China, had already approached him before leaving the States.

It was my mother's music that crossed cultural bounds. A skilled pianist, as well as being competent on the organ, my mother connected through her playing. Her only disappointment was her inability to bring a child to term. In January of 1932, while in Ichow, she had a near-death experience as my father rushed to get the station doctor. "When I got back," my father wrote Marjorie on her behalf, "it was all over, she had had a miscarriage. She has been wonderful about it all, and we have no complaints against our Heavenly Father for not answering our prayers as we wished."

Two years later, pregnant again, she travelled to Tsinan (now Jinan), the capital of Shandong, for its good medical care and boarded with veterans Charles Ernest and Clara Scott. Their daughter Betty had recently married John Stam. They were CIM missionaries in Anhwei province. Like my mother, she too was pregnant and Betty gave birth to Helen Priscilla at the time my mother also should have had her child. It was all very painful. After John and Betty's martyrdom by the 19th Division of the 10th Red Army Group on 8 December 1934 the infant was found unharmed. Publicised as a "miracle baby," she was placed in the care of her maternal grandparents who paraded her in many churches in the States until finally Betty's sister (married to a Presbyterian USA China missionary) rescued her and gave her own last name as protection. In 1949 Helen Priscilla Mahy and I were evacuated together and I got to know her later in Hong Kong, though she was four years older. The whole Christian world, the China missionary community, and particularly nearby Tenghsien station where my parents worked, were deeply affected. Meanwhile my mother waited every month for good news but none came. Why should that baby be deprived of her parents while I am deprived of a baby? It seemed so unfair.

Further along in her pregnancy than the previous time, in spite of some excellent medical care (a doctor came down especially from Peiping), my mother miscarried again. "I had the experience of blackness" she wrote with unusual candour. "I didn't have it the other time. I think the Lord allowed it this time because he wanted to show me that His arms are <u>always</u> underneath and He will <u>never</u> fail to lift us up. I reached the end of myself as I never have before, and abandoned myself to crying. At the end I felt myself coming into a peace, without deserving it, or having any known reason for it. Next morning I woke with such a wonderful song in my heart and said, 'Somebody has been praying for me.'"

The two miscarriages had an enormous impact on our family. I was brought up to regard them as my dead siblings. They were not just unborn fetuses, My mother regarded them as real people. Just before she died at 92 she said she was looking forward to meeting them in heaven. Some Christians find that a difficult inference from their position on abortion. I was chairing an InterVarsity Staff Conference when word came that the wife of one of our workers had had a miscarriage. I called out for prayer stating that the couple had "lost a baby". The guest speaker, a well-known Evangelical leader, roundly criticised my statement, calling it an exaggeration. While not going quite as far as Roman Catholic theology would take us, my mother's similar conviction had a profound influence on the way she raised me. Ensoulment - the moment the fetus becomes a living being with a soul - was not an academic or theological question. Her conviction that ensoulment takes place at an early point in the first trimester of pregnancy powerfully affected the way she raised the child of her, this time successful, third pregnancy. I was told that I had two sisters now in heaven. It explained her intensity as a mother. She felt that finally my birth, after nine years of marriage, vindicated her maternal qualifications, providing a third and final opportunity at motherhood. It helped explain the level of commitment as she brought me up.

Third time lucky. While my father was completing his doctoral thesis at Edinburgh in 1937 on a delayed furlough my mother discovered she was pregnant again. They were boarding with Tom and Annie Torrance. My grandfather had set out to China in 1897 with Mr. Torrance as fellow CIM'ers from Scotland. Later associated with the Bible Society in Chengdu, the Torrances had six distinguished (and brilliant) children all of whom were either Church of Scotland clergy or had married one. By the end of September, under the excellent care of Dr. Graham Brown, to whom I owe my life, and constant liver injections, the pregnancy was progressing well. "I am not worrying at all," she wrote her sister in mid-September, "and not counting too much on it. I hope somebody must be praying for me somewhere." Six weeks later, bedfast all day, she wrote: "a few extra days in bed, even when one is left pretty well alone for twenty-four hours is a small price to pay for so large an expectation of special happiness." On 10 December they sailed to New York, and took the train directly to Philadelphia where they spent the winter as my father edited his thesis and my mother typed the manuscript. Finances were a major concern as the Mission Board had stopped paying his salary and he had to borrow money from his mother. But a baby was on the way and in spite of all the depressing news from China, they were as happy as a couple as they had ever been or would be.

I made my first appearance at 6:54 on the evening of Mother's Day 1938. Children born on the Sabbath Day are supposed, according to the old rhyme, to be "fair and wise and good and gay." The arrival on Mother's Day of a child she had prayed for so many years seemed a special acknowledgement of God's faithfulness. The delivery was quick and comparatively easy for a mother of 36. Her first impression on inspection was that I was "as homely as a mud fence." Barely coherent, her parting comment as my father left her room that evening was "I've done a big day's washing." The washing might have been big but, except for my fingers and toes, I was not: an average seven pounds, eleven ounces and twenty one inches long. On a scale of one to a hundred the obstetrician said the delivery should be graded a seventy.

My place of birth anticipated a lifelong denominational identity. Presbyterian Hospital, then at 39th and Filbert Streets, Philadelphia, was established by well-heeled Presbyterians half a century earlier. Beds had been endowed by various churches and my mother, as a member of the wealthy main-line Narberth Church, had a claim on their charity. Philadelphia represented the heartland of conservative "Old School" Presbyterianism. Eleven years earlier my father had been ordained an evangelist by the Presbytery of Philadelphia in the redoubtable and well-endowed Arch St. Presbyterian Church whose pastor, Clarence Edward Macartney, was about to leave for Pittsburgh. Macartney, the moderator of the 1924 Presbyterian General Assembly, had jousted with Harry Emerson Fosdick in the conservative liberal controversy then roiling the denomination. My father, both as a Macartney protégé and a Princeton Seminary graduate, was a clear target in the battle lines then forming. And the seminary where he taught was not popular with the Board which was riven by charges of heretical teaching and accusations that their leadership was not theologically reliable and was unwilling to take a stand.

Shortly after the article in the Worcester paper appeared, the three of us left for the West coast, stopping off at 156 Fifth Avenue, Manhattan headquarters of the Board of Foreign Missions and seeing family along the way, all of whom were apprehensive on our behalf and tended to cling to us as we said our last farewells for what was for him to be a seven year separation. "I am trying not to think of the separation aspect of this trip" she wrote her twin, "but only of the opportunities and the joy of going back 'home' again. If only you all could come and visit us!" Mother MacLeod, as my grandmother was known, accompanied them as far as her Indiana family home and there was a grand reception with warm Hoosier hospitality. Friends met them at stations along the way. As the train passed Wheaton College in the night it slowed but there was no light in the Tower. We were wafted across the United States with love and respect. Missionaries were the churches' super-heroes (and regarded as super-saints). And I appear to have been a gorgeous and irresistible baby who greeted everyone with a wary smile. My mother was in heaven.

On 23 September 1938 the three of us sailed out of San Francisco on the *President Coolidge*, a Dollar Steamship liner, for of all places, Yokohama. The two countries we were sailing to were at war. Constant stories of atrocities committed by Japan in China were cabled to us and circulated in daily news reports. In our cabin there were two bunk beds: my mother was on the lower one and I filled part of the other, with my father having to hoist himself above. I appear to have been a good traveller, not reacting to my vaccination too badly. My parents took turns in the dining room, one staying with me all the time.

Their vessel was redirected to Manila, the Philippines. Its sister ship, the *President Hoover*, had earlier that year been strafed while docked in Shanghai and they were taking no chances. The inexperienced (and party-loving) substitute crew of the *President Hoover* drove it on the rocks off Formosa (Taiwan). This was the final journey for the *President Coolidge* under the Dollar Steamship Company flag. Shortly after its return to the United States its owners went bankrupt. Investing in the Far East was a risky business. At Kobe we were transferred to the Messageries Maritimes steam ship *Jean Laborde*. "We were in France again," my father wrote, "French meal times, French menus, French language, French stewards and stewardesses. It was quite jolly." It was another world, far removed from the storms swirling around them. They were in a bubble, a world of normalcy and culture, little anticipating the time six years later when the *Jean Laborde,* back in Vichy France, was scuttled and burned by the Germans.

From now on my parents' correspondence would be censored. Nothing could be written down that might mark them as subversive aliens in the so-called "Greater East Asia Co-Prosperity Sphere," taking sides against the Japanese occupiers of China. My mother, in her final letter with an American stamp posted on board ship, described an elaborate code she had developed. References to the Japanese were to be disguised as comments about Jackson or Jacqueline, the Chinese became Chinto or Chezubah. Paragraphs in code began and ended with "Thus and so." Messages for the New York Board were identified as "Let Aunt Rebecca share this news." It was all very cloak and dagger, a spy thriller.

Like all Americans at the time, she shared a simplistic naiveté about Japan's real intentions.

With what confidence they set sail and how little they seemed aware of what lay ahead as they docked. Just over two years later my mother and I were to return in a boat crowded with fatherless evacuees. Seven years later, after terrible privation, my father returned on a U S Navy troop ship, fifty pounds lighter.

CHAPTER 2:

In Japanese-occupied China, 1938-1939

"We are in China and we are thrilled!" As the *Jean Laborde* reached the yellow waters of the Yangtze River on 11 October 1938, my mother wrote her sister on first sight of land. But it was a country at war. On either bank of the Huangpu River trucks full of Japanese soldiers could be seen tearing along the roads. "We saw for the first time the results of war," my father observed, "buildings demolished and a pile of bricks, other buildings with great shell holes in them." And in Shanghai harbour the river was "jammed with Japanese shipping – cargo boats, battleships, [a] big hospital ship with the huge painted red cross." The next day the USS *Augusta*, flagship of the American Asian fleet, arrived from north China where it had been patrolling for the past five years. "The decks were lined with white sailors (referring to their uniform, not their skin colour) on parade, a beautiful sight," he wrote. It would later be the boat on which Churchill and Roosevelt signed the Atlantic charter.

At the wharf buses took disembarking passengers to the customs jetty on the Bund, Shanghai's iconic business and banking centre. The ride took them through Hongkou where there were streets with blocks of burned out shops, soon to be rebuilt by Jewish escapees from Nazi Germany. When they crossed the Garden Bridge into the British concession, Scottish Highlanders in kilts, bayonets drawn, greeted them. "Oh boy," my father exclaimed, "it surely looked good to us to see them." British and French tanks guarded their concessions in a fatuous effort to preserve an illusion of security. They arrived at the customs jetty an hour late for my two o'clock bottle. "His latest stunt is to stick out his tongue – and he's so cute," my grandmother in Philadelphia was informed. As she knew well, a foreign baby in China was a magnet for the curious and a real show-stopper and door-opener.

People, some agitated and fearful, others confused and lost, were everywhere. They were overwhelmed by the crowds. There were people everywhere. Shanghai had swollen to three times its previous size. All streets were clogged and congestion was at a standstill. Accommodation was at a premium. My parents had counted on being able to stay at the China Inland Mission headquarters on Sinza (later Xinzha) Road but it was fully booked with their own missionaries who were in constant flux. Eventually, after many attempts, they were able to reserve a room (but only for a few days) at the Elim House of Rest on Avenue Joffre, a major road through the French Concession. Their large room on a corner overlooking one of Shanghai's busiest intersections belied the "rest" their boarding place had promised.

Death was everywhere. The Rape of Nanking had taken place earlier in the year with thousands, if not hundreds of thousands, slaughtered when the city which had been the Nationalist Capital fell to the Japanese on 13 December 1937. The day after their arrival in Shanghai my father went to the China Inland Mission headquarters to deliver parcels for his sister Annabella, one of their missionaries in the interior. He learned there of the death of her son, his nephew John Maxwell Parsons, two weeks earlier in Shangtsai, Honan, as his parents, his mother five months pregnant with their third child, were fleeing Japanese invaders. John had just celebrated his first birthday and his particularly gruesome death – he was dropped in a bucket of night soil and died days later of dysentery

— was a sobering reminder of how perilous it was to bring infants into a war-zone.

Eager to leave the congestion, we remained in Shanghai for only two days; The trip north to Qingdao was ordinarily only twenty-six hours but the treacherous Yellow Sea held us back with a typhoon and instead of arriving at one in the afternoon it was midnight before we came within sight of land. Our host, Arthur Owens[2], met us at the wharf and took us back to his home where mother and I would be their guests while Father went up country to "spy out the land." Having got all the necessary passes from the Japanese military, he took the train, full of Japanese soldiers, first to Jinan (where he stayed overnight at Stein's Hotel) and then on the next day to Tenghsien. With marauding bandits making rail traffic an adventure, trains never travelled at night and only proceeded cautiously and slowly during the day.

He had let no one know of his arrival but on the platform, much to everyone's surprise, he was greeted by three colleagues waiting for another missionary. A rickshaw carried him and his baggage from the station to the compound outside the walls through a devastated and empty city. Inside the walls only a quarter of the usual inhabitants remained. "The rest had fled or been killed," he noted. "Large sections are in ruins." Friends Ken and Kay Kepler, who lived in the south compound, welcomed him but their young daughters were bitterly disappointed not to see the baby, as was the whole station. He had long conversations with the other missionaries about "conditions of the church, and station and missionaries and China."

"Do you advise Dorothy and the baby to come to the interior?" he asked everyone. "The station was evenly divided between those who said 'no' and those who said 'yes.' So we have to decide for ourselves." Arthur

---

2   Arthur Owens (1890-1987) went to Hunan in 1921 with the PC(USA), transferred to Shandong 1938, returning to America in 1940. Appointed as Principal of the Shanghai American School in 1948, my mother served as his secretary while in Shanghai. He went on to Woodstock School Musoorie, India, in 1949, retiring in 1957.

Romig, chairman of the American Presbyterian Mission, was consulted. He had considerable experience and wisdom: Romig's father had come to China in 1901, serving in Tenghsien for half his career, and had another son in Yunnan. The final decision was to return to their original posting and resume their teaching roles at the North China Theological Seminary, at the time the largest of such institutions in the country, out pacing the more theologically liberal schools. As a school denigrated for being backward and non-intellectual, my father's newly minted Ph. D. made him an important asset for the faculty's credibility.

The controversy then roiling the PC(USA) back in the States was never far away and made "the Board" suspicious of the denominational loyalty of the missionaries serving the North China Theological Seminary. The newly established Orthodox Presbyterian Church in the States had sent out to China Richard and Polly Gaffin who were in Qingdao at the time. My parents valued their friendship (which lasted a lifetime) and reached out to them in their ecclesiastical isolation. But in such relationships there always lurked the danger of misunderstanding and for some colleagues in the PC (USA) Mission questions about denominational and institutional loyalty. In Tenghsien neighbours Albert and Mabel Dodd had joined the Independent Board when it was formed by Gresham Machen and his friends in 1933. In March 1940 Gordon Holdcroft[3], who had resigned from the Korean Presbyterian Mission to become Secretary of the Independent Board, visited the station. "He wanted to see the work here before he went home," my father reported, "so we showed him everything and told him of our plans for the future." My father's ambivalence was apparent.

Four days after arrival in Tenghsien my mother wrote in the first of her circulars to family: "It was a long, long trip but all along the way, things smoothed out, and we felt God's hand in guiding and anticipating all our needs. I don't know I have ever felt so strongly such guidance

---

3   (James) Gordon Holdcroft (1878-1972) Graduated Park College 1903 (DD 1922), PTS, 1908; appointed PC(USA) in Korea Pyongyang, Seoul, 1909-34; helped found IBPFM and serving as its 3rd general secretary.

and such assurance." They needed divine protection. As my father wrote: "The countryside is very disturbed – guerilas and bandits everywhere, robbing people's bedding and money." One night they entered the compound and took Elder Chang away for a ransom of $30,000. "Between the Japanese and the bandits things look bad, but we carry on. Country itineration seems to be next to impossible, not only here but elsewhere in Shantung."

By 28 November we were back in our own home. In preparation for winter, which in North China can be very severe, a new stove had been installed following complicated negotiations. Some scarce material for the tin smith to restore and recreate the necessary piping had been allowed into Tenghsien. A limited amount of coke was available for burning but as the winter progressed soft coal was the only option, leaving a sooty atmosphere throughout the house. One of the earliest words in my vocabulary was the warning "Hotch, hotch" as I got near the potbelly stove that stood in our living room. I learned early that fire can provide needed heat but it can also scar.

One of the immediate personnel concerns was the lack of a Mission representative at the hospital in addition to. Dr Chang the resident physician and Mr Ho the head nurse. "But the mission wants some foreigner to have a finger in the pie to keep in touch with things and see that everything goes along OK," he reassured his mother lest she be anxious about his evident lack of medical knowledge and experience. So from 9 to 10 o'clock every weekday he would walk around the building and say "Good morning" and appear official. My father's time in the hospital greatly increased when Dr Herbert Alexander, a Jewish refugee from Nazi Germany, with his musical wife joined the staff at the end of May. Dr Alexander had adequate English but no Chinese. My father served as an intermediary as patients described symptoms and Dr. Alexander provided a diagnosis. Dad was OK with "Where does it hurt?" but was stumped with "Inflammation of the kidneys."

The anomaly of a Jewish doctor in a hospital created by Christians as an outreach for the gospel was not lost on the compound. There were constant prayers for conversion but, given the circumstances in Europe and the complicity of some Christians in the Holocaust, it was not to be. My mother referred obliquely the following March to some attempt at witnessing which backfired. It was fortunate that she and Mrs. Alexander had their music as a bridge and together they planned musicales for the missionaries. The Alexanders were, of course, not interned and remained at the Hospital after Pearl Harbour and kept in contact with my father in his concentration camp, an experience of which Dr Alexander had first-hand knowledge. He died tragically in the Hospital basement escaping the battle between Communists and Nationalists a year after the war with Japan was over which ironically he had survived. Today in the city now named Tengzhou, other than a crowded church, the Hospital is the one visible reminder of foreign Christian missionary work.

My first Christmas was memorable. Christmas day being that year on a Sunday, the traditional feast was held mid-day Christmas Eve. Of the five member women's planning committee my mother was "the youngest, the most artistic, and the best housekeeper," as my father proudly informed his mother, "so our place was chosen." Sixteen people sat down to eat. The English Christmas Day service, usually taken by someone off-station, was conducted at 4:30 in the afternoon by Earle Woodberry of Ichow. His wife Ada had grown up in the other half of the duplex where my mother was born 37 years earlier in Worcester, Massachusetts. Ada and the children (including Dudley, born in 1934, later to become the well-known Islamic scholar and missiologist at Fuller Seminary) had stayed in Baltimore so Earle was on his own. Boxing Day there was a gift exchange at the Kepler's where Earle was staying. The Keplers' home had been chosen because their two daughters (the only foreign children left on the compound) were of an age when Christmas celebrations meant the most.

The Christmas service that year in the Chinese church in the North Suburb stood out. A building that comfortably seated 500 but could crowd in 600, was packed with 800 or 900. Many came out of curiosity but political uncertainties had created a great interest in Christianity. The pastor, Mr. Kuo, an NCTS graduate, had baptized 33 converts at communion earlier that month. "It gave me a real thrill and uplift," my father commented. When the service ended the gates were thrown open. Beggars, the aged, the infirm and the challenged all crowded in for their Christmas treat– mo-mo (steamed bread) along with other edibles provided by parishioners, who had raised thirty or forty dollars for the poor, a huge amount given sacrificially in uncertain times.

Christmas over, Earle Woodberry and my father set off for Yihsien south of Tenghsien. Yihsien was an important city in south Shandong where coal was shipped by rail from nearby mines to the Grand Canal nearby and then went on to urban centres. American Presbyterians had established a work there in 1904, initially staffed by a doctor and a couple, the husband a minister. They had grand ideas and seemingly unlimited funds from wealthy Presbyterian churches in America, and set up a medical facility, then a day school, and finally a women's training institute and an industrial school, just prior to the outbreak of war in 1914. The extensive property was abandoned in 1927 when political turmoil sent China missionaries packing. Four years later there was an attempt to reopen the station but it lacked personnel. Yihsien had close links with Tenghsien as two of the missionary couples there had served previously in Yihsien

My father was summoned to maintain the work and, it turned out, spent the whole of January providing a male presence in turbulent times. He became increasingly involved in property matters, hardly something for which he was qualified as well as being a frustrating distraction. The redirecting of missionary effort after the 1900 Boxer Rebellion from evangelism to social service, education and healthcare reflected the new priorities of the homeland denominations and decreasing conviction about the missionary task as bringing people to a personal faith in Jesus. Institutional aggrandisement was not what had sent my parents to China.

Their train ride to Yihsien reads like a saga. The Nationalists had scored an impressive victory over the Japanese at nearby Taierzhuang the previous March and early April, one of their rare (and unheralded) victories. Their triumph however affected rail travel. Woodberry and Dad missed their scheduled train (nothing ever was on time) hustled onto the last box car of a freight train with their bedding and suitcase and arrived at Linchang, seventy li^4 south, at 5:00 pm. Their connection left at 2:40 am the next morning so they took the time to see the chapel and other mission property, then in ruins. Rather than staying in a dirty inn the two men took advantage of a cross-eyed Cantonese-speaking station master who, seeing an opportunity to practice his English, offered the use of his office. They talked into the night, playing chess with a portable set that Dad had brought, a single bulb providing unreliable light. They were completely unfazed by all the chaos.

Tiring of the tedium, since the train was already in the station, my father took his bedroll onto the platform in order to fold it out on one of the wooden seats in their railway car to get some rest. As he did so a Japanese guard lunged at him with a bayonet until he discovered it was a *Yángguǐzi* or foreign devil. Eventually, many hours late, the train set off for Yihsien filled with Japanese soldiers. "We were mighty glad to see Mr. D'Olive with a lantern to welcome us." Walter and Lottie D'Olive, stationed in Tsining, were China veterans. They left as soon as Dad had distributed in the countryside the $10,000 in Red Cross relief funds he had been given. Earle Woodberry returned to an empty house in Ichow.

My father was now solely responsible for the safety of four single women missionaries. He used the time with his customary self-discipline, reading the Chinese New Testament. He kept a tight schedule: he had started on Christmas Day with the gospel of Matthew and by the end of January, when he returned home, he was well into the gospel of Luke. He had also brought a set of Chinese primary school readers. He reckoned, as he wrote his mother, that he was now at the level of an eight-year old boy. The irony was that, having been born and raised in China, he returned to the land of his birth as an adult without any knowledge of the language because he had received all his education in a top-notch school that had prepared him perfectly to be a loyal subject of the British Empire.

---

4   A *li* was then a third of a mile, now standardized at half a mile.

He was constantly interrupted in his studying by the "pestiferous" Japanese soldiers. Interpreted by a Chinese familiar with their language, they pummelled him with queries: "How old is your child? When did you come to China? What did you do your first year? After that where did you go, what did you do? When you came out did you stop in Japan? How long were you in Shanghai? Where is your wife? How long have you been here? How long are you staying?" With that not so subtle hint, by the end of the month Dad journeyed home. But no sooner had he left than he was summoned back when in early February Nettie Junkin, one of the single women at Yihsien, was held by bandits in a three hour ordeal. She had only days previously been roughed up by the Japanese.[5]

Meanwhile my mother was negotiating for an amah, the great boon of expatriates with small children in China. She was not particularly warm or cuddly, I suspect because her own mother had farmed her and her twin out to a strong-minded paternal grandmother as children. It took four months but by the middle of February I had my nanny. Mother felt the need for explaining to family at home how essential this was to allow time for her ministry and she was doing the locals a great service by providing employment. The amah chosen was a young widow from the country, one of many whose life had been disrupted by war. She appears to have been a lay preacher whose pastor recommended her highly. She apparently took an immediate shine to me which was just as well as I had acquired my first tooth, had a blocked tear duct, and must have been a bit cranky. My mother also noted that at nine months I had a temper. She blamed herself for handing on that genetic gift to her son. For the rest of my childhood she was anxious for me to suppress my feelings and always turn the other cheek. An only child is at a disadvantage. Retaliation and self-defence, physically or verbally, was drummed out of me at an early stage of life. Christians aren't supposed to talk back.

---

5   See Nettie Dubose Junkin (Sarah Woodard, Ed.). *Bits of China*. Self-published, 1986, 45.

With my beloved amah, winter 1939

In early April further tragedy struck my amah. Her village was burned to the ground by bandits. Those who escaped were shot, including her mother. Fortunately her father and brother were away at the time. Destitute, she found solace in me, developing a close bond. I am glad my mother was not jealous: "The baby is such a comfort to her, and she slips around at every odd time to find things to do for him and to discover a time when he needs attention. He puts his arms around her and makes such a fuss over her – it does my heart good and it is helping her so much."

Not being naturally maternal, the hiring of an amah meant that my mother was free to pursue her real interests. Against my father's advice (fearing she was overloading herself), she gave a course in Doctrine at the Women's Bible School once a week, teaching "salvation and growth in the Christian life" which meant for her "more victorious living and more close contact with the Lord." Her pietism was at variance with my father's stern Calvinism. And almost on arrival Mother acquired thirteen advanced organ students, so anxious were they to take lessons from her each week. She had brought back to China a rehabilitated organ for the Seminary Chapel. Badly damaged in transit, it required total reassembling on arrival. A gifted local carpenter retrieved all the screws, broken bits and pieces and my mother, to her great relief, was finally able to get sound out of the instrument after an anxious time. "Taking it all apart this way," my father wrote, "has given one the satisfaction of knowing that the organ really was completely renovated in Philadelphia as the Estey Co. told us." "I believe it means more, too, to the worshippers here, than some of the organs which cost tens of thousands of dollars to the people in big churches at home." "And when they heard of its cost, they gasped and looked with greatest interest on all its complexity -- two manuals, sixteen stops, and keys which one plays with one's feet!" Mother added.

Surprisingly my father's teaching load was not at the seminary but primarily at the MMI, the so-called "normal" school set up in 1913 which had been the reason NCTS had located in Tenghsien a decade later, turning a sleepy South Shantung town into an educational hub. He taught theology at MMI first class Monday through Thursday. At NCTS he taught Peter's epistle at 1:10 p.m. Friday and Saturday. He also conducted a practice preaching session on Wednesday evenings. His duties as hospital superintendent took up the rest if his time. For his class on Peter he used the Socratic arrangement, questions and answers. He also published syllabi in Chinese for his classes. It was ten years since they had left for China and they were still struggling with the language. My mother, in spite of her musical ear, still required a lot of language coaching.

A change of scenery and release from the daily grind, combined with a promise of tutorials in Chinese, seem to have been the motivation for a three month excursion to Chefoo. "I didn't tell you," she wrote confidentially to her twin, "that I prayed very definitely that if it were the Lord's will or permitting, we might go home this summer." She claimed it was neither discontent nor homesickness but a desire to bring her largely non-Christian circle of friends and family in New England to faith by her personal witness, something she had been unable to do during furlough. "I only pray now, if I failed my responsibility, that the Lord will send somebody to them more faithful than I," she confided.

Her anxious state of mind reflected the high level of stress all missionaries and Chinese believers were experiencing at the time. In Xuzhou, a southern Presbyterian mission centre a hundred miles south of Tenghsien, the Japanese had taken away thirteen local leading pastors and elders and there were rumours of torture as nothing had been heard from them. A notice had appeared, posted on one of the buildings in the compound warning people to be patriotic to China and resist the Japanese occupiers. Gangs of workmen that May of 1939 were building a nine foot high wall around our compound, replacing the barbed wire fences. In the other compound in the North Suburb the walls had been extended to twelve feet. As my father reflected "One enjoys walls out here, when one wouldn't in America!"

The Japanese had, like Mussolini, made the trains more efficient and five of us in our party risked a special Nanjing to Peiping night train that went through Tenghsien at eleven at night. It was preceded half an hour earlier by a so-called pilot train – a boxcar with loopholes for firearms - to ensure the safety of the tracks. As we boarded our second class car it was pitch black, with no light and the windows shrouded. The only exception was a great headlight at the front on the locomotive. The train was packed - they always were in China in my childhood – but a small cubicle provided space for my carry-cot and my mother beside me. By 8 the next morning we were in Jinan and by 6 we'd arrived in Tianjin in time for supper at the CIM home. Here for the first time my parents' two nationalities were a disadvantage and my mother's American passport was the only way to proceed. This was the summer of 1939 and Dad's British passport was a liability as Japan and Germany grew closer.

Two days later my father put my mother, myself, and my amah, on a launch at the Tianjin Bund or waterfront to catch the boat to Chefoo, where we were to spend the summer. My father wrote: "Donald didn't like the launch's harsh whistle one little bit. The last I saw was when the whistle blew, and he was a picture of misery – eyes shut tight and mouth wide open." As my father wrote his mother, addressing letters to us in Chefoo would bring back many memories. He had spent most of his childhood at school there, from age 7 to 17. His three sisters had followed him, though only allowed to see him an hour Sunday afternoons. Aside from a new preparatory school erected in 1934, the property looked the same as it had thirty years earlier. Chefoo was nestled next to what was from 1898 to 1930 the British leased territory of Weihaiwei. The Royal Navy fleet that docked there would only finally abandon it months later in 1940, leaving 350 foreign school children and staff unprotected after Pearl Harbor. They would spend the war in Weihsien prison camp located on the railway line between Qingdao and Jinan.

Soon after arrival in Chefoo and we had been parked at the Missionary Home, my mother was hit hard with bacillary dysentery. She was taken to the Presbyterian Temple Hill Hospital. Fortunately one of the doctors, Paul Adolph, lived next door. He had been my father's roommate at Wheaton College and Dad had officiated at his wedding to Vivian Antoinette MacDougall in Tianjin in 1931. Vivian took my amah and me in as guests, not the last time she would do so in an emergency. I needed a firm hand as I was starting to walk and didn't like being left in a play pen.

By mid-July, seemingly recovered from dysentery, my mother was getting anxious to discover when my father was coming, hopefully "within the next week or ten days." My father had again gone to Yihshien. There was a heatwave as he returned home to police the Tenghsien property. Towards the end of July Mother wrote complaining to her mother-in-law who was used to long separations on the mission field: "Alex does not expect to be here until August. I hope he won't be delayed too long. It is pretty lonely without him – we haven't seen him for six weeks and do not expect to see him for another week or more – my, won't we be thrilled when his boat sails in, and he sees Donald all brown and plumper, and strong and husky, and peppy! I wonder what Donald's reaction will be?"

Dad was by now in Tenghsien, oblivious to her angst and completely unaware of the gathering storm in Chefoo. He was absorbed creating a new moon gate outside our house and kitchen renovations both of which he thought would delight her. It was a busy summer for construction. At the Hospital he was building a new out-patient department. As NCTS registrar he was receiving registrations for the coming academic year. Meanwhile in Chefoo a child in the Missionary Home had whooping cough. Soon all the children were infected. I had a particularly bad case. The mother of the infecting child gave my mother a bottle of lilac scented *eau de cologne* but it did not compensate for the anxiety a parent completely on her own must have felt.

On 20 August Dad finally left to join us, intending to meet up with us in Qingdao, having abandoned any idea of a family holiday. Except for telegrams, communication was uncertain and unpredictable. By that time my mother and I were both in Hospital in Chefoo but he seemed totally unaware of our plight. My situation was fairly dire, at least so it appeared to my mother. "I think I never saw a harder case of whooping cough," she observed. The symptoms of my sickness had worsened: up all night but I was unable to whoop which mother thought would have provided some relief. As the cough worsened my mother came down with a second type of dysentery, first bacillary and now amoebic. From the hospital she wrote her sister: "Because the amah couldn't manage 24 hour duty for both Donald and me, we have come to the hospital, and she cares for him days, and the nurses do it at night. And here I can have rest and proper diet. I hope I'll be recovered and Donald over his worst in another week." My father had by now reached Qingdao, and telegraphed that he would be with us in two or three days. I assume that he had finally learned about our hospitalization. "It has been a long, long ten weeks since I left him," Mother commented.

"Dorothy acted awfully glad to see me!! Was she surprised!" he wrote his mother. To her own family she wrote: "When I had really decided that Alec couldn't get here at all, I looked up from my bed in the hospital, and there he was." Physically she was a very different woman than the one he had left: she had gone down to 115 pounds and was unusually listless, if not depressed. I was in my amah's arms in the Hospital hall when Dad arrived and was most unfriendly and didn't recognize him.

"After a while he was quite delighted to have me around" my father reassured his mother. "They were not seriously ill – Donald has an ordinary case of whooping, and is now 4 weeks along and we think he is over the worst. And Dorothy left the Hospital yesterday." My father, either through guilt or ignorance, made light of everything. My mother never forgot the summer of 1939.

As our family's domestic drama played itself out the world was in flames. "We are living in troubled times, and with a madman in Europe," my father observed in a letter home. A typhoon cut us off from the news that Germany had invaded Poland on 1 September 1939. My father had already been prepared for what lay ahead. On a quick trip to Jinan, capital of Shantung, early in August, alighting off the train at the station, a huge banner greeted him: "Get rid of the British and the Chinese people will be able to live in peace. " He described that as "a lie" but because he was a British subject he was particularly vulnerable. Prior to World War 1 Germany had claimed most of Shantung as its own sphere of influence. Now as one of the three Axis powers, Japan was reclaiming the province for the Third Reich. British subjects were particularly singled out for harsh treatment. First the Japanese held an anti-British rally which was followed by an anti-American one. It was an anxious time for expats.

On our return journey we were fortunate to get a reservation for a berth in a steamer for Qingdao. Since 1 September the two British shipping firms (Butterfield & Swire and Jardine Matheson) were no longer accepting any passengers. Qiingdao, as a former German colony, was bristling with Japanese boats in the harbour. We were heavily laden: mountains of luggage necessitated regular counts at each stage of the journey. At one point I was seen on top of a pile using the potty "with great tranquillity and poise in spite of being held in a very undignified position." No one paid any attention to me as I relieved myself. The cabin reserved had, for the first time, neither cockroaches nor bed bugs. My amah got terribly sea sick.

Enjoying the new moon gate autumn 1940

After a few days in Qingdao, acquiring the necessary papers and certificates of inoculation, we arrived home by rail. As we came into the station in Tenghsien we passed the remains of a train that guerillas had blown up a few days before. One of the missionaries, Martin Hopkins, had just gotten off that train and was walking to a neighbour's house when he heard a massive explosion. It was a narrow escape and a warning that we were all in constant danger.

Chapter 3:

In the Shadow of
Impending War, 1940

On her return home to Tenghsien, my mother was delighted with "her" moon gate. Not a gardener, Dad had still managed to plant an oleander bush alongside it to welcome us. It encouraged big plans for her garden: she had acquired many bulbs during the summer. And the kitchen renovations were impressive: a new refrigerator room had been added. Her teaching load was substantially increased: she was to cover in Chinese John's gospel with a class of Bible women and she now had thirty-five eager organ pupils. My father's responsibilities remained unchanged, though with a recently purchased second-hand motor bike (which was always breaking down – Dad was no mechanic) he was hopefully able to itinerate in surrounding rural villages on Sundays. Meanwhile I was learning to talk in two languages. "Thank you" greeted any item placed before me but whenever my mother spoke in English I reverted to the language of my amah, expressing my gratitude in Chinese which at the time was my preferred tongue. "He is picking up lots of words, Chinese and English, with plenty that only he seems to understand," my father reported.

My mother's teaching schedule was heavy. Fifteen of her organ pupils had individual lessons with another thirty in an introductory music class twice a week. Preparation for that class was demanding. She memorized her presentation after acquiring a whole new Chinese musical vocabulary. The demands on her time were intense: one day that October she worked solidly from 6:30 in the morning to 9:30 at night. There were three male servants to do the cooking, washing the adults' clothes, and gardening. My mother described the number of our staff as "ridiculous." "However, I am thankful that we do have people to do the work – otherwise I could not teach classes." And they were grateful for any employment. Numbers were reduced in November when an efficient and energetic cook was hired, someone to whom she could leave the management of the home and its continuous flow of house guests. Just before 8:00 each morning (after my father had gone to 7:30 chapel at the seminary), there would be servants' prayers lasting fifteen or twenty minutes. "We are reading through Acts now and each day I give a bit of teaching or explanation and we take turns in prayer."

My father's English class at the MMI consisted originally of going through Catherine Vos' *Child's Story Bible* and later an adaptation of a book surveying the Bible by Reuben A. Torrey, an editor of the Scofield Bible. "The students are not very bright and responsive but the chief difficulty seems to be with the textbook," he reflected. They were also asked to write a letter in English to a missionary either requesting tracts or hymnbooks or inviting the recipient to preach in their chapel. These classes took place for several hours Monday through Wednesday mornings. Wednesday evening preaching classes continued to be a challenge, providing an opportunity to critique a student's message. "We certainly need to develop a higher grade of sermons," was his reflection. But it was his Thursday and Friday morning class on I Peter that was his particular delight. Sixty-five or seventy had enrolled in this class and, using a syllabus he had had printed, he went through the epistle carefully clause by clause, verse by verse. This took time and so, by the end of October, he was only at verse 20 of chapter 1 but he picked up speed as the semester progressed. His students were introduced to a thorough and painstaking exegesis which would have been unfamiliar to them previously.

Franklin Roosevelt enhanced Thanksgiving 1939 creating a family holiday, a time to get together and reconnect. He pushed the date back a week ensuring a good run up to Christmas and providing longer time for Christmas shopping the final year of the Depression. Hearing reports from the States of "Franksgiving" (as the new holiday was nicknamed in honour of the President), brought mixed feelings: homesickness as Mother missed traditional family reunions and turkey but also frustration at the insularity of her isolationist compatriots. It was the time of the so-called phony war in Europe and Japanese belligerency in Asia as America stood on the side-lines. She detected a lack of comprehension or even care about her own family's present vulnerabilities in China. Her immediate family failed to grasp the peril the three of us were in, lacking any awareness or comprehension of our precarious situation. Letters were infrequent, took a month, and seemed to suggest business as usual. Her frustration showed how far she had travelled personally in the previous decade. Acquaintances in her small town New England had little or no post-secondary education. None shared her intense faith. China was a long way away. How could they relate to her as they corresponded? They were simply on different planes.

To add to the communication challenges there was evidence of Japanese censoring of their letters. My father was remarkably free expressing his feelings about the Occupier. In one article he submitted to *Christianity Today* (a magazine edited by his friend Samuel Craig of Princeton) he spoke fearlessly of "this iniquitous war of aggression, with all the suffering and sorrow it is bringing to the Chinese people is being carried on with American supplies." Japanese Protestants, forcibly merged with the new name of "Kyodan" in June 1941, were pleading "for a charitable judgment of Japan" citing the old canard of "judging not lest one be judged." The American Presbyterian Mission in Japan, unlike its Korean counterpart, was regarded as hopelessly compromised theologically and now politically. My father saw a connection between theological woolliness and political naiveté.

That was definitely not true of the Presbyterian mission where we were. From 7 – 16 December 1939 the Executive of the Shantung Presbyterian Mission visited the station and were greatly impressed with what they observed. "Several had never been in Tenghsien" Mother wrote after they left, and remarked that "it did them all good to see our work here. It results in larger sympathies and corrects station-mindedness." The Shantung Mission, with its comprehensive list of ministries, was a showpiece of the American Presbyterian China Mission. It had adopted (from Korea) the Nevius Plan for self-governance, self-propagation and self-support. "As I visit and see other stations I am increasingly glad that I am in the work that the Lord would have me do," Dad declared after the delegation departed. He would never be as settled, or as happy, as he was during his decade at NCTS.

Not that there was always harmony among the missionaries but disputes were resolved in a biblical manner. Just before Christmas a dispute arose among the missionaries over the boundary line between the Hospital and the MMI. Dad wanted to build a new kitchen and dining room for the Hospital "to take the place of the hole they call by those names" (my mother's description). It meant taking a small slice of the MMI property. Words were said, my mother went into a prayer and fasting mode, and the next day the atmosphere was completely changed. The irony, of course, was that not long after the entire property was destroyed with only the Hospital and the Church a reminder today that Christianity had once come to this city to bring healing and hope.

Christmas 1939 – the last "normal" one we would have as a family – was still somewhat surreal. Four days previously there had been gunfire. Bullets ricocheted off our property. My anxious mother suggested that their bed should be moved so that they would not be in the line of fire. Dad slept through the whole fray and by morning we were ready for celebrating the season as the conflict moved on. Christmas Day started with the servants and their families, all opening our gifts to them ("mostly Bibles and hymnbooks" my father explained), though the children got something more exciting by way of edibles. Later on our own (to avoid comparisons) I opened my gifts, the largest of which was a small table and chairs made by our carpenter. At 10:00 a service was held in the Seminary Chapel followed by entertainment. Music was provided by student quartets. Mother conducted a choir. Bachelor missionary Oscar Walton played the newly acquired organ. Ken Kepler sang several solos. Dad's contribution was gramophone music from Handel's *Messiah*, winding up the machine for each 78 rpm recording. At 1:00 o'clock there was the station's traditional Christmas dinner, with a gift exchange. Roy Allison[6] was Santa Claus. As the only infant present I was the centre of attention, grabbing all the presents I could from under the tree. My own gift was a cloth bunny rabbit, a copy of which (after some depredations) I received the next Christmas. The neighbours dropped by in the evening for ice cream and more music, played both on our piano as duets and again records on our gramophone. Who would have known the world was caving in around us?

Our Christmas celebrations that year were enhanced by another German Jewish couple that had joined the station. Dr Eisenberg, married to Dr Alexander's sister, was a dentist and had brought his own dental equipment to Tenghsien to set up a practice. With their music the Eisenbergs were warmly welcomed by my mother. Their Jewish faith was a concern to Mother who issued an all-points bulletin to her sister to join her to pray for their conversion, not a likely response as again the Holocaust in Christian Europe made acceptance of our faith difficult if not impossible. The two couples participated freely in the religious life of the station. "These four Jews," she wrote with great admiration and respect, "are certainly an unusual group – they show that they are from a background of real refinement – and they never complain or sigh about their lot, living on a terribly small amount, and helping their

---

6   Roy M. Allison (1876-1974) a graduate of Washington & Jefferson University, Harvard Law School (1903), PTS (1906) & Princeton University Graduate School. Appointed by PCUSA to Shantung 1910. Assigned to the nascent MMI in 1919 - 1942. Gifted rural evangelist. After repatriation, he served churches in PA & IN.

fellow sufferers from their own pittance." At the time no one knew the full horror which they had escaped.

As the New Year 1940 arrived there were some encouragements. A student came up to my father after a lecture and said "Praise the Lord, I have been helped so much." This kind of accolade, my mother noted, was unusual for the Chinese and meant a great deal to Dad. But there were also reminders of the perilous times in which they were living. A country pastor came to him recounting how his ten year old son had been taken by bandits for ransom and in the process of negotiating his son's release had been forced to give up everything that he possessed. He could no longer support him, the brightest of his boys, so would my parents take him in and educate him? The sheer weight of human misery everywhere could be overwhelming.

Winter that year was bitterly cold. There were two heavy and unusual snowfalls in February, further compounding the general distress. The moisture was, however, welcome after months of drought. At the end of the winter in early April, Henry S. Little, a wealthy Presbyterian layman visited the station at his own expense on a fact-finding mission. Little was very much a denominational man and therefore initially suspect. "He seemed rather impressed by the program of work and the normality of things in contrast to other stations, and I feel that he was really benefitted by his visit to us," my mother commented in that somewhat condescending way that infuriated more mainline Protestants. After the *de rigueur* musicale for visiting dignitaries, the missionaries let fly about the need for "a truly Christian college in China" in contrast to the present educational work which was described as "top-heavy." Then my father and Ken Kepler made a presentation about the priority of evangelism in mission work. "Little was more (apparently) open-minded and fair than anyone who has yet visited us, and seemed to be really impressed by the presentation of ideas," was my mother's assessment of the visit. I grew up in an atmosphere of theological conflict and denominational suspicion. Enemies lurked on every side and they had the power and the money.

At the same time a revival was going on in the Leper Colony attached to the station. A patrician man from Jinan had contracted leprosy and was very bitter. He came to faith and promptly discovered a gift for evangelism, not only among lepers but in the wider community. There were four meetings a day. The missionary in charge (Dr Dodd) was initially anxious about over emotionalism but was so impressed when he heard him preach that he released him for ministry in the colony. "We are very glad to hear of such work, and pray that a similar reviving may take place right here on the campus."

"We are thinking of going to Peitaiho this summer," my mother wrote the end of February. The resort had been set up in the 1880s by missionaries anxious to find a place to restore themselves after a strenuous winter in the interior and to avoid the heat of the summer. Destroyed during the Boxer Rebellion, the cottages were soon rebuilt. The one our family rented – shared in by other members of the Tenghsien staff – had a large veranda looking out over the five miles of pristine sandy beach. Ironically it is now a resort reserved for the ruling elite of the Communist party. At one point during the summer my father almost offered to buy one, which would have equalled in folly my grandfather speculating in south Florida real estate. The summer of 1940 became a kind of talisman for ever after, the happiest time of my parents' marriage and (like the summer of 1914 in Britain) a time with its carefree life which would never be repeated but was often invoked.

It did not start all that well. I had become increasingly deaf and unresponsive, quiet and withdrawn, quite different from my usual chatty self. Fred Scovel[7] of our Mission from Tsining, who gave us our annual physicals each spring, advised that I have my adenoids and tonsils out in Peiping *en route* to Peitaho. At that same examination Fred Scovel assured my 39 year old mother that she was not pregnant, scoffing at the idea. When her period finally came, it ended any lingering hope of

---

7   Fred Scovel (1902-1985) Graduated Hamilton College 1925, Cornell Medical 1929 where he met Myra (1904-1995) They went out to China under PC(USA) in 1929 and appointed to Tsining, Shandong. Repatriated in 1943, returned China, Anwei & Canton 1946-1951. Reassigned India 1953-1959. Stony Point, NY, in private practice.

having another child. In mid-June we set out for Peitaho only to return to Peiping in early July when I was booked to have surgery in Douw Hospital. The facility, now called Beijing No. 6, was originally the 1880 gift of an Albany New York socialite, later linked to the Rockefeller Foundation-funded Peking Union Medical College. Dr John Young, recently arrived from America, performed the operation. In spite of my mother's apprehension, I bounced back quickly.

The summer was judged (in contrast to the previous one) "a great success. Busy, happy healthy, spiritually profitable," my mother wrote. The spiritual profit came from a Korea missionary, Ned Adams[8] of Taiku. "I wish I could begin to tell all it meant to us," as she shared with her sister the contents of his messages. The meetings were held on the porch of the Blackstone "cottage" at Peitaho. Bill and Betty Blackstone[9] were one of the few missionaries who seemed to have generous financial resources. Bill was the grandson of William Eugene Blackstone, the Christian Zionist who had made a fortune both in real estate and eschatological speculation (his book *Jesus Is Coming* was an all-time religious best seller). My father was never clear as to who posed the greater danger to faith: liberal or dispensational Presbyterians.

---

8   Edward (Ned) Adams DD (1895-1965), Roseburg, Oregon, MK returned to Korea under the PCUSA in 1921, set up the Taiku Evangelistic Fund in 1925, expelled by Japanese with the other Korean missionaries in Oct. 1940. Returned after the war and finally retired 1953. Received ROK Presidential citation and a Cultural Medal.

9   William Treman Blackstone (1904-1992) attended Occidental College & USC, then Princeton Seminary (1927-1929), graduated Westminster Seminary 1930. Ordained LA Presbytery, 1931, assigned by PC(USA) to S China, During WW2 was chaplain to Claire Chennault's Flying Tigers, Returned in 1950 to First Church Hollywood staff. His wife, Betty Shirk Blackstone (1905-2009), proved the longevity of the China missionary community.

Peitaiho, Summer 1940

Letters home disclose that one of the reasons we went to Peitaiho that summer was increasing anxiety that I was growing up without any contact with Western children of my own age. Aside from the Kepler girls who were five and six years older there was no one else on the compound. At Peitaho that summer I had a whole range of missionary children as we played together on the beach. "Donald," it was observed, "enjoyed swimming—in fact he was thrilled by it." Swimming became my lifelong passion. We returned to Tenghsien at the end of August. Rail traffic in wartime China was always harrowing, crowds everywhere, and rail schedules meaningless. At one point my mother boarded the train but then realized I was still on the platform with my amah who was coping with numerous packages and suitcases. She shouted out hysterically in Chinese "My baby is outside and I must get to him," which brought unexpected assistance. We finally arrived at our destination, greeted by my father who had left two weeks earlier to calcimine the walls of our home and prepare for the beginning of classes as NCTS Registrar.

At the start of the academic year 1940-1941, registration of students proved a daunting challenge. My father was caught up in the general instability of China. Some of the challenges he faced were predictable, given the inexperience and immaturity of youthful students, but the whole process reflected the chaos of the times. Students registering would arrive late or change courses. It was payment in particular that proved a nightmare. Instead of cash, sponsors, family or missionaries had subsidised students' tuition (or facilitated their payment) with cheques from banks located in both occupied and "Free" China. Inflation was out of control. Running a school with a large student body requiring daily feeding and the cost of accommodation was a constant test of the administration's flexibility and ingenuity.

On 9 October 1940 the American State Department issued an urgent bulletin. Sent to every American in Tenghsien from the U. S. consulate in Shanghai, it advised "all Americans living in the Japanese Empire, China, Hong Kong, and French Indochina" to return immediately to the United States. The word came on the Patterson's radio at ten that evening and they called around the station (using the new security phones that had been installed for safety) waking up people and "the ladies didn't sleep all night - I wished the word had been held till next day" my father reproachfully noted. Earlier that same day my mother wrote: "I am hoping that I can soon accustom myself to the new uncertainties and inconveniences and stress so I can be a help to others. I am ever so certain that the Lord is protecting and guiding and truly 'going before' and that is all we need to know from day to day."

Days before, a tricycle had been ordered for me for Christmas and when it arrived it was decided realistically that "we are likely not to be here then, he might as well get some use out of it!" With all the uncertainty my father withdrew: "I really don't know what he plans," my mother wrote, "I think he is just waiting. He is very calm and always takes plenty of time to decide things." But being a British subject at the time was a definite liability. Meetings were being held by both American Presbyterian Missions, Southern and Northern, as to what to do. The Southern Board told all their women and children to leave, their Northern counterpart was more restrained. My father mused that "It is hard to plan when you don't know what to plan for. And we rather expect that what we leave behind will all be looted. And if we go, how soon can we get back? We ask ourselves many, many questions." "It is certainly sad that we have all to break up this way."

Meanwhile, classes had never been larger. The 1 Peter class had fifty students and Colossians seventy. "It's hopeless to teach them, one can only lecture. And I haven't got to know them personally." He was working on syllabi with a Chinese helper, attempting to improve the "awful Chinese" of the first edition. His helper had links with his own father's ministry in Zhejiang. Between registration, lecturing, and the Hospital my father was completely preoccupied. I was the only distraction: "Alec can certainly let down and really play with Donald and make the most terrifying roars as well as the most delightful play ideas."

On 8 November the Kepler family joined the many that were leaving the station. "Donald will miss his little playmates – he calls for 'Jean, Jean' and 'Mei, Mei' or 'Kay.'" Kay Kepler was five months pregnant and her husband Ken pledged himself to return once he had taken them to America. There was enormous psychological pressure, particularly for the men to remain at their post of duty, and latent criticism when they abandoned their work. For those who stayed there were great rewards beyond feeling that they had stayed the course: "Classes are going along with increased pleasure, at least on the part of the teacher." But the Chinese were also asking questions about the missionaries: "The Christian community here, and the student body, have been very much perturbed over the evacuation advice from [the] U.S.A. We are hoping however that we can carry on through this present semester, at least."

In the midst of all this disruption, my mother required dental work and the nearest place was Peiping, though I was never told why she didn't use Dr. Eisenberg. She took seventy-four year old Mrs. Hayes with her so that she could spend time with her son and his family. John Hayes was doing student ministry there. Both she and her husband, Watson Hayes, had come to China in 1882 and had no intention in going anywhere else. My mother having departed, for nine days I made the most of having my Father to myself. "He had an especially great deal of time with him that he'd not have had if I'd been here," my mother explained. Her faith sustained her during the separation: "I am going step by step and am beyond planning," my mother said on her arrival home, but she was already thinking of what she would do when she returned to America, balancing the demands of both sides of the family and tactfully suggesting to her own family that she would not be returning to life with them. They had no comprehension of what she had been through, and very little sympathy. For that she looked to her mother-in-law who understood her life in China as no one else in her family could.

By 1 December word was received from New York. The Foreign Mission Board had changed its mind from "No hurry" to "Strongly advise early withdrawal of mothers and young children." On 7 December we got word that my mother and I were booked on the *President Coolidge* the last day of 1940. "It is the saddest date we have ever had, and we cannot even take it in," my mother wrote. They were fortunate to get a passage, as all steamers across the Pacific were fully booked. My father reflected on the unexpected calm of those final days of 1940 ("the Japanese piped down"), attributing it to the evacuation declaration of 9 October. But it was not to last. Some missionaries with large families were being sent on to the Philippines with Manila regarded as the "safest place in the Far East." They were to pay a heavy price for that irresponsible advice.

Edith Allison had arranged a farewell dinner for all the expatriates remaining on the station. Their home was the only missionary residence within the city walls and thus was a good place from which to catch the train at night and avoid the inconvenience of the curfew. Sixty-five years later I visited the building, the only structure (other than the Hospital) remaining of all the pre-war foreign missionary construction. As we said our good-byes I was tucked into bed briefly and roused after midnight to board the 1:41 am train south. "A horrible time to catch a train" was my father's comment. A procession of lanterns accompanied us to the railway station. I was lodged firmly on my father's shoulders. It is my earliest memory and made an indelible lifelong impression.

So it was that two days before Christmas 1940 we left Tenghsien, left the only "normal" life I would ever know as a child, closed the door on the first and most important stage of my life, lost the stability of a settled existence that would never return, and a natural father-son relationship and started out on an uncertain future. How little any of the three of us knew what lay ahead.

CHAPTER 4:

Evacuees, 1941

It was a Christmas unlike any other before or after. Arriving at the Shanghai railway station that Christmas Eve, Dad hailed a taxi which took us directly to the China Inland Mission (CIM) headquarters on Sinza Road. In spite of the size of the building and the number of rooms available for guests, every space was taken. As we entered, a large Christmas tree loomed in front of us. Gifts were scattered underneath. Children were everywhere, predictably excited by the season but also aware of the adults' preoccupations. They could not grasp why grown-ups were locked in serious conversations but hushed voiced did convey tension and fear. At the end of 1940 no one knew what lay ahead: apprehension about the future charged the air. "Peace on earth, good will to humankind" was an oxymoron: the words seemed almost to mock and jeer us. We went to our room.

Gift giving was announced for "tea-time," the CIM being dominated by Brits. We came downstairs and, with my anxious mother in tow, I joined the crowd of children seated on the floor. I looked around, saw all the stuffed animals by the tree, for later distribution, and marched up to the very front and, much to my parents' embarrassment, snatched a knitted grey bunny with pink ears. Taking it captive I marched back with my trophy to a deeply embarrassed mother. Growing up alone in the interior I had no idea of waiting my turn: the rabbit caught my fancy, I wanted it, and I would grab it no matter the onlookers. My mother, always concerned about appearances, was mortified. The story became the stuff of family legend. I had my comforter: that rabbit was a constant companion for the next years of change and uncertainty. Linus might have his blanket but I had my rabbit - that is until someone trying to be helpful accidently threw it into a washing machine. It immediately shrank and expired, leaving me distraught.

Final family portrait before separation and departure for America, 23 December 1940

That final week in Shanghai was frenetic. With Christmas coming on a Tuesday, there were only three days for shopping and settling accounts. I enjoyed every moment of it: sitting in my father's lap in a rickshaw I called out "Mota ca" as vehicles passed. "Oh my, my, my" I exclaimed, each pronoun spoken a little louder. A check-up at the doctor's showed that I needed immediately to have my ear drums punctured. Three days later, as my father held me down for inspection; the procedure was deemed a success amid cries of "huitch", an expression of pain I had made up. I was obsessed by seeing for the first time in months, children of my age and race, "so different from Tenghsien" was my father's observation. Dad went on in a letter to his mother: "He seemed especially fond of me these past 2 weeks & we wondered if he sensed we were soon to part." A poignant recognition that our relationship was soon to be significantly altered.

At 8 in the evening of New Year's Eve I was wakened. A taxi driver took us to the customs jetty where we caught the 9 o'clock tender. The Bund was ablaze with lights as we steamed down to the *President Coolidge*. Only my mother and I were granted an embarkation ticket but because he was carrying me in his arms my father got on the boat and settled us in our cabin. By good fortune our reservation had been upgraded from third class steerage, to second class. Swarms of children were everywhere. Two hours later my father caught the 11 o'clock tender full of other "papas and husbands." From the boat Dad had one last glimpse of my mother and me. I was easily identified with a fuzzy red top knot. I did not see him, however. "I was so glad we went to the upper deck to wave again, and also glad Donald didn't see you" she wrote the next morning in the first sentence of her first letter to Dad. He got back to Sinza Road just before midnight as the church bells rang in 1941. He had mixed feelings. He wrote that he was not "particularly cheerful about seeing in the new year – thought it was a strange way to be spending the end of 1940, & the beginning of 1941."

We returned to our small stateroom with its two bunk beds, Mother on top and me below. We were awakened at 1:30 by the arrival of the first of our two cabin mates. As she entered Anna Louise Strong turned on all the lights. Two hours later her travelling companion, a Miss Bitmann, settled into the remaining bunk with greater concern for the others in the stateroom. I was coughing and my mother's frequent ministrations from her upper bunk must have been an annoyance. At 4:00 she accidentally crashed into my bunk and remained with me the rest of the night to avoid further interruption. She was unfazed by the two now sharing our stateroom: "I am not going to be too nervous about them. They are decidedly not missionaries." True to her calling, my mother strategized as to how she could bring them to faith: "I am going to be cheerful and thoughtful and not over-concerned about them otherwise."

Anna Louise Strong had recently been in Yenan, the Communist redoubt in the mountains of Shaanxi. She went on to Chungking, wartime capital of "Free" China. She had then flown out to Hong Kong where she met the man handling foreign relations for the Communists. Liao Cheng-chih had told her to delay submitting an article about an explosive interview she had had with Chou En-lai, the Communist number two (after Mao Zedong), both good friends of hers. She then had journeyed on to Shanghai where she embarked on the *President Coolidge* for America. A greater contrast between two women in a cramped Second Class stateroom could hardly be imagined but there were similarities in their heritage and motivation for being in China

Journalist Anna Louise Strong's father was a Midwest Congregational minister. As an adolescent she dedicated her life to service overseas in the name of Jesus. As she explained her motivation: "It seemed to me that I could see the influence of Christ reaching out to all the lands, and that the reign of love had begun." [10] She graduated in 1905 from Oberlin College, the school identified with evangelist Charles Grandison Finney. Twenty years later her social gospel took her to revolutionary Russia and made her an apologist for Joseph Stalin. She subsequently identified and met up with the Chinese Communists, taking a circuitous route to West China. There she interviewed Mao Zedong and Chou En-lai, then holed up in Yenan in the mountains of Shaanxi.

The zeal of Anna Louise Strong typified the ideological alliance between many American Protestant liberals and Communism in the 1920s and 1930s. Mother also saw her mission to save China and specifically, as she wrote home, since God had placed them in the same stateroom, to witness to and hopefully "reconvert" Anna Louise Strong as they crossed the Pacific. Strong's mission, on the other hand, was to convert Americans to Communism, convincing them that whether

---

10   Strong, T.B. and Keyssar, Helene. *Right In Her Soul: The Life of Anna Louise Strong*. New York: Random House, 1983. 24.

Soviet or Chinese it was redemptive, benign and empowered the weak and the disenfranchised. She spoke little Chinese so her journalism was heavily filtered (if not delusional) and very dangerous. She sold Communism to a generation of the gullible.

Her vaunted concern for the disadvantaged did not transfer to sensitivity for a two-and-a-half year old evacuee. Anna Louise Strong stayed up late and then slept until noon. At both times she would turn all the lights on, interrupting my sleep or nap time. She challenged my mother's Christian forbearance. When I got up in the morning I would point to her bunk and say "in a loud mysterious whisper 'Shh! Quiet!'" But I apparently passed muster: Mrs. Strong's travelling companion, Miss Bittman, said as we were about to disembark at San Francisco that, instead of making their life miserable as I very well could have, I was "a model child."

As we said goodbye that morning, our lives took radically different turns. Anna Louise Strong remained a Communist sympathizer and stayed with Mao Zedong throughout all the twists and turns of his career. For her services in old age Chou En-lai provided a rent-free apartment in Beijing, created from the old Italian Legation. There she had a ring-side seat from which to observe the abuses of the Cultural Revolution. No longer welcome in America, and realizing that, should she ever return, her passport would be confiscated, she remained in China until she died in 1970. That same government was responsible for my mother fleeing China in 1949, never to return. Both American women gave their lives idealistically for China but each served a different Master.

At 5:30 on the morning of Thursday 16 January 1941, as my mother and I slept, we sailed under the Golden Gate Bridge. She was disappointed to miss the sight. It was a rush all that day for her, going through quarantine, customs and then buying tickets and checking baggage. Fortunately I missed the "whirlwind" as a Presbyterian ladies group took me away with the other missionary children on board. I was learning some social skills, allowing another child to take away a toy truck without complaint. My immediate preoccupation was the "Choo choo" which I vociferously demanded. My childhood had taken a sudden lurch. I was back in the country of my birth but those initial two and a half years left their mark. A small boy and an anxious mother were setting off on a new adventure together but without a father.

CHAPTER 5:

Fractured Family, 1941

"This room certainly looks large and empty today," my father wrote my mother on his return to the place where he was staying, surveying the realities of his new solitary existence. Poignant reminders of his family's rushed and wrenching departure were everywhere: a stuffed animal, a drawer full of children's socks and the cork for a thermos flask. He seemed lost that New Year's Day. Wandering aimlessly down to the Bund, he met a party of CIM missionaries who were oblivious to the wrenching pain of separation he had just experienced. He stopped at a cinema to see a half hour of British war films. A turkey dinner had been arranged for husbands of evacuees, Presbyterian missionary fathers were now suddenly left on their own. With no better alternative Dad joined them

In their eleven years in China, Shanghai was not a place my parents were familiar with, choosing rather the northern cities of Peiping and Tientsin. For him Shanghai was a city haunted with memories, a place of separations where his parents put him on the boat for boarding school in Chefoo. It was also the location of the final night of his father's life twenty years earlier. He had taken the ferry to Ningbo, transferred to a sampan to reach his station further south, and on board had died a hideous death of cholera before any medical aid could arrive.

For missionaries "the international homeland of *vice*" (as Shanghai became known) was hardly the kind of advertisement they sought as Westerners for their Christian virtues of chastity and restraint. It was there that Wallis Simpson learned, it was rumoured, the art of the so-called "Shanghai squeeze" which so allured Edward VIII and for which he gave up his crown. There was always a tension between those who came to China for Christ or for commerce. "We're not like them," the missionary would say to Chinese who found it hard to make distinctions. Surely all foreign devils were the same: from the opium wars to extortionate indemnity for the Boxer Rebellion to the notorious sign (which Dad claimed was a myth) forbidding entry to the park beyond Shanghai's Garden Bridge to "dogs and Chinese." The business class in the Treaty Ports often set an example of racism, self-indulgence and excess. Mao's description of their Chinese allies as "running dogs of the imperialists" had some resonance. China was a place to get rich quick if you had the right contacts. Even Stornoway Castle on the Isle of Lewis in Scotland was built on the proceeds of the Opium Wars. In their perception all foreigners in China were there out of self-interest and for profit.

One visit before returning to Tenghsien was mandatory: a trip to the post office to mail letters and a parcel. Catching the departure to America of the *President Pierce*, one week after the *President Coolidge*, as duly recorded in the *North China Daily News*, was a priority. For the next eleven months postal schedules dominated his life. The Shanghai General Post Office, he reported, was mobbed with anxious customers despatching precious letters and parcels overseas. The building, erected only two decades earlier, dominated the skyline of Shanghai as, appropriately for its reputation, statues of Eros and Aphrodite gazed down from the clock tower on nearby Soochow Creek and the Garden Bridge. While there, Dad bought U$109 worth of postage so that the entire station could take advantage of more favourable Shanghai dollars. He also asked my mother to save the stamps he had just used. His son, he was determined, would be a philatelist.

His errands completed, my father met up with E. H. Hamilton (known as "Ham"), a Southern Presbyterian missionary in Hsuchow, the last major city before Tenghsien on the main Nanjing-Peiping line. His wife Estelle and their five children were also on board the *President Coolidge*. "Ham" was best known for his poem about the 1933 martyrdom of colleague Jack Vinson. Titled "Afraid of What?", it described the bravery of a China missionary when challenged by a bandit who raised his gun and asked whether the missionary was afraid to die. "Ham"'s account of what might have gone on in Vinson's mind at that moment as he faced death was in the mind of every China missionary at the time. Vinson had demonstrated a confidence in immortality and life beyond the grave that was a powerful testimony to the faith of missionaries who daily confronting death and danger.

But life was not all dark. "Ham" was also known for his keen sense of humour and also being notoriously penny-pinching. The two men, bereft of their families, returned to their stations together. "Ham" proposed that they share a room together in a Chinese inn in Nanking[11]. My parents had spent forty-four Mexican dollars (the currency of the time) for accommodation going south. "Ham" now reduced the overnight accommodation cost travelling north to a single Mexican dollar, much to their mutual delight. The cockroaches were free, my father reported later. There was a camaraderie that developed between men whose wives and families had returned to America, mutually supporting each other in their solitude.

It was 20 minutes after midnight on Thursday January 9 when Dad finally arrived in Tenghsien. At the railway station he was met by his cook and a helper carrying a lantern. They escorted him back to his house through a variety of security barriers: street gates, North Suburb gates, and finally campus gates. The next morning visitors came to welcome him home. My two "sisters," Wei and Ch'en, asked about our embarkation, the size of our cabin, and "they gurgled with delight and

---

11   Now Nanjing. I retain the pre-1949 spelling for historical accuracy as used at that time.

were so pleased to hear everything" my father reported. The campus was deserted: students were still away for the holidays. By now few foreigners remained on the station. Craig Houston Patterson, in China since 1923 and about to leave permanently, was the only foreigner who greeted him. Watson and Julia Hayes had gone to Jinan for dental work. At the house they were staying in, Dr. Hayes had missed a final step while coming downstairs and broke his leg. At 83 he was still unstoppable. He would return to Tenghsien within the month for a lengthy convalescence. He, the oldest, and Dad as the youngest missionary, had remained at their post of duty while others had left or were leaving. But those remaining were not real company for Dad, now pretty much left on his own.

*   *   *

Meanwhile, along with six other China Presbyterian missionary families[12] my mother and I were taking the *Challenger* across the United States, leaving from Oakland, California. The *Challenger* was a 1935 partnership between the Union Pacific and the Chicago and North Western Railway and mission boards were grateful for the savings that resulted from the merger. Pullman sleepers as well as meals cost a dollar a day. The observation cars were the great attraction. Sitting there on my mother's lap, while passing through Salt Lake City, I "wrote" my very first letter to my father. "Aunt Marjorie," it said (in a poor imitation of a childish scrawl) "sent a box of books and toys for me to play with on the trip." On a brief stopover in Chicago, prior to taking another train to the East Coast, my mother made a nostalgic journey out to suburban Wheaton where my parents had first met as college students. It was her first visit since graduation in 1924. We arrived finally in Philadelphia and went immediately to my paternal grandmother's apartment in Germantown. Rather than return to her native Indiana after Cathie and

---

12   Ervine & Gertrude Dungan (Shanghai), Dr Wm & Mary Cochran (Paotingfu, Hebei), Dr. Wallace & Signe Merwin (Paotingfu, Hebei), Wm & Harriet Mills (Nanjing), Harry & Lucy Romig (Shandong).

Mary graduated from Wheaton College, she had chosen to settle near the American headquarters of the CIM where they had more prospects and opportunities.

Picnic, Carpenter's Woods, Germantown, PA Summer 1942

My mother had told me that I was going to see my grandmother. Confused, I thought that I was returning to Tenghsien. As we walked to grandma's apartment I kept exclaiming "Going home? Going home?" Then I turned to my mother and quizzically said "Daddy? Daddy?" But there was no father and I was soon distracted by a ride in the "moto ca". The next morning looking out the window I turned to my grandmother and said "Daddy far far away, gone back home." All this was reported to my father. It would not be long before he would disappear from my consciousness. My Chinese was also rapidly vanishing. Leaning out of a window I was warned of danger and I replied "Donald all gone, *mei yu* [no more]?" It was hard for a two and a half year old to bring all the parts of his complicated life and language together.

We left Philadelphia by train in early February and were met at Pennsylvania Station in Manhattan by my mother's twin, Marjorie, and their sister Priscilla. Throughout their long life "the twins" (as they were known in the family), had a complicated and mutually dependant relationship. Priscilla was a beautiful free spirit whom her sisters felt needed protection and support. One of the things that the three sisters discussed that day was the nomadic existence of their parents who seemed, in their poverty, never to have settled anywhere permanently. For almost the next half century, until his death at 97 Grandfather lived off the generosity of others in the family. Marjorie had married before the change in the family's fortunes and she had married well. Her husband, Carleton Campbell, was a surgeon who at the time, as we have seen, practiced out of a five story brownstone at 886 Park Place in Brooklyn, New York city. A single floor just below ground level was his office and clinic. There was also a pre-Revolutionary War farm in Wilton, Fairfield County, Connecticut, which the family had bought in 1908 and which is now in the midst of some of the more expensive real estate in the United States.

My uncle Carleton's affluence, in marked contrast to the rest of the family, was an unspoken *leit-motif* throughout the years. His mother was a German woman of strong religious commitments, probably "Plymouth Brethren," but aside from a brief incarceration in Leavenworth Penitentiary in 1917 for his youthful pacifist (and possible pro-German) convictions, "The Doctor" as he was always deferentially referred to, was reluctant to affiliate with any church. Many of his patients chose him as their doctor because they felt more comfortable with a physician who shared their values and their faith. It was into these complicated family dynamics that I, as a two-and-a-half year old, was thrust. But it was the silence, the inability to discuss the obvious dysfunctionalities of the family situation, the pretence, which made everything confused in my childish mind. Too often the maternal religion I observed was a religion of denial, a kind of piety that papered over the cracks. It was the cult of niceness that most bothered me as I grew up. Questions were never welcomed. My father's family would have been more realistic, with their robust Calvinism, and wholesome recognition of human brokenness. But they were all in Scotland. It is little wonder that my father, away in China, soon counselled us to move to Philadelphia rather than staying on in Brooklyn and Wilton where we had first lighted down.

My mother and I first settled at 1239 Pacific St. in Brooklyn. It was a ten minute walk from Marjorie and Carleton's home. We had stayed at the Sudan Interior Mission headquarters nearby but this three room basement apartment, at a rental of $12.50 a week, seemed ideal. Marjorie shared some of her domestic help, particularly baby-sitters and house-cleaners. It was a far cry from the home we had enjoyed for the previous two years in Tenghsien, the only house we lived in throughout my entire childhood. Our furniture was either provided or second-hand. But my mother had a talent for domesticity and she soon made it attractive and home-like.

It might be our home but it was home without a husband or a father. Like many other fragmented war-time families, emotions could rise to the surface quickly and unexpectedly. "We moved in here on Friday [14 February 1941] and it was a hard, hard thing to come in here alone without you," she wrote my father. "Even though I was glad and thankful to be at last settling down with Donald for a while, I shed quite a few tears too. I started to tell Marjorie about how nice it was, and suddenly found myself gulping - she was a peach – didn't put her arms around me and get me completely out of control, merely said 'I've got plenty of handkerchiefs' then later when I was a little better off, showed me she was really wasn't hard-hearted." Really?

CHAPTER 6:

Creating Normality in Abnormal Times, 1941

For a seminary professor who was also registrar, January was always a busy month. Marking papers, turning in grades were routine, but registration for the second semester was complicated by the political situation. Students from so-called "Free" China could not always get across into Japanese-occupied China. And there was the difficulty of students who were able to attend classes, paying for tuition with so many different currencies in circulation. A cheque in Peiping currency had to be bartered with someone there for goods purchased. In spite of obstacles Dad reported that "Registration was the most efficient we've ever had" and by 3:00 in the afternoon he and his four helpers could celebrate its completions as they prepared class lists.

Finances and monetary chaos affected other ministries as well. The Tenghsien Leper Home had been operated for many years by the powerful Alma Dodds (not to be confused with our next door neighbours chaplain of the home Albert Dodd and his wife). Alma – who always signed her letters "Dear Love Alma" – was a remarkable, if somewhat eccentric Minnesota farm woman who had been in China since 1910.

Almost on arrival she was involved in humanitarian work among orphans and lepers. In 1939 there were ninety-one men and thirty-eight women in the Tenghsien Leper Home. Located a mile out of the city, there were two houses, one for men and the other for women, and they had provided a refuge for neighbours during the 1938 battle for the city. Then, in spite of fear of the disease, many sought shelter there. Ninety per cent of those in the home were professing Christians. Everyone received regular medical care. Some could be discharged as symptom-free, others remained bedfast. It was a model for Christian outreach and caring.

At 4:30 Tuesday, 4 February, Miss Dodds summoned the missionaries and some local Christian leaders to discuss the future of the Leper Home. Subsidies from the Mission to Lepers in London had dried up, the Home had a debt of U$2000 and little prospect of any more money being received in the future. "Like other dictators," my Father commented drily, "Alma has no use for a Board of Directors in ordinary times but wants everyone to tell her what to do when she's in trouble!" After discussion my father recommended that the institution be "curtailed" (his euphemism). "It will surely be hard to tell the lepers that they are going to be turned out to beg or starve." My father, always the realist, could sometimes come across as rather hard. My soft-hearted mother wrote unrealistically on hearing the news six weeks later: "I wept over the lepers and feel so badly. I hope they may all come back soon." My Father admitted that "It pulls on one's heart strings." Later my father noted: "If we have to evacuate the Japanese will probably, as they have done elsewhere, shoot them all."

The next morning the Seminary President, Chang Hsueh-kang, described at Chapel the response when a delegation of six went out to the Home to tell the lepers the outcome of the discussion. "When they got there the lepers were assembled in a prayer meeting, & after the meeting they told them they would have to turn them out as funds had given out. There was a stillness over the group (about 120 men), then one got up & thanked the Directors in the name of the group for their kindness. They left the Home while some of the lepers were crying and wailing, & others were singing Christian hymns." The lepers were each given enough to go home (if they would be welcome) and also $5. The following day a collection was taken which netted $250 for them, a huge sum for the students and faculty to raise. The war, and its elimination of all Christian mission work in the interest of so-called "Co-prosperity" (as the Japanese called their new order) had taken a heavy toll.

Relentlessly the Japanese advance proceeded and appeared to be gaining momentum. News came from a noon-hour broadcast from Shanghai. The missionaries would huddle around the wireless at Craig Paterson's home after eating lunch together. News also came from reading the *North China Daily News* out of Shanghai which took three days to come in the mail. They first heard and then read about the ominous conversation between Matsuoka, the Japanese Minister of Foreign Affairs visiting Berlin, and Ribbentrop on 27 March. More directly Presbyterian missionaries in Korea were arrested for refusing to allow shrine or emperor worship in their schools. Most of them now in jail were well known to my father so the conflict became very personal. Japanese soldiers now occupied the land immediately west of the seminary compound. "Are they permanent or temporary?" he asked nervously. "What are they here for?" "We are not going to be surprised if before very long Japan and USA. are at war." "It will be a naval war," he predicted. "Meanwhile we thank the Lord for protecting us, & giving us 'peace' locally. We will seek to follow His leading, & do His will." They were living in ominous times.

Morale among missionaries was plummeting. Each person had their own private struggle with anxiety and depression. On 31 March my father reported two suicides in the month of February within the Shandong Presbyterian mission, both by hanging. John Heeren of Qilu University had been struggling for some time with the thought of suicide. One of the most highly educated of the missionaries, with a Ph. D. from Halle-Wittenberg University (following undergraduate work at Grinnell and theology at McCormick Seminary, Chicago), he had written the definitive history of the Shandong mission. His wife left their apartment for a short walk and on returning found the door locked. Fearing the worst she summoned both the police and fellow missionary Courtland

Van Deusen. Breaking down the door, they found him already dead. Father speculated that Heeren's close links with Germany might have pushed him over the edge. At the same time, news about Margaret Speake came from America. She had gone home on furlough in 1938 after seven years identifying closely with her students in the Christian high school where she taught. She had chosen to live in the dormitory with her students in order to identify with them in their struggles and suffering. Now working temporarily with the New York office of the Associated Board for Christian Colleges in China she likewise hanged herself. "She gave of herself and substance without stint" her obituary stated. The cost of missionary service in China amid rampant suffering was very high.

Missionary children were particularly vulnerable. The seventeen year old daughter of a colleague known to my mother from childhood was sent home to America following completion of her high school studies at Chefoo. Escorted by two women, she informed them as the boat left China for America that she was now independent and free and would do whatever she wanted. She connected with a Marine on board. When her family met her at the pier in America she told them she intended to marry him. They cabled her parents. When the news came, her father was out itinerating in the country and couldn't be told immediately. Her life has followed a predictable pattern: three marriages (that first one very short), a single child from them, blighted potential and broken-hearted parents. It was often the children who paid the price for their parents' missionary call. When the news spread, every parent of a China mishkid must have asked: "Could that next be mine?"

*　*　*

My father was making every effort to ensure that it did not happen in our family. Each letter to my mother was accompanied by a message to me. On 18 March he wrote: "Tell Donald that Daddy loves to hear from him." A fortnight later: "Tell Donald I love to hear all about his growing and talking & pleasures with the things he sees. I am very interested to hear about the apartment you have found." My mother's parents were not so understanding: my grandmother found me a wiggly child while we were driving and made frequent unsuccessful attempts to bring me into line. Mother tried to excuse her: "Grandma hasn't impressed him very strongly yet with her good discipline," my mother apologetically told my father in China.

Eleanor Searle Whitney with Cousins Marjorie & Dorothy,
Old Westbury, LI, NY, October 1959

In contrast to our straightened circumstances was my mother's cousin Eleanor, daughter of my great grandfather's half-brother George James Searle, a country doctor in Plymouth, Ohio. Dr Searle and my grandfather were near contemporaries – and the death of his father when he was still young – meant that the two had been raised as brothers. Eleanor, on graduation from college in Florida where she had studied voice, came to New York (one version says) to join the Metropolitan Opera and soon caught the eye of Cornelius Vanderbilt Whitney. His second marriage was crumbling. Eleanor and "Sonny" (as he was known) Whitney were invited to 886 Park Place ostensibly to discuss renting "The Barn" an auxiliary property on the Wilton compound which my grandfather had turned into an award-winning home.

The real reason for their visit was to calm the family's apprehension. For all his wealth twice married Sonny was risky in the marital stakes, damaged goods. Eleanor, strikingly beautiful as she was, at 30 had almost run out of options. It was the catch of a lifetime. My mother, in awe ("they live in a different world"), described to my father a success-ful Sunday dinner on 18 April. Eleanor came with her new beau after singing at a church. Marjorie and Carleton were on their best behaviour as hosts. But my mother was sad: "She has certainly missed out on the spiritual experience she might have had." Sixteen years later, at Madison Square Garden with Billy Graham preaching, Eleanor had that experience. Sonny was suing for a messy headlined divorce to marry for a fourth (and final) time. Eleanor's conversion caused almost as much publicity as his avoiding her lawyers by holing up in Flin Flon, Manitoba to escape a New York state court summons Eleanor had initiated with her lawyers. Instead of playing the role of a castaway wife, she became a major speaker on the women's so-called "celebrity spirituality circuit" of the 1960s and 1970s. She had finally, as the title of her autobiography said, accepted *An Invitation to Joy*.

Aside from my mother's nieces and nephews there was little social contact for me and I was as circumscribed in my circle of playmates as I had ever been in Tenghsien. My childhood would increasingly be a solitary one. My cousin Carleton, two and a half years older, would have been a logical choice as we were both destined to be only children and our mothers were identical twins. But as my mother wrote, "Carleton is not an easy child to manage - he has a peculiar nature – he can be as sweet as an angel, but he seems to enjoy teasing Donald and really hurting him. I try not to let Donald be a 'mamma's boy' and come crying to me all the time." Carleton had a stutter which I started to mimic, thereby drawing more attention to his dysfluency. We two cousins were inevitably compared and my aunt became wistful on those rare occasions. In all their correspondence little was said about their sons. It was unspoken but nevertheless apparent that I was the kind of child Marjorie wished she had had, which helped neither of us as we grew up. Only children have their own unique struggles and in our case they were compounded by our mothers being identical twins.

I was however emotionally unstable and vulnerable. Mother hesitated to tell my father about a revealing incident ("it will make your heart twinge"). One night at bed-time, feverish, I was sobbing. My mother picked me up and held me, sat by my cot, and held me as she sang to me. I got quieter and then suddenly looked at her and said "Want see

Daddy." She hesitated, not knowing how to respond and then I repeated "Want see Daddy" and began to cry in what she said was "a grownup way" as my lips trembled. I seemed a much older child. My mother, fighting back her own tears, tried to speak in a matter-of-fact way. "I was thrilled to think he still realized you met a need in his life," she wrote "and he remembered and wanted you then." And she concluded: "He doesn't forget but he's usually very cheerful & happy about talking of you. I'm so glad."

To help celebrate my third birthday Mother accepted an invitation to her sister's parsonage in Port Jefferson, out on Long Island, the terminus for the Bridgeport Connecticut ferry. She had been asked to speak at the local Presbyterian Church where the father of one of Dad's classmates at Princeton Seminary, Thomas Coyle, was supplying the pulpit. In the evening she spoke at her brother-in-law's Baptist church. The tensions in their home could make visits to Wesley and Priscilla fraught. Mother got into a theological debate with him over a book given his young communicants as they were about to join the church explaining Christian belief that she felt was weak on the atonement. Personally, she stated to her brother-in-law, she had found the word "substitutionary" helpful ("met a spiritual need of every day for me") while Wesley wanted other adjectives to describe what Christ did on the cross. Like other Christians at the time, there were three non-negotiables for Mother: "the book, the blood and the blessed hope."[13]

Our time in Brooklyn was coming to an end. The prospect of moving out of the city for the summer proved very welcome. Sharing rent with my grandparents would reduce the cost of living for both of us. On 30 April my father wrote to my mother about the future: "In a recent letter you raised the question of where to live in the autumn. It **is** a problem. I'm afraid that I can't see much chance of your being here or my being there by then. But by the autumn we ought to be able to see

---

13   The book meant the authority of the Bible as God's inspired Word. The blood represented the blood of Christ on the cross which alone could bring salvation. The blessed hope was Jesus' Second Coming.

the evident drift of world events and the war. It seems to me that by then the outcome of the war (which I have never had any doubt of) & how far off the end of it will be, should be much more obvious than now. And I am thinking of Europe primarily when I mention the war, though it involves every continent. Everyone is bound up with one side or the other. And the future will be more clearly seen in the autumn than now."

How little he, or anyone, knew what was ahead.

Chapter 7:

A Day Living In Infamy, 1941

My parents' twelfth wedding anniversary came on 26 June 1941 and it occasioned on Dad's part an outpouring of love. "I have been thinking a lot about you all day – thinking very loving thoughts about how dear you are, & how very much I am in love with you, & how happy you have made me these past 12 years. Lots of things have happened in those years, and we have travelled far from Holden where we joined hands."

At the time my mother and I were back in New England. In early May 1941 we had joined my grandparents in renting "Pondwood," an idyllic cottage in Ridgefield, Connecticut. My Father described our situation in the New England woods as "enchanting," contrasting it to Shandong's "brown flat earth, sun-baked adobe villages, & absence of flowers & wild vegetation." He added: "That you would exchange that for this I consider to be about the highest possible expression of your love for me & home!" He was delighted that she would have found such a place and hoped that "Donald would develop a love for nature & beauty."

There was little of beauty as summer approached in China. Dad sent on a packet of clippings from the *North China Daily News* because he had heard the American press was playing down the Japanese conquests ostensibly to keep the United States in a state of blissful ignorance. One clipping featured the Japanese capture of Ningbo (where my grandfather was buried) on 20 April. Subsequently Wenchow, further down the Zhejiang coast, was also seized. To my grandmother, this was familiar territory. For over twenty years she and my grandfather Kenneth had planted a church at Ninghai, midway between the two cities. They had also served briefly in Wenchow, now called "Jerusalem of China" for its large number of Christians. They were covering for George and Jessie Seville, parents of Edith Schaeffer[14], during their furlough. The Japanese conquest of Zhejiang province signalled for many that they were now unstoppable.

In Europe there was a major invasion with implications that went all the way to Tenghsien. On 22 June Hitler launched Operation Barbarossa, surprising Stalin by launching a military offensive against the Soviet Union. My father wrote: "The outbreak of the Russian – German war cuts the Far East off from Europe by the short Siberian route. This directly affects merchants, & only indirectly affects us although our Hospital will find it difficult soon to obtain medicines. But we are all waiting to see how Japan's policy will develop in these new circumstances. We are all for a strong U.S. & British foreign policy." Those on the ground saw the looming crisis as few in the United States did and were under no illusion about the ultimate goal of Japan as a member of the Axis powers.

At least there was no interruption in the routine of academic life. His work as a professor and as registrar continued. Exams started on 15 May and continued for a week. Students then "piled out" (his term) to trains heading north and south for a very uncertain future as he "morning noon and night" marked papers and set grades. Four men and four women graduated that year and he made out their diplomas. Their future for ministry in wartime China was difficult and precarious if not

---

14   Edith Schaeffer (1914-2013), wife of Francis with whom she cofounded L'Abri, Swiss Christian retreat centre.

impossible. But nothing would interrupt the rhythm of seminary life and their calling. He set an example of disciplined work as everything seemed to be in transition and flux.

At the same time he was increasingly isolated. All the President Ocean liners had been requisitioned by the American government, thus taking them out of the Shanghai postal run and leaving mail to America totally dependent on Japanese vessels. Bookings to America, previously made, were cancelled. Many were feeling trapped. "I don't see that Americans who stayed on have anything to complain about," he wrote his mother, "they had been warned." He had initially hoped to spend part of July in Shanghai but as more and more foreigners left the station, it was apparent that his presence was urgently required.

Without the pressure of classes, he was also now free to get on with class preparation, focussing on the book of Romans. His summer schedule he told his mother was "almost as regular & unexciting as the clock." Up at 6 or 6:30, the next four hours were focussed on Romans verse by verse – by early July he was into chapter 6. The middle of the morning was spent with the mail, the postman arriving about that time. Usually it was only the newspaper, but he allowed half an hour for this daily exercise. At noon lunch was prepared by his cook, eaten either at his place or shared with other male missionaries also on their own. The news came on at 12:15 and he was the self-described "station news spreader," the first to tell the other missionaries of the German attack on Russia which created great excitement. In the afternoon he cycled or played tennis after an hour's postprandial nap. There was also his hour's typing lesson – he had promised my mother, who had typed his Ph. D. thesis, that he would learn to type and thus relieve her. Evenings he devoted to reading - at the time he was into Williston Walker's definitive 1909 *John Calvin, The Organizer of Reformed Protestantism* which is still on my shelves replete with his neatly pencilled annotations. He lit his lamp at 8:00 and was in bed by 9:00. "I find the days go so swiftly & uneventfully by, that I lose track of the week and have to ask my cook." As his world was crumbling around him the discipline of a set routine kept him sane and at peace.

One day a Japanese guard dropped in unannounced and peppered him with questions for an hour. "Why have you not taken a Chinese wife since yours is now in America?" was one of his questions. My father had been interrupted in writing a letter to my mother, passionately describing how he thought of her every day as he used the shaving lather she had sent from a Brooklyn department store. It was four years and two days since the Marco Polo Bridge Incident that had started the second Sino-Japanese war. The visits continued and on 2 August my father described a scary encounter: "The Japanese *t'uan chang* – head military official in the city – came out this morning, a little man on a great big horse, which he left at the gate. He was taken to Father Hayes. He asked Dr Hayes if we were all going. Father Hayes said we had no such intentions, whereupon the pleasant little man dropped the subject, stayed half an hour, sipped tea, and talked pleasantly about this & that & then left, with his great big sword, 2/3 of his height banging against the calves of both his big leather boots. Father Hayes summoned us half way through his visit, so we escorted him to the gate & bowed profusely."

Later in the afternoon, the President of the Seminary, Chang Hsueh-kang. and a Rev Ting met with the Japanese *t'uan chang* for two hours. He complained about the freezing of Japanese assets by the Americans and then inquired as to what was specifically American mission property. This, he warned, would later be sealed. "He said that America was treating Japan very badly and they intended to treat us the same way! Bur he hasn't told us to leave & we don't intend to until and unless he does but it looks as if the chances are not very bright for opening school in the fall." The Hospital, as American property, would also be affected. Dr. Alexander would not be allowed to use the building. As the only medical facility in the city it seemed very short-sighted and a self-inflicted wound. No property could be turned over to the Chinese church for others to use or maintain. The Nevius Plan that the Shandong churches had been attempting to implement for the past quarter century proved its value and hopefully would help the church and its ministries to avoid the worst consequences of Japanese occupation.

To counter the rumours that all the foreigners had fled the station Dr Alexander suggested that foreign staff should parade through the streets of Tenghsien. As August began my father wrote my mother's aunt Grace that "we live at high tension and no sense of security" and continued "we see the wicked flourish and are daily confronted with sufferings & wrongs which we are powerless to remedy. Only one's Christian faith can give one peace." The Japanese invasion of French Indo-China in September of 1940 had further isolated foreigners making them "prisoners where we are." He set the odds at 95% that the situation would become worse. And he concluded with the dire prognostication that "war with the Allies before next winter looks extremely likely." But he had no plans to flee.

It was not just the Americans that the Japanese were against. A graduate of the seminary, one-eyed Evangelist Pang Chi-lin, was flogged in Hsuchow "to within an inch of his life." Reports of harassment came in from everywhere. In nearby Tsining when Myra Scovel returned from Qingdao the Japanese obligingly vacated their living room where they had taken up occupancy. The Presbyterian Hospital in Ichow was closed briefly by the Japanese. And in Tsinkiangpu the Southern Presbyterians missionaries were herded into the Hospital and kept under confinement by armed guard. Rumours circulated that another missionary was strangled, later disproved but it was hard to sort fact from fiction. In Tenghsien at midnight 12/13 August there was an armed robbery as twenty to thirty men armed with guns and knives invaded the compound, opened the big gates, and stripped four of the servants' housing units of all their possessions. Our cook was left with only a pair of trousers "and looked pretty glum" my father reported as he foraged around for some old clothes to replace those taken. This was the third robbery in eight months. Violence was endemic everywhere and it was hard always to know who the players were. It was thought that the armed robbery at the seminary compound was done with the collusion of the local police.

With permission being granted by their Independent Board in Philadelphia, our next-door neighbours, Albert and Mabel Dodd, were told they could leave whenever they thought appropriate. My father was, as always, defiant: "But we are content to leave before we are interned – except the Hayeses." Watson and Julia Hayes, as we have seen, had come to China in 1882 and had no intention of ever leaving China. Her nephew, Dr. James Young, who had removed my tonsils the previous summer, stopped by and pronounced the elderly couple in good health. At the same time, he gave physicals to all the missionaries on the station and said that my father was in "tip-top shape" except for low blood pressure. At the end of a harrowing summer he reported, weighing in at 158 pounds, he had had "excellent health for months and no summer complaints." But as he wrote his mother, he did have a personal gripe: "I sure get tired of this cook's monotonous diet. Wish I could drop in at my mother's & get some of her good food and cooking!"

On Monday, 22 September 1941, classes began for North China Theological Seminary's final normal year in Tenghsien. Registration, which had taken place over the previous weekend, stood at 132 students, slightly down in number because several students had encountered financial difficulties. At the start of the school year which would be so soon interrupted, he wrote: "It is a joy to be meeting classes again. I love to teach. And I find myself coming out of classes walking on air, feeling good all over. It seems good too after the long 4 months of the summer to have a change of occupation. But I look back at the past months with a good deal of satisfaction for the work that I got done, only interrupted by 2 or 3 days all summer." What my Father could not anticipate was that the countdown to Pearl Harbor had begun.

* * *

Our summer had been uneventful. My third birthday had passed and I was going through the usual childhood growth pattern. Reading between the lines of her letters (unsaid because it was so painful), my father was increasingly far off and absent from my thinking. I transferred my feelings about my own father to mother's father. I wanted to be near him all the time and when he went for the day down to Brooklyn I went into separation anxiety and kept saying "Where's Grandpa?" and finally

"Tell Grandpa stay right here." Unfortunately he was not particularly responsive to my longing for a father replacement and kept his distance. Our time at "Pondwood" went all too quickly.

In early October we completed our move from Connecticut to Philadelphia. Of all the choices we could have made this seemed to both my parents the best. Philadelphia was a Presbyterian city, a centre for the Old School Presbyterians. Its regional body, Philadelphia Presbytery, was the heartland of the evangelical Presbyterianism my Father related to. Its women's missionary society, the Philadelphia Presbyterial, had supported Mother. My father held out the lure of more studies at Eastern Baptist Seminary paid for by an educational grant from the Mission Board. The Seminary had recently moved out to Overbrook from downtown Rittenhouse Square. There she could take courses in Bible and, most importantly, continue her music with their excellent organ and choral program. Proximity (but not too close) to Mother MacLeod in Germantown was a bonus. Father's sister Cathie had graduated from Drexel Library School and was now Librarian at the Episcopal Theological Seminary in West Philadelphia at West 42nd and Chestnut streets. Mother and she agreed to share the expenses of a modest two bedroom apartment in a house at 507 West 42nd Street.

One emotional evening in mid-November there was a rare and unusual moment of self-disclosure. Cathie, usually a very private person, shared her highly conflicted feelings about growing up as a China mishkid. With floods of tears she gave full vent to her feelings as she spoke to Mother. When my grandparents had gone on furlough in April 1919 they had left the two younger girls, aged 8 and 14, in boarding school at Chefoo while they were on furlough in America and Scotland. They reunited in Shanghai in the summer of 1921 but shortly after their return to school that autumn my grandfather suddenly died of cholera on the boat as he returned to his station. My grandmother stayed on with her two younger children until the mass missionary exodus of 1927. The three returned to Canada, but being British in their citizenship, they only got into the United States after a long delay. Eventually both sisters, as their older siblings had, graduated from Wheaton College. Their studies were financed by their mother who ran a boarding house for Wheaton students. The sisters were the housekeeping staff. Graduating in the Depression with an arts degree from a small Midwestern Christian college gave them few employment options. Cathie sank into depression, her weight ballooned and she felt, rightly or wrongly, that her mother favoured her younger sister. It was only in 1936, when he returned to America and saw the situation, that my father suggested Library School at the Drexel Institute and loaned tuition money so she could attend.

While working at the Protestant Episcopal Library, Cathie met Paul Hart Ruby, the brother-in law of one of the students there. He was a salesman who was subsequently transferred to Des Moines, Iowa. At the age of 35 she fell in love. Evangelical Christianity was new to Paul Ruby and the romance met with stony disapproval from my grandmother. Surprisingly, my mother favoured and encouraged the relationship. Cathie and Paul eloped to Chillicothe Missouri. Four days later, she wrote my mother all about it, concluding "Well Dorothy, this is a long letter but there was so much to tell – still is! Will you give Donald a big hug from his Aunt Cathie and ask him to kiss you from me! Thank you for so much Dorothy." The bride and groom set up house in Des Moines where Paul worked as a salesman for Burry Biscuit Co. They had an idyllic marriage but in spite of his professing faith and being baptized by the well-known and beloved Rev. Will Orr[15] in the Westminster Presbyterian Church in Des Moines, under the pressure of Sunday sales conferences their links with organized religion became tenuous until cancer struck her down fifteen years later. Because she had suffered so much as a misunderstood missionary child, she had a compassion that resonated with me. Her accepting love was totally non-judgmental.

It was fortunate that Cathie had been with my mother when the blow came that Monday 8 December 1941. The announcement of Pearl Harbor crackled over our new Philon radio as we listened breathlessly.

---

15   Will W. Orr (1904-1994) of Charlotte NC. Graduate Erskine College, Pitt-Xenia Seminary. Ordained UPCNA 1931. Westminster, Des Moines 1939-1949; President Westminster College, New Wilmington, PA 1949-67.

We were told by the President in a never to be forgotten speech that it was "a day that would live forever in infamy." My mother had had four speaking engagements the week before but on that Wednesday, when her husband turned forty, she made time to reflect: "Today is Alec's birthday and I have been thinking much of him. I have been forced to put other things aside and pray for him and keep on praying with fasting. I feel a real burden for him – and have not reached the assurance I want - but of his safety I am assured. I have such confidence in the efficacy of your prayers and want to especially ask you to pray for him." A week later, after the news had sunk in, she wrote "I have been grateful to God for the way He has helped and strengthened and given me peace. I have shed many tears but they have been the right kind. The whole situation is so terrible and yet we can praise Him constantly."

My father was teaching I Peter that Monday morning when an armed Japanese soldier, one of fifty that descended on the compound seemingly from nowhere, entered his classroom while others gathered the rest. Proceeding to the podium where Dad was standing, my father was ordered to leave his classroom. All the missionaries on the compound were then summoned to Watson and Julia Hayes' home where they were informed officially that Japan was at war with America. Within two or three days all the student body had departed. The following Sunday, when Dad was ushered out of a packed church in the North Suburb by another armed guard and told to stay in his house, he knew that a long period of confinement was beginning. He was a prisoner of the Japanese "for the duration."

"If I could tell you how much I think of you and about you and how I pray and how much I love you, I would. You must know and I won't fail you in all I can do here in prayer and thought and love, my very Dearest Dear." The quote comes from the first letter my mother wrote after Pearl Harbor, dated 10 December. Six months later, after being approved by Censor 1657, it was sent back "Return to sender service suspended." Like millions around the world our lives and our future had been irretrievably altered that Sunday morning as the Japanese air force circled over Hawaii and left its cargo of death and destruction.

CHAPTER 8:

Christmas 1941

For Americans, Christmas 1941 was a sobering time for reflection. Two weeks into a world war the reality of global conflict was beginning to sink in. The Japanese strategy carefully crafted years ahead, was becoming apparent in places within the wide reach of the land of the rising sun: Midway, the Philippines, and Hong Kong. The tentacles of Nippon seemed inescapable and the cruelty and rage that my parents had experienced in their small city in North China were now apparent to all. Americans were learning that the "business as usual" policy their government had pursued recklessly for the past decade was a costly error, exposing the naiveté of isolationist politics.

Three days before Christmas Mother and I set out from Philadelphia for Long Island in her newly purchased 1936 Ford. I have a vivid memory of turning off into Fairmount Park on our way north as we crossed the bridge over the Schuylkill River. For this three year old there was a strange sense of utter abandonment and foreboding. My mother and I were now on our own. But there was always, it appeared, family to provide support and solace. Her big hearted sister Priscilla's invitation to spend the holidays with her could not have been more opportune. The Baptist parsonage in Port Jefferson provided a refuge and in the midst of limited means it was warm and welcoming. We arrived on Monday 22 December and the next two days were spent in frantic pre-Christmas activity. "It wasn't easy to enter in fully to the children's fun, but they were very sweet", my mother opined later in a letter to my father he never received. My three cousins - Duncan, aged 10, Fay aged 8, and Bruce, aged six - burst into a spontaneous "Happy birthday to Jesus". Their devotion consisted of earnest prayers that none of the celebrants focus solely on gifts.

The children were all marched off to bed but the grownups continued until 2 in the morning preparing for the holiday. We woke to open gifts - mine was a building set from my father, a set of blocks with pegs that could be assembled into buildings or houses or boats. "Donald is very good at imitating the pictures shown for examples, and building and really shows constructive skill" my mother reported. The most significant gift that Christmas was my uncle's recently published *Fair Are the Meadows*, a sequel to his 1930 blockbuster novel *Silver Trumpet* which had defined a whole generation of fundamentalist young adults and sent many of them off to Wheaton ("Wharton") College as a major recruiting tool. The first edition of *Fair Are the Meadows* had quickly sold out to eager fans patiently waiting a decade for a sequel to *Silver Trumpet*. A second printing had made possible several corrections. His writing this time showed "advanced thinking" with a risqué reference to "making love" appearing on page 137. My uncle Wesley had a way with words and his gift of a second revised edition, dated Christmas 1941, was inscribed "To Dorothy and Alec whose faith and courage in these fateful years will remain a constant inspiration. Affectionately Wesley and Priscilla."

The first giving gift giving over, all seven of us set off in two cars for 886 Park Place, Brooklyn. There a large group was assembling: three sisters and their families, their parents, and three other distinguished members of the wider family circle. Rev. James Ingles, Wesley's father, was for thirty-five years prison chaplain in Sing Sing, the notorious prison on the Hudson River. Dr Ella Alexander Boole, Ph. D., was, with her unmarried daughter Florence, a feature of Campbell family gatherings. At the time she was 82, and still had three more years to go as the head of the Women's Christian Temperance Union (WCTU). Associated with Frances Willard (with whom she cofounded the WCTU in 1879), she was an early leader in the women's movement. Today feminists have difficulty with the so-called "temperance" of those early women pioneers but still accept them as sisters. Dr Boole, as she was always known in the family, was a woman of steel who had placed third in the Senate race in New York in 1920. Five years later she became national WCTU president, and in 1931 International President, an office she held for 16 years retiring in 1947. She died in 1952 at the age of 92. She was a formidable woman who had a distinct aura about her. I kept my distance from Dr. Boole.

We children sat a table in the living room but, my mother reported, "Behaved beautifully." As a single parent she lacked confidence and seemed anxious about her child rearing skills. The exchange of gifts was followed by 78 rpm records played on Marjorie's new radio gramophone. There was a musicale presented by the grandchildren. The highlight was cousin Duncan's solo sung behind a curtain and accompanied by his mother on the piano. His clear pre-pubescent boy's soprano voice brought tears to my mother's eyes. The whole event, with three generations present and staff to do the work, celebrating the holiday in a five- story Brooklyn brownstone, with a tree piled high with gifts, was in marked contrast to our and the Ingles' very straightened circumstances.

My father never described his Christmas 1941 experience. Totally cut off from the outside world (other than occupied China) foreigners on the compound must have had a solitary celebration. They were prohibited from mingling with Chinese Christians so there could be no joyous celebration of the birth of Jesus. They would have gathered, as they often did, for meals and singing and worship. Two days after Christmas my mother and I headed back to our apartment in Philadelphia.

CHAPTER 9:

Father under House Arrest, 1941-2

The day after Pearl Harbor the Japanese gathered all foreigners and introduce them to the new order. They were now part of Japan's Greater East Asia Co-Prosperity Sphere. Western white, imperialism was forever gone. A new order was being established and they should be proud to be a part of it. "All was done in a dignified, serious, and courteous manner by the highest officer here."It took seven weeks after Pearl Harbor before that first report trickled out from Tenghsien. Martin Hopkins[16] managed to get a letter to his wife, Bessie, in America. It was then copied and passed around to families and supporters eager for any news. It was apparently sent through a contact in West China (the mails within the country still being operational) and forwarded out of China "over the Hump" through India to the United States. The first letter Mother received was dated four months after Pearl Harbor and

---

16   Martin Armstrong Hopkins (1889-1964) (PCUS China, 1917-1951). His aunt,
      Mrs J. J. Kelso, left a collection of family correspondence in the Archives of the
      United Church of Canada (CA ON00340 F 3135). See his "A Fourth of a Century
      in China" (1942) published by First Presbyterian Church, Knoxville, TN.

was hand delivered on the pier in New York by one of the fortunate missionaries who was among the first to be repatriated.

Martin Hopkins reported that all gates in the seminary compound had been barred except the front one which was heavily guarded. He had moved in with my Dad. Those outside the campus retreated to the seminary grounds: Alma Dodds abandoned the now empty Leper Colony and the Allisons vacated their home in the North Suburb. Today, alone (other than the Hospital and Church) of all the thirty-five buildings erected by the foreigners in the city now known as Tengzhou, their residence still stands as a ghostly (and run-down) reminder of what used to be.

Edith and Roy Allison's Tengzhou home in 2006, the last place I stayed before boarding the night train to Shanghai 21 December 1940.

Martin Hopkins, a genial southerner, had joined my father, occupying my bedroom. And until food ran out in March, our home became a communal dining hall with our cook catering for the whole compound a meal a day. Fortunately the seminary had cash which eventually could be replenished in small amounts from the Hong Kong and Shanghai Bank in Qingdao, now "consolidated" with the Yokohama Bank. My father's salary stopped being paid directly the end of 1941 and my mother allowed it to accumulate in a New York bank throughout the war unspent. A half century later it formed the basis of his estate.

"We get no news only rumours, mild and wild, and all kinds," my father wrote. The noon broadcast from Shanghai, and the relay from California which had brought the compound daily to our house had been silenced. There was no news as the Japanese juggernaut swept over East Asia and across the Pacific. Instead, the nine gathered in the home the Allison's now occupied each afternoon at 5:00 for communal prayer and worship. And my father maintained his own personal devotional life: "You may be sure," he wrote mother, "that I constantly pray for you that you may have every needed grace and physical strength and that the Holy Spirit of God may bless you mightily in your spirit, that God will raise up friends who will be good to you, and that you may have the peace that passes all understanding." And he added: "Don't be concerned about me, The Lord will watch over us while we are separated, and bring us together again in His own time. I daily pray for Alistair Donald and your training of him."

He maintained a rigorous schedule with no interruption in the routines of his life. In the morning he continued his exegetical study of Romans, reaching the last chapter (16) and the last verse (27) at the end of January. He then went on to read his Chinese Bible, starting at Genesis and getting as far as the end of II Samuel. His disappointment was that, cut off from the Chinese, he did not have a language teacher to guide him through the more difficult parts. His routine was interrupted in April when he was told to get ready to leave. From then on he lived out of a suitcase. In the afternoon and evening, aside from games of chess with Dr Dodd, he would read, reviewing each book in a notebook with meticulous notes. From the end of January to the day in June when he wrote, he had gone through thirty-two tomes, each of which he listed for my mother.

Martin Hopkins was the first to leave. He was followed on 10 June by the others who were escorted to Shanghai by armed guards. My father was not among them. Being the sole British subject on the compound he did not qualify for an American evacuation. So it was that my father, five days after the last of the evacuated missionaries left, sent the following message to Albert Dodd in Shanghai, awaiting deportation to America:

"Tuesday I had the gate by Oscar's house pulled out and the place walled up. This may or may not save some of the trees and shrubs in these grounds from being cut up and destroyed while the owners are away. Sunday especially this place swarmed with boys with sickles. It also makes it harder for 'others' to get in and out. All have now to go through Hayes' yard as the old gentleman sits in his window looking out - makes things safer.

Wednesday graduation ceremonies, and thereafter students began leaving by all trains. So summer holiday quiet is settling down over the place - except in this one respect. This is Friday morning; visitors are spending the morning out here stripped to the waist, working like Trojans. By now all your furniture is out in your yard and there is dulcet music from the piano. Carry carts will I think if no rain comes out this afternoon, transfer it all. They have already made many trips with sacks of smaller movable things. Soon we will have it all empty for you.

Then they passed my house – I in there as still as a mouse and are now in the north house. Already tables etc. may be seen in the yard. It is rather awkward that my moon gate is locked and one has to go around. But they've learned the way.

No forced sales in Tenghsien - - free taking. Hayeses staying tight in their house and I in mine, expecting to be visited any moment. We feel so happy in our hearts and buoyantly expectant you know. It has been so quiet here for several days."

Since the Japanese had taken over an American golf course in Shanghai as their collection base for enemy citizens about to be expelled from China, Dad concluded with a note of humour: "I hope you are having a not-too- hot week of fragrant golfing at the Country Club and then the wonderful sea breezes! Boy isn't life worth living! Bon voyage to a world free of worry and care about things left behind and people."

My father was not altogether honest about his fears. He had been in touch with the Japanese consul in Jinan pleading not to be abandoned in Tenghsien as the sole remaining foreigner. Other, that is, than Watson and Julia Hayes who had refused to budge. At the age of 84 he sat by his study window and watched the looters come and destroy the institution that he had worked so hard to create, "the child of his old age" as he described the formation of North China Theological Seminary in 1919. Now it was being destroyed. His carefully selected foreign faculty departed, his compound looted, his graduates scattered. And his vision seemingly blindsided.

CHAPTER 10:

Stenographer's Error? 1942-3

Philadelphia's Eastern Baptist Theological Seminary, where my mother had enrolled, was (like North China Theological Seminary) a product of the split between modernists and fundamentalists in the 1920s. The "Northern" Baptist Convention (ABC) had been roiled in controversy and its theological seminaries, particularly Colgate Divinity School in Rochester but also Crozer outside Philadelphia (which joined Colgate in 1970 and whose most famous graduate was Martin Luther King), had been stigmatized as "liberal." In 1940 Eastern Baptist seminary moved from its location on Rittenhouse Square in downtown Philadelphia out to the suburb of Overbrook, acquiring property at the northwest corner of Lancaster Avenue and City Line. It was an easy commute for Mother and the Presbyterian Church Foreign Missions Board paid her tuition, particularly since she was upgrading her qualifications in musical instruction for the seminary. A Miss Snyder was her piano composition teacher as she sought to develop skills in preparing a Chinese hymnbook with indigenous rather than imported musicology.

Meanwhile my academic qualifications were being honed three days a week at Nursery School. Mrs. Shaw, married to a professor at the University of Pennsylvania, was my first teacher and I loved her. The report after my first days at Nursery School in November of 1941 was promising. Mrs. Shaw had said to my mother that I "showed great cooperation." And then the inevitable response of an anxious single parent "I was pleased." Appearances mattered a great deal then and my mother was no exception. One thing that Mrs. Shaw flagged was increasingly apparent that "he has a very quick temper," as she reported to my father. Redheads are supposed to have a quick trigger but was there something going on here, was I internalizing all the changes, frustrations, and disappointment of my life? Was my mother using denial as a coping mechanism? Was conflict being internalized?

Our apartment at 507 South 42nd Street was close to Woodland Presbyterian Church, at the corner of Pine and 42nd. The minister there was a returned missionary from the Ottoman Empire. J. Ramsay Swain was an institution in the community and in the Presbytery, an Old School Presbyterian minister. My mother started our long link with Woodland Church by teaching a class in the Sunday School. "I love the Junior boys, and am so glad that I didn't turn that opportunity down" she reported to her sister. One was a Mormon, another a Jew, and there was a know-it-all who tested her patience. Several in the class came to a personal faith through her prayers. That faith was a preparation for what awaited them ahead as conscripts in the armed services. There was a general seriousness as the nation got caught up in conflict overseas. Subsequently Mother was interviewed for a position as church visitor and secretary to Dr Swain, a job she found rewarding until arrangements for my care did not work out. She also had the use of the church's organ for practice. Many friends from the congregation enriched our lives. One, Gertrude Quick, became my mother's regular prayer partner. Dr Swain served for forty years, retiring in 1944. I remember him vividly for his annual "The Lord is my Shepherd" demonstration, wearing the turban and staff of a Bedouin shepherd.

From March on, our lives were dominated by lists. Was my father on the list to be repatriated or had his name been left off we would ask, overwhelmed by the uncertainties. An exchange had been arranged between the combatants, exchanging Japanese diplomatic and consular staff for prisoners of war caught behind enemy lines when hostilities broke out. The American government rented a liner from a Swedish American cruise company. With its yellow and blue colours, its search lights left on day and night and huge signs on both sides "Diplomat Sverige Gripsholm" it was able to avoid unfriendly U-boat attacks successfully but there was always danger. The exchange actually took place off Lourenço Marques in the Portuguese colony of Mozambique, Portugal being a non-combatant and presumably neutral.

Woodland Presbyterian Church, 42ⁿᵈ and Pine Streets, Philadelphia

The first inking my mother had that Dad might be coming home was three months after Pearl Harbor, though that first intimation suggested only those over sixty would be included. On 20 May 1942 a bulletin from Lloyd Stanton Ruland[17], Foreign Missions Board secretary, went to the families of those missionaries caught behind enemy lines. "The Department of State," it began, "has made public announcement of the chartering of the Swedish motor ship 'Gripsholm' for purposes of repatriation." It continued "We are informed that probably no definite lists of persons included in the first civilian exchange will be available until the ship arrives at an American port, but if we are able to secure such information earlier it will be send out promptly in a bulletin."

It would have been best if they had kept to that decision as rumours and half-information took a heavy toll on our family. After one such disappointment, at the end of May, I turned to my distraught mother and said "Perhaps God has something for Daddy to do in China." Then on 23 June, at about midnight, my mother received two calls in our apartment in Philadelphia "telling me that Alec is on the Italian repatriation boat which has left China, and the ship that meets it is expected in New York around the 20th of August. Of course, I was simply speechless." Then the next morning a letter came with the names of all on board listed and though every other American Tenghsien missionary (excepting Dr and Mrs. Hayes) were included, my Father's name was not there. Dad, being British through his father's nationality, was in a different category for repatriation.

Still she continued to hope. At the end of June she wrote my father (letters only being penned when there was some hope of delivery) "I am looking forward to seeing you, my dear. And know that the Lord is able to bring you safely and uneventfully to us – and if that is His will, and somehow, I feel that it is! We shall have a 'glorious' and happy reunion. Donald and I both will be waiting eagerly for the definite news, and I do hope it will be possible to send a cablegram or radio message from there,

---

17   Lloyd Stanton Ruland (1889-1953) Graduate Westminster College, 1912 (DD 1932), McCormick Seminary, 1916. Decade with PC(USA) in Shandong. Returned to US in 1926 and pastored West PC(USA) Binghamton, NY until 1938 when he was appointed Board Secretary for China, leading a delegation there in 1946. "There were many and heady decisions to be made, involving inescapable responsibilities." (Rev. Wm. P. Schall)

or at least before you reach home. However, we will be patient." But that glorious and happy reunion seemed elusive: appearing, disappearing, and then reappearing.

Uncertainty was taking a toll on my mother, though she was not eager to admit it. Five days after that midnight call she told her sister "I seem to have developed some difficulty with my heart and have had one or two rather nasty little times. The electrocardiogram shows damaged heart muscles but evidently not serious enough so that I can get on top of it with some reasonable care." Throughout the rest of her long life to her death at the age of 93 this "condition" seemed to come on her at times of great stress but with little ultimate physical effect other than making her family less sympathetic than we might otherwise have been.

Arrangements had been made for us to spend the summer in New England. In July we would be in the Berkshires in western Massachusetts and in August in Maine. "Mountain Rest" in Lithia, Massachusetts, where we spent the first month, was one of several turn-of-the-century retreat homes established and endowed by wealthy turn-of-the-century missionary philanthropists. It was an idyllic nature centre. In August we were booked to go to Alna Maine where there was a cottage owned by Grandpa and occupied by his sister Grace Raddin. At the end of our time there I suggested taking the house in a box back to Philadelphia "but not the woodshed or the bathroom." My mother felt sufficiently rested that she intended to meet the *Gripsholm* on arrival in Newark, scheduled for 23 August. Knowing it would be an emotional time for her seeing other families reunited on the pier, Priscilla characteristically agreed to accompany her. Even as late as 10 August she was still hoping: "If I know by that time that Alec is not there, I shall simply go to Philadelphia and when it is in, plan to go to New York for a day of the Conference, to meet the other missionaries and get my news and letters."

Those other missionaries included several who had been evacuated from Tenghsien on June 10. They brought a long and much read and reread letter from Dad for her and another shorter one for his mother both written the day the boat left. There had been some uncertainty as to whether any uncensored letters would be allowed through enemy lines. They were glad finally to join the 600 repatriates on board the Portuguese vessel *Conte Verde* as it set out across the Indian Ocean for Mozambique. But their humiliation was not over. On the pier, as they were about to embark, Japanese officials rifled their luggage, holding up personal possessions for all to see and taking delight in destroying what they quixotically regarded as incriminating: photograph albums, notebooks, diplomas, artwork and particularly Bibles with their family data, shredding them before their eyes as possessions of a lifetime were treated with contempt. However, my father's two long letters, to his mother and his wife dated 7 June from Tenghsien, were safely delivered intact and uncensored and were a rare treat. Though circumspect about what he said about the occupiers, named as "J—s", he was able to speak freely about his own life and circumstances. Letters within China did get through, albeit unpredictably. The postal system there, in both "occupied" and "free" China, appears to have been operational and he was in regular communication with his sister Annabella in "free" China as well as a daughter of Albert Dodd. The infrequent use he made of this means of contact is surprising, though any communication was under considerable restraint and was slow, infrequent and unpredictable.

The fortunate evacuees joined the *Gripsholm* and the transfer was made, successfully choreographed by the Red Cross. It was not until the boat docked in Brazil that word could be cabled to America as to who was on board. Though their careers had been abruptly ended, and they had been thrown out of the country for which they had given their lives often at great personal sacrifice, the missionaries were surprisingly ebullient. My mother was on the pier, bravely greeting many friends in the close bonds of the missionary community. She was presented with her two precious letters and a photo taken on 11 April in Tenghsien by Dr Alexander of the nine who had remained. Her reaction was memorable: she immediately burst into tears as she saw her now bearded husband. When this was reported later I was unsure if her reaction was to the enhanced masculinity of her partner or simply that she became suddenly aware of how many changes had taken place during their war-time separation and would affect their relationship.

Many missionaries having returned, an assessment and strategy conference was now held at the Board headquarters, 156 Fifth Avenue. It
included all the Presbyterian Church USA, mission fields in "war areas":
Japan, Chosen (Korea), Thailand, Philippines, Hainan, Hong Kong and
a seventh category, "other China Missions" brought by Harry Romig of
Qingdao, Shantung Mission administrator. Romig was well known to
the Tenghsien contingent because of his years living there. Other fields
were also covered in the evening: Africa, the Near East, India and Latin
America. The PC (USA) was probably one of the largest, wealthiest, and
most comprehensive Protestant missionary enterprise in the world at the
time and the political situation worldwide meant that it was in crisis. A
second day, of less interest to my mother focussed on "The Church That
Awaits You" with Paul Covey Johnston. "The Women's Viewpoint" was
provided by Mrs. Rex Clements. The meetings represented an attempt
to reintegrate returning missionaries into the denomination, many of
whom had been warned about a perception of theological and strategic
drift in the organization amid worldwide political turmoil. After over
forty years as Board secretary the legendary Robert E. Speer was no
longer at the helm. It had lost both traction and momentum.

Johnston, chairman of the Mission Board, was a well-known
denominationalist with several prestigious pulpits in his resume. Mrs.
Clements was the wife of the minister of Bryn Mawr Presbyterian
Church on the Main Line in Philadelphia. Both Johnston and Mrs.
Clements represented the big wealthy establishment with which the
Tenghsien contingent would not have felt at home. Ever since Pearl
Buck's notorious 1933 Astor Hotel Manhattan speech to Presbyterian
women, denouncing China missionaries (other than medical and educational) and the perceived weak response to it and to the Layman's Report
on Foreign Missions by Robert Speer, most evangelical missionaries in
the Presbyterian Church (USA) felt increasingly marginalized and some
even alienated. I grew up with the idea that the people who employed
my father were unreliable and unfaithful, choked by institutional
loyalties and an uncertain theology. The ultimate criticism was that a

missionary was "board-y," signifying an uncritical acceptance of edicts from New York.

Evangelical missionaries were now forming their own alliances and coalitions in self-defence. On 29 December 1942 the Tenghsien missionaries and their American supporters organized a so-called "Home Council" for the North China Theological Seminary "to ensure the continuation of the work that has proved so valuable and to provide for a full resumption of activities at the earliest possible moment." My mother became secretary of the Council which frequently met in our apartment in west Philadelphia, being closer to rail transport than the Berwyn mansion on the Main Line of the chair, Horace G. Hill, secretary-treasurer of the Atlantic Refining Company. Hill gave time and expertise over the next two decades to the organization and was a major donor and fundraiser. The money thus raised meant that our ministry could thrive without being accountable to an unsympathetic Foreign Missions Board and formed a significant counterweight to its power.

That conflict between "liberal" and "fundamentalist" caused me no end of confusion. As a very small child, I decided that a liberal missionary could be detected if "she" wore open toed sandals and "her" toe nails were painted red. But on a more serious level the fact that my father's employer was suspect and even fellow members of the same sending organization needed to be treated with caution, if not suspicion, was a continuing reality in my growing-up years. The fundamentalist-modernist controversy was being played out in our own circles. In both Shanghai, and later in Hong Kong, our family identified with fundamentalist English-speaking spin-off congregations much to the puzzlement of our more traditionalist colleagues. I was raised to be, in Bunyan's words, a pilgrim who was "Valiant for Truth." Growing up fundamentalist was a heavy burden to place on a child and very isolating.

CHAPTER 11:
Reality Sinks In, 1942-1943

"I left Tenghsien on August 8ᵗʰ [1942]"my father wrote my mother almost a year later, the first full description of his whereabouts she had received. To avoid a censor destroying his letter he continued cryptically and elusively: "The circumstances of my leaving were not happy, but they are now far in the past." He never provided details. He left behind Watson and Julia Hayes, the last foreigners remaining on the station. In March the following year these two octogenarians were forced out of their home and sent to Weihsien concentration camp where Dr. Hayes died a year later. Before Dad's departure, to avoid the same looting of surrounding homes that he had watched helplessly, he built seven concealed places in the house to hide our belongings. In behind closets and our WC, hidden walls were constructed by our carpenter to protect and preserve our possessions from vandalism in the anticipation that we would be returning after the war was over. There was always a touch of innocence about him and presumably the moment he left, the carpenter disclosed exactly where he had built the false walls and our possessions quickly disappeared. Then in 1946 the house, along with all the others in the compound, became a battleground between the KMT and the Communists and wholesale destruction ensued.

The train that he boarded, filled with expats, preceded to Jinan where it joined an even larger train coming down from Peking and Tientsin. It was filled with "compatriots" who were promised immediate evacuation. As it turned out, only seven of the seventy-seven actually sailed. Four days later they arrived in Shanghai early in the morning and were sleepily escorted to the Columbia Country Club out on the Great Western Road. There, amidst the luxurious pre-war trappings of Shanghai's American elite in a 1931 Spanish Revival building standing on five acres with sports facilities and a swimming pool, they settled in. Crammed into every available corner, they bedded down behind the bar, on the dance floor, along the bowling alley, and in the lounges. "For the great majority of us," my father wrote, "the promise of repatriation was not fulfilled, hopes died a lingering death for two months and when the mourning was over we settled down for the winter." Powerless, there was a savage irony in being housed amid such ostentatious wealth accumulated by a business community who earlier had seemed oblivious to the suffering all around them.

"Father MacLeod is a trump – no complaining although he is probably here for the duration. He does more reading than most of us and has been in a long continued chess tournament and generally keeps cheerful but his cheerfulness takes on a special aspect when he has heard of his wife from A. B. Dodd." That report by Margaret Frame, Secretary for Women's Work and a Board loyalist, gladdened my mother's heart when she received it in late October. But the thought of waiting "for the duration" obviously upset her. "It has been a new thought, preparing for the duration absence, and I am not clear as to what to do or whether to go or to stay here in Philadelphia but I am finding it is possible to live one day at a time, and being reassured as to his state both of mind and body, and feeling increasingly that opportunities are surely opening up to him there for service for the Lord, makes the whole thing more obviously a 'blessing in disguise', though often the disguise seems very evident."

For seven months my father was free to make a life for himself in Shanghai in a kind of time warp bubble. He preached occasionally in city churches, frequently visited friends in the China Inland Mission home on Sinza Road, kept regular appointments with a Swiss lady, a Mrs. Bober, who became his German tutor, and had the freedom of a fascinating and cosmopolitan city, but always under the eagle eye of the enemy occupier. Had he the money, many valuable antiques and other chinoiserie objects could be purchased at rock bottom prices, sold by stranded refugees and other locals eager for immediate cash and prepared to sacrifice family heirlooms for a song.

That relaxed period came to an abrupt end at 9 o'clock in the morning of 12 March 1943 when he was summoned to register at Church House on Kiangsu Rd.: "By military necessity you and your family are hereby ordered to live in the Civil Assembly Centre. Necessary preparations shall accordingly be made by you as follows" and two sheets of instructions itemized what could and could not be brought with each prisoner: "in small portable suitcases." The list included "items of daily use," "beddings and clothings," [sic] "tablewares," and "goods for sport and amusement." Jewellery and other valuable were to be left with "the Protective Power" and keys to any real estate should be turned over to the Japanese consul.

The night before his final departure from the Columbia Country Club, 17 April 1943, he wrote his sister Annabella in "Free" China: "This is my last day here before my translation. Baggage went this morning, I'm off to the Pootung camp tomorrow morning early – exactly 7 months since I came down here from Tenghsien, So a new experience in life. I'll be thrown in with thirteen hundred and we'll have to cook, do washing, barbering, etc. etc. all for ourselves. And mending clothes & darning socks. I'll have to learn – have bought the necessary materials. I was around the C. I. M. today saying 'good-bye,' Many have already been removed, almost everyone else now instructed to disappear next Wednesday, Hope it won't be for too long." Cheery, upbeat, but unrealistic and naive, my father was crossing a threshold in his life.

The so-called "Civil Assembly Center" to which he was to go the next morning was the warehouse ("godown") of the British American Tobacco Company in Pootung, across the Whangpoo (Huangpu) River. The company dated from the turn of the twentieth century, and with the business acumen of a man from North Carolina familiar with tobacco marketing, by the time war broke out and the company was seized by the Japanese, it was selling 55 billion cigarettes in China. Today China has the largest number of smokers in the world – 53% of all adult Chinese males - and it is a national health catastrophe, a lasting impact of the West on China. It was there that 900 non-compliers with the Greater East Asia Co-Prosperity Sphere, as the Japanese called their new anti-imperialist order, were to be incarcerated. Again, as with the Columbia Country Club, there was a savage irony in the choice of venue. The warehouse had been abandoned in 1932 as unsafe so an advance party of fifteen "pioneers" had been at work since 31 January trying to get the building ready. "The cavernous rooms were dank, filthy, and filled with an almost unbearable stench," one early arriving POW reported[18]. Rats and vermin were everywhere. Behind the building there was (in addition to a sports field) an open space where there had been a small village destroyed in strafing when Shanghai was attacked, what was soon known as the "Happy Garden" with plots assigned POW's by a lottery. My father was no gardener, alas.

"I shall never forget my first sight of Pootung camp," my father wrote in a Christmas 1945 letter to several hundred supporters in prose which has haunted me the rest of my life. "I was in the third batch to go in. Our guards led us a devious course through a large factory compound and suddenly, on rounding the last corner, we saw a large drab three-storey building. The windows crowded with the faces of bearded men peering at us from behind iron bars. The sudden sight sort of left one cold. Then around to the main entrance, where the iron gates creaked open to admit us and clanged shut behind. So this is it!"

On arrival one of the first things he had to do was to settle where and with whom he would bunk. The lines of 600 cots in the men's dorm provided little space between them. At such close quarters you needed to be next to someone congenial. In Ian Morrison Dad found such a

---

18   Leck, Greg. *Captives of Empire: The Japanese Internment of Allied Civilians in China 1941-1945* Shandy Press

man, someone with a remarkably similar background and highly congenial interests. Ian, a decade younger than Dad, was a Gaelic-speaking
Highlander, a crofter's lad like my grandfather, who went to Glasgow
at 14, joined the Glasgow Tabernacle and heard the call pf God at the
age of 20. He attended the Glasgow Missionary Training Institute from
which, like my Grandfather, he went to China under the National Bible
Society of Scotland. After eight months there he married Rachel Nicoll
in her family home in Chefoo. Five years later, and just before Pearl
Harbor, Ian had gotten his family off on one of the last boats to Canada
to live with Rachel's single sister Cathie Nicoll.

Both men were missing their families. As he was about to enter concentration camp, Dad struck a plaintive note in an otherwise upbeat
25 word message: "Lack only news of you, wonder so much." Those
Red Cross monthly missives encouraged creativity in evading the censor
and brevity to comply with the twenty-five word limit. In September,
shortly after entering the concentration camp he wrote me the following
message which I think was facilitated by another family giving up one of
their children's allocation: "Dear Donald- Daddy thinks of your every-
day – wonders how fast you are growing – hopes to see you before long
– Be a good boy. Whole heaps love Daddy" To which I am reputed to
have replied: "Dear Daddy – I am fifty-one pounds and forty-six inches!
Learning to write a book. Helping mother lots. No asthma this winter.
Hugs kisses. DONALD."

My mother's attitude towards my rearing was summarized in a letter
she wrote to my father the summer of 1943: "I am trying to fill my days
full, to make up to Donald for not having you these many days, so that
we can take up threads, and see the Lord bring out of the very distresses
and hard things a deeper experience in His service, and in our family
life. I know that your prayers are responsible for much of the peace and
the victory of most of the long times and I count very much on them.
You know my prayers are unceasing." Many families during those war
years were deprived of a strong male presence. Often a grandfather or an
uncle could provide an alternative. In my case as an only child, with a
strong-willed older mother, a grandfather who was weak and wounded,

and a plethora of aunts and few strong masculine role models, I was at a distinct disadvantage as I grew into young manhood.

On arrival at Pootung each POW had a work assignment and my father's was KP duty. He became an expert in scrubbing the large bowls that were a part of the daily cuisine. Initially there were elaborate menus prepared by prisoners who had been among the top chefs in pre-war Shanghai. The fiction only survived a few days and then the words "SOS" appeared on the notice board: "Same old stew." The kitchen squad was headed by a chairman with whom alone the Japanese commandant dealt and there was no other communication. The food, such as it was, was left at the gate. In his second year at the camp Dad was promoted to cleaning up after meals. Eventually his love of books was recognized and he was appointed camp librarian. He sorted out the many volumes looted from the homes of foreigners in Shanghai, as well as confiscated stock from Kelly and Walsh, the famous Far East bookseller. These books were then distributed to the six concentration camps in the city. Lectures were also provided by former professors from St John's University speaking on various subjects about which they were experts. Services on Sunday were provided by a rota of clergy. When the Yangchow camp was closed following the second repatriation, remaining families were sent to the other camps. "From then on," my Father wryly noted, "the improvement in our manners and morale was noticeable."

Among the families sent to Pootung camp were George and Beatrice Scott and their two children, Margaret and Basil. George Scott was originally assigned to Szechuan but had been appointed to the Shanghai headquarters of the China Inland Mission where my father had met him during his time in the city earlier that year. George and Beatrice came in September and in December, in time for Christmas, their children joined them, having been sent down from Weihsien concentration camp in Shandong where they had been incarcerated along with the other 300 students at Chefoo School. As the reunited family settled into the newly set-up "family wing" my father attached himself to Basil, immediately bonding with him as a sort of Donald substitute.

George had had an unusual childhood himself, being at Chefoo school from seven to seventeen, and had little concept of normal childhood. Seventy years later Basil would write me: "Whenever I think of your dad, I think first of his amazing kindness to me – and then of the way he lavished his love on me as he could not be with you." In August 1944 Basil became gravely ill with pneumococcal meningitis. The camp doctors decided to try a new and still unknown antibiotic called suephedrozine that had come in a parcel from America. Miraculously Basil came back from near death and my father being there to minister to him, the bonds becoming ever tighter. The Scott's returned to England at the end of the war and we met them at the CIM Home on Newington Green London in 1948 and again in 1953 when George Scott had recently become Home Director[19].

At the end of the summer of 1943 it was announced that there was to be a second *Gripsholm* repatriation. On 24 August Mother sent out, at the government's suggestion, an all-points bulletin for her friends and family to write Dad, providing the Pootung address and adding "Via M. S. *Gripsholm.*" She prepared a box of things he might enjoy and need. Helped by her brother-in-law doctor, medicines, nutritional and dietary supplements were all crammed into the small parcel and sent to the boat. There is no indication that the parcel ever reached him. The letters that she encouraged family and friends to write and send were unpredictable in speed and whether they ever reached their destination. One letter Dad got came from a family connection in Worcester, Lillian Cunningham, whom my father had not heard from in years and had little in common with. It was greeted by him with consternation but also appreciation. What "pull" did Cousin Lillian have that others lacked, my mother puzzled. She clung to hope. In that same letter she wrote: "There are a number of omissions from both British and American lists,

---

19   Succeeding the much loved Fred Mitchell following Fred's tragic death over India in a *Comet* aircraft crash as he returned from meetings in Singapore. When we visited, everyone was still in shock. See Phyllis Thompson's *Climbing on Track: Updated Biography of Fred Mitchell*. Manila: OMF International, 2014.

which are going to be very hard to bear, and I think we should all pray both for those who are still left in concentration camp, and also for those in this country who are deeply disappointed, that they might right away accept His lifting power above the disappointment into the blessing He has for them all."

On 20 September the second *Gripsholm* contingent left Shanghai on the *Teia Maru*. By 24 October they were in the Portuguese colony of Goa in India at the port of Mormugao, where the prisoner exchange occurred. A week earlier the *Shanghai Post and Mercury* (published out of New York for expats and funded by the US government as being useful for intelligence purposes) had reported breathlessly that "1236 Americans are Included on Teia Maru List" and took three full pages to name them with pictures of several notables, reminiscent of press coverage of the sinking of the *Titanic* but this time with a more cheerful outcome. My yellowing copy is full of notations and checks made by my mother. When the *Gripsholm* got to Rio de Janiero many were able to communicate with family for the first time in two years amid much excitement. On 1 December the *Gripsholm* docked in New York. Many stories were told about the joyful reunions. Myra Scovel, wife of our doctor in Tsining, was rushed from the boat to Columbia Presbyterian Hospital where she delivered her sixth child (the other five being with them on the boat). When asked what the baby's name would be she uttered the memorable line: 'What else could we call her but Victoria?"

"Victory" was not a word that first came to mind to describe my mother's feelings at that point in her life. She was feeling desperately disappointed. Where was God in all of this she asked? Dad had now missed a second *Gripsholm* repatriation and it seemed unlikely that there could be any more opportunities until the war ended, if it ever would. Through her brother-in-law, an approach was made to Senator Robert F. Wagner who had represented New York State for the past fifteen years in the United States Senate. Wagner a Lutheran turned Methodist, was a Sunday school teacher and a man of faith (who converted to Catholicism at the war's end under the influence of Cardinal Spellman). He in turn approached Cordell Hull, the Secretary of State who three days after

Christmas wrote a three paragraph letter to mother in which he stated that for repatriations the American government cooperated only with those governments within the Western Hemisphere. "The Department of State can therefore, give no encouragement that Dr MacLeod may be included in such additional exchanges as the United States Government may be able to arrange with the Japanese Government." Case closed.

On Hull's suggestion Mother wrote to Edward Wood, Lord Halifax, British ambassador to the United States. It was a wise choice: The Wood family had dealt with tragedy and adversity all their lives and the one armed Edward Wood rose to the challenge. In a courteous and pastoral response, Lord Halifax stated his inability to help. There were so many British families also praying for a similar release and reunion. Wood's Anglo-Catholic Christian commitment made him gracious and under-standing but regretfully unable to help. My mother's encounter with him verified the nickname Churchill gave him. To my mother, in her deep distress, Lord Halifax was truly her Holy Fox.

Chapter 12:

A Home for the Homeless, 1943-5

At the end of the summer of 1942 my mother and I had moved three blocks further south on 42nd Street. It was an indication that she had recognized that this could be a longer separation than earlier anticipated. It was a two bedroom ground floor apartment in a turn-of-the-century four story building with a living room facing the street from which the "dinky," as the 42nd Street trolley car was affectionately called, could be seen (and heard) making its hourly trips. Mother had the gift of turning it quickly into a comfortable and homey place, filled with hand me downs and furniture bought at second hand stores on Market Street. The living room rug, a loan from my grandparents, featured an aquarium-design with tropical fishes in the pattern. They provided endless fascination and a welcome distraction for me during what seemed to a pre-schooler endless adult Bible study and missionary meetings I was expected to sit through.

For my mother it was the first time she had had a place of her own in America. Her considerable skills as cook, hostess and homemaker were fully utilized. She went out and bought a second hand player piano which, when it arrived was placed in a commanding position in the entry hall. She set about acquiring a library, most of our books being left in China. A family in the church was relocating and their move provided us with a selection of classics such as Jane Austen and travel works such as Stanley's account of David Livingstone's journeys. From January 1943 Freda Schenkel, described as "a most satisfactory roomer" boarded in one of the bedrooms. Freda Schenkel, a student and then staffer at the Philadelphia School of the Bible came from nearby Maryland. She took me to her family farm one weekend, giving me a new experience of rural America. She provided practical common sense when needed. Freda's sunny personality was a welcome contrast to my mother's intensity and our current preoccupations with war and death.

Mother's busyness seems, in retrospect, to have represented overcompensation. The first weekend of February 1943, for instance, she had two Sunday speaking engagements and six dinner guests including two couples from Tenghsien. It is hardly a surprise that she eventually ended up in hospital "sick from overwork" as she described it to her twin. Her mother-in-law, a sturdy no-nonsense farmer's daughter from Indiana who, as we have seen, had had her own travails on the mission field, came down from Germantown and promptly established order in our apartment with the help of Freda. Mother reported to Marjorie: "This is the first time since coming home from China that I've fallen down on my job!! But I had a good rest in the hospital, got my blood tests, other exams, my electrocardiograms etc. and now I shall be 100%."

Just after my fifth birthday I had a major asthma attack. My mother, as a single parent, reported: "I had 24 hours of anxiety - he had such difficulty breathing, his heart pumping, breath whistling, and part of the time grunting with his breaths. He was so miserable and I was really troubled. Every once in a while he'd catch my eye and pull his face into a reassuring sort of made up smile ... The doctor says we are going to try to find the cause." Indeed, we were fortunate in having the legendary Elizabeth Kirk Rose as our paediatrician. She practised out of the Hospital of the University of Pennsylvania, just blocks away from our apartment. Dr Rose, a committed Presbyterian, was a year younger than my mother and was a no-nonsense kind of physician who was caring without pandering to my mother's hyper anxieties. She lived to be

106 and was designated in her nineties as a "Distinguished Daughter of Pennsylvania". The Foreign Missions Board was exemplary in securing the best medical help for its employees and generously underwrote all costs, perhaps because medical missions were so much a part of its commitment.

One of mother's greatest challenges was the monthly ritual of filling in the twenty-five word communication that the International Red Cross was allowed to send to civilian prisoners of war in concentration camps. These so-called "telegrams" could take over a year to arrive so much (if not most) of the information was stale and dated. Limited to twenty-five words they could only contain family news and were heavily censored, thus raising many questions and uncertainties. Citing a Scripture verse resulted in the censors cutting out all numbers which might be code. Dad's 10 July 1942 message conveyed his isolation as he asked mother to contact family in Scotland as well as Clarence Edward Macartney. In another he referred to a Christmas message received via his sister Annabella then in so-called "Free China". Mother's replies tried to buck up his morale and provide family news:"Keep writing. Sister Cathie married. Son garrulous, charming, kindergarten." The sheer emotional trauma of trying to compress everything you wanted to say into a twenty-five word "telegram" was emotionally draining and drew attention to the separation and lack of communication, but the alternative of having no communication was even worse. "It seems as though I should have been able to say a lot more in 25 words, but try and do it!" Mother exclaimed to a friend.

Professional photograph, 1944. Mother justified the expense because she wanted Dad to have the best record of the years he'd been a POW

By the summer of 1943 my mother was emotionally and physically exhausted. Six weeks at "Mountain Rest" gave her a needed time for recuperation and restoration. Situated in the New England countryside she loved, it provided an emotional catharsis. I was instructed in nature, with three texts about birds, trees and flowers, helping me to identify each. I assembled a scrapbook with pressed flowers. A 25 word Red Cross "letter" came near her birthday (July 19), the first she had received since the previous October. My mother was also writing down for my father some of my childhood sayings so that later he would know something about what he had missed. A prayer of mine that she recorded (and later reported to him) went: "Dear Lord, we thank Thee for the things that we've been doing today. Make it the same way tomorrow. We thank You for dying on the Cross. Take away all my sins. Make Daddy come home if it be Thy will. Amen." The juxtaposition of Biblical "thee" and "thou" with ordinary "you" and "yours" represented my linguistic dexterity between the King James Bible English and ordinary language.

We returned to a busy autumn. I entered first grade at Illman-Carter School of the Faculty of Education at the University of Pennsylvania, my mother apologizing for the expense of private education and assuring my father that a year later I would be in the public school system. My report card stated positively that I enjoyed reading but negatively that I showed an unfortunate tendency to "help other children more than is necessary. I feel that this is due to his new found confidence in himself" according to my teacher Margaret Zeigler. The only "very satisfactory" pluses I received were in language ability and creative arts. My mother predictably blamed my being below par as being due to my allergies. A further health complication occurred when I spent the Christmas of 1943 in hospital with an appendectomy.

Her anxieties over my health made life for both of us very serious. "I am taking your advice heart to heart to be less serious and more light-hearted about things to do with one's child!" she conceded to her sister. There were many worries other than health: finances were a constant concern. My mother would not take my father's stipend so we survived on her half salary together with my dependent's allowance. The car was one expense that she could eliminate, first returning the car for the summer of 1943 to the man who had sold it to her, and then finally, just months before the end of the war, relinquishing ownership to the "candy man" across the street. At least she no longer had to deal with gas rationing but the lack of wheels further constricted our movement and my father never picked up driving when he returned. Filling in income tax forms also foxed her. Like many women on their own during the war, she had to take initiative and responsibility. The balance of power in their marriage was shifting.

Mother was by now busy supplementing her income with a part-time position with the Presbytery of Philadelphia's Summer Evangelistic Committee, working out of the denomination's Witherspoon Building downtown. "It's interesting and worthwhile! Mostly secretarial and later interviewing applicants," she explained. She was also busy speaking with enthusiastic responses, particularly in theologically sympathetic churches such as Westminster not far away. She had been elected President of the Woodland Church Women's Missionary Society, a task which surprisingly for a capable woman made her feel "fearful" and inadequate. She found herself in the thick of denominational politics. "Now that I have come to a certain position in the church, comes the necessity of expressing myself on these difficult situations which arise with literature, speakers, budget and doctrinal standards for members. Please pray" she asked her sister "that I may be firm and loving and uncompromising but sweet and Christ like and loving at the same time. I do not desire to please everyone, but I want to suggest and teach and help in love, even when it's necessary to appear critical. And it amazes me almost, how responsive the group is, even to criticism; there is a real desire to know more and to clearly discriminate."

She made many friends there. One of them, Gertrude Quick, an active and long-time member, lived with her mother and an unmarried sister (and several boarders) in a large detached home a block down from Woodland Church. She was a soulmate of my mother, based on the intense faith they both shared. She was another of the many courtesy aunts I acquired throughout my childhood. But she was an exception as the neighbourhood and the church were changing. Dr Swain had delayed retirement because of the war and the shortage of clergy with so many going into the chaplaincy. "I did not feel like quitting in an hour of crisis when America expects every one of us to do his duty." He wrote in a letter to members in the military, typed by my mother. "In all my years at Woodland, I had never been obliged to miss the sacrament of the Lord's Supper by reason of sickness or accident," he gratefully noted. He finally retired in 1943 after over forty years of ministry. In spite of my mother's probing questions at the congregational meeting that chose his successor, Stanley Kiehl Gambell was called from Hightstown, New Jersey, a year later. Although he was a 1936 Wheaton College graduate, mother felt his theology was uncertain. He remained at Woodland for nineteen years, a flamboyant but warm-hearted pastor to our family. My mother reciprocated, drawing close to Violet Gambell when their son Jeremy died as a child. As Gambell developed into a parody of Liberace, famed for his acting *The Christmas Story* each holiday, rumours abounded but my parents were loyal, if somewhat innocent. He left for Binghamton, NY, changed denominations, and crashed his car onto a bridge over the Northeast Extension of the Pennsylvania Turnpike in 1966.

We followed the fast changing war in Europe during the summer of 1944 with family in Maine. My mother sublet the apartment, displacing Freda Schenkel, and returned to Philadelphia for what turned out to be the final year of the war. We were all getting weary. As I "wrote" my father: "Thinking of you on my [sixth] birthday Happy time construction toys, bird and animal books, Planning summer way down east with aunt Grace [grandpa's sister], Priscilla [Mothers sister]. Donald." One day I announced that I was going to write a book about God and read it to the Japanese. The defeat of the European Axis took place on my seventh birthday, a date which I shared with President Harry Truman. I was showing signs of the stress we were all experiencing. My second grade teacher noted that "Let Donald be on his own as much as possible this summer. Tears are too near the surface. He seems tense." My mother asked at the beginning of 1945: "All my thinking processes seem dumb and I have to push myself to do the next thing. How long will it last?"

I can only speculate what made my mother decide to register for Wheaton College summer school during what turned out to be the final summer of our separation. Was it to prepare herself for a return to China, taking advantage of the Board's educational grants? Or was it to recreate those halcyon years of her youth, to return to the place she had first met my father? Suffice it to say she and I bundled ourselves off to Chicago when school let out (after Hospital tests Dr Rose ordered for me to learn if I had rheumatic fever, a false alarm). Memories flooded back: as she wrote her sister Priscilla "every once in a while my stock goes up when it happens that somebody knows that Wesley is my brother-in-law!" The continuing closeness of the alumni/ae of those classes in the mid-'twenties flooded back on her return.

Revisiting the scene of her courtship did not help to allay her fears about my father. In early July mother woke up in the middle of the night "with a great sense of pressure and urgency about Alec." Their courtship at Wheaton had not been an easy one and she had turned down my father's earnest proposals only to accept them five years later. Was she ruminating over "what might (or might not) have been"? In her distress she found help in the Daily Light reading for the evening of 24 July: "He staggered not at the promise of God through unbelief." (Romans 4:20) She went to church with me and during the service I leaned over to her with my Sunday School book and pointed to the question: "Is anything too hard for the Lord?" and asked "What is the answer?" and she replied with a resounding "No." It was that summer of 1945, at a Daily Vacation Bible School at Wheaton Bible Church, that I first made my faith commitment. The program was based on Psalm 107 in the King James Version and God's protection amid the perils of sea naviga-tion. It all seemed so relevant.

And then it was all over. On 14 August 1945 I was chosen to ring the bell in the iconic Wheaton College tower. The war was over. There would be no invasion of Japan or, for that matter, of Shanghai. The city where my dad was imprisoned would not be bombed. Hiroshima and Nagasaki were a terrible price to pay but it meant my daddy was safe and coming home. But before we had even had a reassuring word from the Far East we had a conflagration of our own.

Six days after our return to Philadelphia we made our way to New Hampshire to the old family cottage at Alton Bay. The campgrounds there had been originally set up in the 1860s by disciples of William Miller, the millennial speculator who took hundreds of people to a Vermont mountaintop in 1844 to await the Second Coming of Christ. These Adventists, as they were called (not to be confused with Seventh Day Adventists), had been the catalyst for my mother's family's Christian experience. The family cottage was in a circle of 300 frame buildings, each about ten feet apart, around the so-called "Tabernacle" where "revival" meetings were held every night in the summer. Cottagers were located as near to the so-called sawdust trail as was possible, perhaps to make non-attenders feel guilty.

Although the family cottage had been the site of my parents' honeymoon before they set off for the mission field sixteen years earlier, it was perhaps just as well that Dad was not there. Alton Bay stood for everything in American fundamentalism that made him uneasy. The cottage had not been open for several seasons (neither of my mother's brothers found the atmosphere congenial) so we spent the first three days on arrival scrubbing floors, cleaning up rat and squirrel droppings, and airing bedclothes. I was looking forward to using my new pair of roller skates which I had brought with me.

At 11:45 on the morning of 23 August 1945 I heard from the porch of our cottage a woman screaming hysterically. Blossom Batchelder had upset her stove and the gas canister had exploded. The fire spread quickly from cottage to cottage enveloping the whole campgrounds in a matter of minutes. It then spread to The Grove, the holy place for prayer and meditation, flames travelling rapidly from tree to tree. My grandfather, mindful of his arthritic wife, hurried the four of us into his Ford, barely allowing time to collect any of our goods, let alone my roller skates. We sped around Lake Winnipesaukee, dodging fire trucks and curiosity seekers, hastening to the opposite side of the lake where we watched in horror the terrifying inferno, the flames reflected in the water.

The toll was massive: 300 cottages, the Assembly Hall and all the adjacent buildings were destroyed. Fortunately there were no fatalities but the fire had a purging effect on our small family removing a final reminder of my mother's chequered religious background and eliminating the last piece of property that my grandfather had been able to save after his bankruptcy. Gone was the reminder of Grandmother Ella Miles and her hymns full of pious but predictable verse.

The view across Lake Winnipesaukee as we sat in Grandpa's car watching the inferno left an indelible impression on the overactive imagination of a 7 year old boy. I saw it as a grim reminder of John's words in Revelation of "the lake that burns with fire and sulphur, which is the second death", the fires of hell that await the ungodly at the return of

Christ. Adventist end-times speculation may have been discounted but the fires of Alton Bay that summer's morning in 1945 were a warning of what I had been taught lay ahead. As my Adventist Great-Grandmother Ella E. Miles wrote in one of her better-known hymns:

"How far to the City of Gold?
Thy waiting church would know;
Each day Thy children upward gaze;
Each day more anxious grow;
Blessed Savior, cleave the sky,
And quickly, quickly come;
We long to see Thy blessed face,
And dwell with Thee at home.
Press on, press on."

With the eyes of a chid it seemed to me, looking back on the incinerating campground, apocalypse was very near and very real. The atomic age had begun and we were called to press on.

CHAPTER 13:

A "Red Letter Day," 1945

"November 15 was a red letter day—when I stepped out of the train in Philadelphia and was joyously welcomed home." My father's use of the word "home" struck me as strange. "Home?" It was my home not his. And the two page 1945 mimeographed Christmas letter which I helped to fold, stamp, and place all two hundred copies in the mailbox – the lot of every missionary child as his or her parents unpaid assistant – introduced me to the idea of a "red letter day." I remember that day well. Mother had retrieved our car from the person to whom she had recently sold it and we set off early that Thursday morning for the North Philadelphia railroad station.

She had done a lot of preparation for my father's re-entry into my life. "I read," she recalled later, "articles in *Parents' Magazine* and other magazines about how to prepare a child to become reacquainted with a Father whom he hardly knew. And I studied and prayed about all the details." Those details included being carefully tutored as to where to put my father's things on his arrival. I was instructed about how the breakfast table should be spread, ready for our return to being a threesome for the first time in five years. And, anticipating that the train might be late, instead of bringing one of my favourite books, my mother brought a series of multiplication cards to distract me, but not too much. Always intense and lacking a light touch, that morning my mother was understandably in orbit, hardly reassuring for a sensitive child.

My father, more measured, reported three days later in a letter to my mother's twin, "Had thought that I would need someone to introduce us, but we just kissed each other, & it seemed the most natural thing in the world to do! We have talked steadily since & haven't begun to get caught up on everything." Three weeks later he wrote "Dorothy & I talk & talk, keep atrocious hours & are only just beginning to get an outline of the doings & thinking of the last five years' separation. I suppose that for some time to come news of forgotten things will be constantly coming out to surprise & interest. This is a second honeymoon. We weren't a bit bored with each other & don't expect to be for some time to come!"

Fortunately I rose to the occasion. After lunch I stood at the door of the bedroom my parents now shared, beckoned to her to come to my room and said quietly, "Mother I'm going to like him." Those six words instantly became part of our family lore. Her concern for my first encounter with my father appears to have dominated the narrative to the point that I wondered later how they now reconnected, what intimacies did they share? I recall a cartoon at the time as a just demobbed sailor rushes through the door of his home as his wife looks on, rushing up the steps to their bedroom, clothes scattered on the stairs as stark naked he rips them off, making his way to their first tryst in years. "Dear I'm home" is the caption. What intimacies did my parents share, how was their relationship affected by their years of separation? Certainly my mother was not prepared, it turned out, to relinquish responsibilities she had assumed for five years to a man whom she described that day as "thinner and shabbier." My father, it became increasingly apparent was, under his tightly controlled exterior, an angry man. There was to be little laughter in our home as I grew up. His wartime experiences scarred him deeply. Only once, in later years, did he divulge (not to me but to his grandsons} some of his wartime humiliations from the Japanese occupiers.

The week before Dad re-joined us, President Harry Truman called Americans to celebrate Thanksgiving as a solemn religious rite: "May we on that day, in our homes and in our places of worship, individually and as groups, express our humble thanks to Almighty God for the abundance of our blessings and may we on that occasion rededicate ourselves to those high principles of citizenship for which so many splendid Americans have recently given all." The words had a special resonance for our family after the years of separation and loss. The three of us as a reunited family rushed up to Brooklyn to celebrate the occasion with the Campbell's. The next day Dad went over to the Board of Foreign Missions headquarters. He had written ahead that "I look forward to seeing you again, & renewing fellowship of sight and hand," Visits there were always a bit fraught but this time he was greeted as a returning hero. Most of the other missionaries, being American, had been released two or three years previously and were redeployed. His situation was unique and called for extensive medical observation and treatment.

Dad's relationship with the man who married his wife's identical twin and *alter ego* was, over the years, a delicate one. Carleton Campbell Sr. was generally recognized to be a difficult man to get close to. His attitude toward missionary activity, following the death in China of his close friend and fellow alumnus of Cornell Medical School (class of 1921), Leighton Payson Rand, was negative. "Sticky" Rand (so nicknamed because his family owned a glue factory) had gone out to China under the China Inland Mission to serve in the Borden Memorial Hospital in Lanzhou, Gansu. During a typhoid epidemic he had taken a young patient to bed with him to provide critically needed medical attention (or so Carleton claimed). He contracted the disease and died on 5 May 1929 and was buried there. Carleton regarded his action as not only unprofessional but incredibly stupid and had no sympathy for him. Rand was engaged to be married to my mother's sister Priscilla, who had postponed their wedding to be trained as a nurse at Presbyterian Hospital, New York City.

Missionaries like "Sticky" Rand who put themselves in the path of danger and took unnecessary risks were not regarded by Dr. Carleton

Campbell with any sympathy, let alone empathy. They were fools, not heroes. Why had my father abandoned his wife and son for a dubious mission in far-away China? While the sisters were close (too close, it might be argued) their husbands remained far apart. Marjorie stayed loyal to her husband but my mother was her safety valve. Now my father tried to reach out to Carleton and start a new chapter in their relationship. He invited the three of them to come to Philadelphia ("outside your parish" was the way he described it to Carleton) and celebrate the holiday with them as families on our turf.

The invitation was not accepted. My father showed little understanding either of his brother-in-law or the scheduling complexities of an urban medical practice. But he continued to reach out, possibly at the urging of Marjorie who felt her husband was isolated relationally. During the time we spent in Brooklyn over the Christmas holiday my father tried to connect by commending a book he otherwise would have had little interest in. The 1940 best-selling *The Doctor and His Patients* was written by Arthur Hertzberg, a Mennonite country doctor in rural Kansas. Hertzler's book is now a classic: misogynist, anti-academic, and at points even anti-Christian, this so called "horse and buggy doctor" advocated a no-nonsense medical practice that cuts through a lot of theories of patient care. It could have provided a starting point as my father attempted to find common ground, hoping to encourage Carleton to examine his own professional and faith premises. "A mixture of good and bad" my father summarized the book. The effort was never repeated again.

I retain two emotional reminders of December 1945, both related to family celebrations. One is a forty-fourth birthday card, presented on 3 December to "My dear Son Alexander" and signed "Lovingly Mother" with "So glad to have you home today." She cites Ephesians 1:3 which the Authorized or King James Version reads "Blessed be the God and Father of our Lord Jesus Christ, who hath blessed us with all spiritual blessings in heavenly places in Christ." She was passionately proud of her only son. Dad became a buffer between her and my mother who at times scarcely understood this heavy- set, practical, no-nonsense

Hoosier farmer's daughter. The other is a New Testament with Psalms presented to me that first Christmas of our re-acquaintance by my father again with a Scripture verse, this time from Psalm 119:105: "Thy word is a lamp unto my feet, and a light unto my path." He had chosen the American Standard Version (1901) as his preferred translation, carefully instructing me on the need for accuracy in the translation of the Bible, and the use of a text closest to the original. I learned for the first time the importance of the *autographa* being as close as possible to the original which God had initially revealed to humankind.

Dad had sent a cheque to cover the purchase of *A Child's Story Bible* for me in 1941. Catherine Vos was the wife of Geerhardus, one of Dad's Princeton professors and mother of Johannes ("Jack") Vos[20]. Dad's friendship with Jack Vos went back to Princeton Seminary days and they were at language school together, both going out to China in 1930. Exiled from Manchuria in 1941, Vos pastored a "Covenanter" (RPNA) church in Kansas and went on to teach at Geneva College in Beaver Falls, Pennsylvania. He and Dad, together with Dr. Calvin Chao, were involved in, and committed to, the Reformation Translation Fellowship (RTF) founded by Sam Boyle in 1949. which continues to provide many useful Reformed books for the Chinese church. Vos also edited *Blue Banner Faith and Life* for many years, tirelessly handling not only content but also the logistics of production. My father outlived him by ten years but throughout their lives they shared a common vision and mutually encouraged each other.

On New Year's 1946 my father introduced me to another of his passions: the keeping of a diary. In my case it was particularly ambitious being a five year one with five lines provided for each day. My father's provided a full page. His diaries would stretch for the next fifty-nine

---

20   Johannes Vos (1903-1983). Graduate Phi Beta Kappa, Princeton Univ., 1925; PTS, 1928.Th.M. WTS, 1937; served under the RPNA in China 1930-41; pastored Clay City, KS 1942-1954; Geneva College head of Bible Department, 1954-1973. Son Mel, my WTS classmate and recently ordained, was tragically killed out jogging.

years, detailing every aspect of his life, letters and literature but without any revealing reflections or analysis or gossip. My first diary lasted to 23 June 1946, setting a pattern for all subsequent diaries. Some of them lasted a week or two, others a month, but usually (until lately) never getting as far as my first attempt. Unlike my father, consistency in diary keeping was never one of my virtues.

On 5 January 1946 I gushed: "It's so nice to have Daddy around." It's fascinating to compare the father son versions of the same day comparing my diary account. The following day he and I went for a stroll: "Daddy and me walked to 51 St. Miss Quick came to have supper. We play Bible families." My father described the route he and I took, down Chester Ave. and then back up Baltimore Ave., with a sense of accomplishment as ten-block hikes had not been something featured when my mother was in charge. I suspect there were complaints along the way. My father soon developed a routine as he settled into his new freedom and the responsibility of a wife and child. We were ideally situated for access to various academic institutions: the University of Pennsylvania and two nearby theological seminaries: those of the Protestant Episcopal (where my father's sister Cathie had been Librarian) and the Reformed Episcopal denominations several blocks further west where Robert Rudolph was professor of systematic theology and Christian ethics. Rudolph gave my father a key to the school, a vast edifice built in 1887. I date my early fascination with Victoriana with my forays around that building. Rudolph was closely identified with Westminster Theological Seminary and specifically Cornelius Van Til, with whose presuppositional apologetics he identified.

Westminster Seminary, out in Glenside, suburban Philadelphia, became part of the schedule my father had now created for himself. Every Wednesday, starting 16 January, he would take the train to Glenside and walk over to the seminary campus. Most of the faculty had been his classmates at Princeton Seminary and he felt theologically safe there. He registered for Ned Stonehouse' s class on Apostolic History, took notes in John Murray's systematic theology and Paul Wooley's Church History. Then he would come home, sit down at the dining room table, and type up his recently acquired material. It was as though he was attempting to turn back the clock. I would travel with him some days, sitting out on the lawn of the grounds as he visited the library, frankly bored with the whole process. We would talk but it was often about church life and politics which for an eight year old was inaccessible.

My father was a seventeen-year veteran of the Presbytery of Philadelphia and Stanley Gambell collected him and took him to the first meeting of the court in the New Year. At noon on 28 January, Ramsay Swain invited him to the monthly Adelphoi Club luncheon, a fraternal of Presbyterian clergy. Although the members of Woodland Church did their best to include him he later said he regretted that mother had not chosen one of the more strategic congregations in the Presbytery. He received few invitations to speak, which is surprising given the adventures he could have shared and his wife's popularity as a guest at various women's and missionary meetings. Finally on 26 May, at the invitation of Donald Grey Barnhouse, he preached on "Jesus the Chief Hero of Faith" (Hebrews 12:2). Barnhouse, who had been a guest in our home in Tenghsien when on a fact-finding trip in the mid-1930s, epitomized a polarised Presbytery. Dad never found preaching easy – he spent most of the previous week in sermon preparation and came across, in spite of the interest of his story, as professorial and stiff. In addition he had lost his connectedness with contemporary American culture.

Meanwhile the invitations for him to take an academic position in America started to arrive. The first was from Merrill Tenney who two years earlier had left Gordon College to teach New Testament at Wheaton College and whose summer school class on Romans the year before had so impressed my mother. On 5 March 1946 he invited Dad to teach Systematic Theology at Wheaton. In his response Dad replied that, having taught history at Wheaton before leaving for the mission field, he had gotten into New Testament as a consequence of the request of the NCTS staff and faculty and an awareness of how crucial Paul's letters were in response to a culture shaped by Confucian morality (the subject of his Ph.D. thesis). "You can see how impossible it is to maintain strict specialization on the mission field. For one thing, one is far removed from libraries. For another, the number of qualified men, foreign or Chinese, available as teachers is so limited that it is hard to departmentalize the curriculum. If there is no one who is specialized in a subject that needs to be taught or if colleagues are on furlough, works against specialization." And he concluded with a telling comment: "To me it is one of the great sacrifices that my call to the mission field has entailed."

The wider question was whether his Reformed position, particularly on eschatology, was compatible with Wheaton's commitment to premillennialism. On such matters as "end times prophecy" he remained undecided. The immediate post-war evangelical scene had been badly bruised by the fundamentalist controversies of the '20's and '30's. In fighting to maintain theological orthodoxy, academic standards had eroded. Even at schools that had a strong academic reputation such as Westminster, few younger professors had doctorates from accredited institutions. My father's Ph. D. from the University of Edinburgh had an immediate cachet.

Months later, while sitting on a rock in Muskoka Canada, Dad wrote a letter to his Princeton Seminary classmate and former fellow China missionary Everett Harrison, declining an offer from the dispensationalist Dallas Seminary. Harrison was about to decamp to become a founding faculty member at Fuller Seminary in Pasadena. Dad would have been theologically incompatible with Dallas and he knew it. Harrison only received his own Ph. D. from the University of Pennsylvania three years later. The Harrisons had been good to mother and me during the war when he pastored Third Presbyterian Church in Chester, Pennsylvania.

My father's decline of both offers demonstrated that he had academic job options at the time. Returning to China, given the dangers, would be sacrificial. But no matter how enticing the opportunities in America, his heart was set on China. The North China Theological Seminary was never far from his thoughts. On 1 April the 1946 annual meeting of the American Council was held in our apartment. The Romigs and the Scotts came for dinner beforehand. The meeting went on until 11:30 p.m. so great was the amount both of business and the interest in events unfolding in China. A memorial tribute to Watson Hayes founder of the school, who had died in concentration camp the year before, was tabled. Things were chaotic in South Shandong, the meeting was informed. The Nationalists and the Communists had recently made the seminary campus a battleground. One fatality during that battle was Dr. Alexander, the Jewish doctor who had bravely managed the Christian Hospital in Tenghsien throughout the war. The special diary entry when that news was received on 23 January 1946 testified to how deeply effected my father was by the tragedy. The annual meeting was told that the seminary "was pushing ahead the door of opportunity in China" and that there was a great need for support as the school relocated to Hsuchow, North Jiangsu. Martin Hopkins was in charge there and he was hopeful for a fresh start.

Visiting Mr. & Mrs. Horace G. Hill at their Berwyn, PA, estate
prior to leaving for China, August 1948

Through the American Council our family was befriended by oil magnate Horace Hill, Secretary Treasurer of the Atlantic Refining Co., who lived in a large mansion (at least to my child-like eyes) in Berwyn on the Mainline. Aside from my uncle Carleton I had had little contact with affluence. I remember being given a very nice gift before we came to their home one time. Mrs. Hill admired it so my mother gave it to her, much to my annoyance. As a mishkid dependent on the charity of others more fortunate, one was taught to be deferential, if not obsequious. For thirty years Horace Hill poured his life into theological education in China and even after the Communist takeover when the Council focussed on the Chinese *diaspora*. My Father, unused to wealth, spent a lot of time with Horace Hill, but they were never close. Frequent references to visiting him at his office on South Broad St. or his home were made in Dad's diaries. Horace Hill opened a whole new world to us.

Aside from the occasional trip to Glenside, my father did his best to form a relationship with me but he had little to work on. His own childhood as a China mishkid, sent away to boarding school at the age of seven, gave him little understanding of family life. As least at school he had had other contemporaries to bond with. As an only child with parents in their forties I was deprived of many things that are part of the culture of American males growing up. Never did my father suggest going to Shibe Park to watch a baseball game. While the A's were suffering from Connie Mack fatigue the Phillies were welcoming a new star, barely 21, a local boy from Olney just out of the Navy named Del Ennis. It wouldn't have been far to travel up to 21st and Lehigh but that cost money and was outside my father's comfort zone. Instead we made trips to famous local museums. On Valentine's Day 1946 I inspected the mummies at the University of Pennsylvania's Egyptian collection gathered by Flinders Petrie sixty years previously. We viewed the Medieval and Renaissance collections at the Museum of Art. (They also showed newsreels, safe for born again Christians because they were not "the movies.") After that excursion I was rewarded by a visit to Shanghai Gardens restaurant for some welcome – and familiar - food.

Holy Week 1946 saw me resuming my diary entries. "It feels funny not to be going to school. I help Dad with some of the NCTS cards," I write. We set off for Connecticut for Easter in Wilton, worshipping on Easter Sunday at Georgetown Congregational Church as there was no local evangelical congregation. The night before, mother wrote that "we grownups had had a long talk". My uncle Carleton had just driven up from Brooklyn with his sister, an unmarried neurologist who lived with them and formed a "ménage à trois" which took on an increasingly complex dimension. Alice had introduced her brother to Marjorie at a landmark 1924 house party in Wilton. She had long since abandoned her earlier simpler faith. She maintained a close, and to me puzzling relationship with the famous sculptress Brenda Putnam[21]

One of the matters under discussion was a projected trip to Canada which my father was promoting. Dad proposed that his mother would come with us and that Marjorie would take her son and we would all travel to Canadian Keswick in Ferndale, Muskoka. Dad had always, since the summer of 1925, wanted to revisit the Dominion. His mishkid experience at Chefoo Schools had made him embrace the British imperial vision of an Empire on which the sun never set. He never, during his decade as a student in America, tried to revert to his mother's citizenship. He paid a heavy price for that during the war, as we have seen, spending three additional (and unnecessary) years in prison camp. He clung to his British identity and Canada was the nearest expression of it. It was only when he had no alternative that he was forced into renouncing his British citizenship and became an American. But that, as we will see, did not affect his wishes for his only child. I think from the earliest moments he wanted me to be a Canadian and that eventually resulted in a crisis in our relationship.

The annual national or General Assembly of the Presbyterian Church (USA) was meeting in Atlantic City in 1946 and my father, as a returning missionary of the denomination, was expected to attend. His diary entry expressed his frustration: "This evening [28 May] was the popular meeting on foreign missions. A great disappointment. No missionary spoke!" And then he quickly adds a positive note: "met many friends." Among those friends was George Vorsheim, who drove him home the next day. Vorsheim epitomized the theological diversity among evangelicals in the Philadelphia Presbytery of the PC (USA).He was a popular dispensationalist, pastor of Westminster Presbyterian Church at 57th

---

21   Brenda Putnam (1890-1975) winner of awards, moved to Wilton CT from NYC
      in the early 1950s until 1971.

and Chester, a few blocks from our apartment. Prof. Ed Clowney, who taught me preaching, grew up in that congregation and later reacted against the dispensationalism of his youth, emphasizing rather the unity of the Biblical narrative and teaching which brought the Old and New Testament together. Vorsheim shared a missionary enthusiasm which trumped such theological differences.

CHAPTER 14:
Canadian Caper, 1946

On June 27, 1946, school being out, we started on our long planned trip to Canada, the country that for my father represented a comfortable combination of his dual identity as a China mishkid: British and American. We travelled out of Philadelphia on the Maple Leaf Express, joined by Grandma at Wayne Junction and at Bethlehem by Marjorie and Carleton Jr.. Stopping over at Niagara Falls we did the tourist thing, travelling on the Maid of the Mist boat to see up close the spectacular cascade. Two days later we went on to Toronto. The connecting train out of Union Station was an hour and a half late so we missed our reservation with the Muskoka steamer, finally arriving at 3:30 Sunday morning. Grandma found her way to missionary accommodation while Marjorie and Carleton Jr. were given a room in the main lodge, a vast wooden Victorian hotel. When we arose the next morning we were amazed by what my father described as "a beautiful place." In searching for their trunks on Monday they enjoyed a cruise around the Lakes.

Canada was *terra cognita* for Grandma MacLeod who had arrived as a refugee from war-torn China back in 1927 with her two younger daughters and had been stuck at the China Inland Mission (CIM) Home on St George St. Toronto until four years later she was allowed admission to the land of her birth. She had been required to renounce her American citizenship when she was married in March 1901 to my Scottish grandfather at the British consulate in Ningbo China. For insular Marjorie, who had made only one short sortie outside the United States a dozen years earlier, it was all very new and broadening.

Many memories of that blissful summer remain. It was then that I was introduced for the first time to *Pilgrim's Progress*. James Hunter who had memorized vast screeds of Bunyan's classic, held this eight-year old spellbound. He recited it with a backdrop behind of the lake in a glassed in extension called appropriately "The Delectable Mansion." As a mishkid I was no longer odd man out but, because of my parents' vocation, honoured and special. I went around, making a nuisance of myself by asking people to sign their name and address in my notebook. I recall that most seemed to be from the city of Hamilton. A fundamentalist (and Presbyterian) enclave. My cousin and I went for swims with my father in the icy Canadian water and enjoyed ourselves thoroughly at the children's program. By 15 July our time together was over as my cousin and his mother returned to the States.

Two days later at 4:00 in the morning we were woken up by shouts of "Fire" from the main building. My father hastily changed from his pyjamas as the flames became more visible. Mother, experienced about resorts on fire, started to pack. Men were throwing furniture out of the windows of the Delectable Mansion. My father was more measured in his response carrying furniture down the stairs. A woman fled down the fire escape with one nylon stocking and a bottle of Sal Hepatica, a cheap well-known over the counter laxative. Never lost for a teachable moment, it was brought home to me, as the motto on the wall of our mission hostel stated, "Only one life will soon be past, only what's done for Christ will last." Storing up treasures on earth was not, I was told, a sensible idea. Moth, rust, and even fire, would take it all away sooner or later.

But the summer activities at the conference centre went on without interruption. T. Roland Philips, a Canadian Keswick habitué, provided the ministry throughout the post-fire week in the Delectable Mansion, oblivious to the smouldering ruins of the once proud hotel. Philips, of Arlington Presbyterian Church in Baltimore, was one of the fundamentalist titans of the PC (USA), a firebrand preacher with a wide national following. His presence was a reminder of how strong the links were between fundamentalists in the two countries. What no one realized at the time was that on 17 July 1946 far more than an old Victorian hotel was destroyed. That catastrophe signalled the beginning of the end of a comfortable Canadian religious conservatism. Canadian Keswick epitomised a whole way of life that flourished during the first half of the twentieth century in Ontario, an interconnected shared religious experience that had its favoured preachers, packed urban churches, filled prophetic conferences, and anticipated the "imminent return of our Lord Jesus Christ." Overseas missions were enthusiastically and sacrificially supported. Canada was more church-going than the Unite States, a reality that coloured my Father's love for the Dominion. He found it a far cry from the polarized religious scene of the United States. Canadians are by nature peace-loving compromisers.

And it was also very British. My Father was always proud of his Scottish roots and felt as the oldest among his siblings the responsibility of nourishing their Scottish ancestry. I can remember pouring over my recently acquired Canadian stamps, the four cent deep red picture of a uniformed George VI standing out in my mind. My father's sentimentality about his British roots was reinforced for his son by a selective choice of reading material: Jane Porter's *The Scottish Chiefs* and *Our Island Story* with its sequel *Scotland's Story* were all required reading. For someone who had spent only a year and a half in total in Scotland during graduate study it seemed rather contrived. But his fixation extended to all things Canadian as an extension of the Empire on which the sun never set. Such are the myths that shape our lives and certainly would determine my future.

Only a year and a half in Scotland certainly, but also a decade at Chefoo School during his formative growing up years. It always struck me as ironic that spending the first eighteen years of his life in China my father had never acquired either the language or the culture of the land of his birth. China and Chefoo were the common bond that drew us back to Toronto where we stayed at the China Inland Mission home on St. George St. Walking west one block and then north on Spadina Rd. we were at the Toronto Bible College. The Principal, J. Bernard Rhodes, had been Dad's roommate when they were together at Chefoo. A child-less Presbyterian minister, he took an interest in me and made me feel at home in the Principal's residence on campus.

The dawning awareness that last week of July 1946 was that Dad might not be allowed to return to the United States. My father haunted the British High Commission office and the American Consulate for permission to cross the border but none came. On the last day of July my father put my mother and me onto a US bound train. He was unperturbed by the prospect of another family separation. What my mother was thinking I can only imagine. She started to pull strings in Philadelphia, having had considerable (and previously unsuccessful) experience in getting my father through the hoops of the American immigration authorities. He continued to enjoy the sights of Toronto, shopping at bookstores and working through a copy of *The Infallible Word* sent to him in Canada, an effort by the Westminster Seminary to assert biblical authority. He visited the churches: Knox one morning, Bloor East the next. He wrote: "Went to Bloor East church this morning. Only songs, no organ, severe and simple architecture and worship and weighty theological sermon." That evening, which he hoped (and was) his final Sunday evening in Canada, he went to Knox Church. Forty-eight years later he would be buried from that same building.

Two days afterwards a call came to the CIM home for him. Typically he was at a bookstore, the Evangelical Publishers, sponsor of Canadian Keswick. The American Consulate was trying to reach him. An appoint-ment had been made for three o'clock that afternoon. He set out imme-diately for the CPR at Union Station and ordered a ticket for the night train to New York. His confidence was rewarded when he received his clearance and he was off that very evening, to be met coincidentally and accidentally at the South Norwalk station an hour after his arrival by my mother and me. But there was a hitch. To become an American citizen, which he now reluctantly conceded was the only course of action possible; he would have to remain in the United States for two years until his naturalization process was completed. That would delay his return to China and his beloved seminary. As events were unfolding there it was uncertain whether there would be any ministry to return to, given the Communists' success on the battlefield. Our lives were now "on hold" and those two years would be a test of their faith and my adaptability to change. A China mishkid had to be flexible.

CHAPTER 15:

Freed POW Tells Story
to US Family, 1946

The summer of 1946 was a time for discovering the New England heritage of my mother. The previous summer I had been introduced to my father's British Empire identity, accompanied by his mother, as we explored Ontario. Now it was my mother's turn and a summer odyssey was planned that would include five of the six New England states and introduce me (and my father) to her relations. This side of the family provided a contrast in cultures, being very different: less religious, less academic, less structured. As August came grandmother's MacLeod's deteriorating health dominated our life. By the end of the summer she was dead, a link with the past forever gone.

As a case in point, winter over mother's parents always seemed to arrive like gypsies *en route* from Florida on a Sunday, missing church and generally being disruptive to our Sabbath routines. Her mother's brother, a railwayman with a free travel pass, would also suddenly show up and then leave abruptly. I found Harold Blanchard's bohemian attitudes intriguing. Grandma Miles appeared to have little understanding of my father's Scottish Sabbath or indeed his sensitivities generally. On seeing him for the first time after his release, she asked a particularly insensitive question: what it was like to be hungry all the time? And her reference to him as a bookworm, as noted previously, seemed to betray insensitivity to his interests and profession.

To be fair, the loss of the family's financial security in 1926 in the real estate bust in North Miami had reduced her in summers to become a travelling saleswoman for Spencer corsets. Grandpa as her driver waited outside in a car parked in the farmyard. Her weight and arthritis meant she navigated with difficulty. Winters in Florida seemed to ameliorate her arthritis and renting cheap furnished accommodation in Bradenton for the first three months of the year became an essential part of the rhythm of their retirement years. Neither Grandpa nor his two sons shared the same religious commitment as his twin daughters. How could they, I reasoned in that straightforward manner of bright children, be sympathize with our China experience and its painful separations for the cause of Christ?

So we first found ourselves that summer in mother's hometown of Holden, outside Worcester, Massachusetts. We stayed with her childhood friend Myrtle Adams MacKay, married to a Canadian. Myrtle's sister Ruth had died in a terrible accident when the twins, on the eve of their thirteenth birthday in 1914, had gone to swim, disobeying maternal warnings, in Eagle Lake. Marjorie watched helplessly as her best friend drowned. She was so distraught that the family despaired of her sanity. She was sent off to Ohio to live with Dr. George Searle, Grandpa's half-brother. I often thought that the accident explained Marjorie's emotional detachment. I loved Myrtle, her unforgettable laugh, her handcrafts, and her large house on Armington Lane where I was always welcomed and accepted for what I was, not what my mother wanted me to be.

After visiting my mother's brothers we travelled to Maine bypassing the ruins of Alton Bay campground. In grandpa's car we were bound for his sister in Wiscasset. "Maine's prettiest village," to quote the town's motto. Grace Raddin, my grandfather's only sibling, had lived there after the collapse of the family business. Howard, her husband, had been its secretary-treasurer, and was a quiet well-meaning person who generally stayed out of trouble. The real focus of the visit was Lawrence Augustus Averill, Ph.D., married to my mother's cousin Esther. Averill was a professor at the Worcester Normal School (teacher training). An educational psychologist, he was a widely published textbook author and an amateur local historian. He was the one who, of my entire mother's family, related to my father as an intellectual. He was full of intelligent questions to my Dad about his past experiences in China and the future of US-Chinese relations. Cousin Lawrence took us around the historic sites of the area, and there were many in a town established in 1663. Fort Edgecomb stands out in my memory, a fortress built in 1809 to protect the coast from British warships prior to the War of 1812. Indeed, the whole trip was my first foray into historical research. I must have caused no end of exasperation in my desire to see all the New England state houses which, with the exception of Vermont, I managed to achieve that summer. On Sunday we worshipped in nearby Alna, which had been the scene of a family reunion a decade earlier when my childless mother, seven years married, had felt a failure surrounded by her siblings' off-spring. So much had happened in that decade and here I was her trophy.

We then drove north through Augusta to Monmouth, where my mother's sister Priscilla and her husband had been offered the use of a cottage that summer. Wesley Ingles had been offered a teaching position at Bates College in Lewiston, a small liberal arts school. Bates had invited him to teach English and creative writing. He was hired in spite of his lack of any advanced degrees but with his track record of two bestselling novels. They had rented the home of a vacationing faculty colleague In Monmouth, thirteen miles north of Bates College. I remember it as the house where I first encountered an early electric dishwasher, a great boon for a child when it came to chore times. My mother could summon by a bell pulley in each of the seven bedrooms non-existent housemaids. A dazzling array of books fascinated my father. As a mishkid I was transported to another world of luxury and excess.

On our way back, through Holden and Wilton, our travels were punctuated by visits to bookstores and academic institutions, with both of which my father was now obsessing. In Boston we went to Gordon College and the famous Williams Bookstore. In Rhode Island we stopped at Wickford where Grandma's sister was married to a funeral director. I spent the night in the coffin room, not a wise choice for an impressionable eight year old. On Sunday morning we visited First Presbyterian Church, Providence, where Frank Suetterlein was beginning what turned out to be a twenty-one year ministry. As a mishkid, with parents wanting to make a good impression, I was always aware of being on display. Presbyterians in New England were so rare that these contacts became very important. We stopped off at Yale as we made our way to Wilton, inspecting the School of Oriental Studies. Dad was getting restless. On 2 September, Labour Day, we set out for Philadelphia to an uncertain future.

CHAPTER 16:

Uprooted By Death
and Distance, 1947-8

It is not clear when or why my father switched his attention from Church History to New Testament. His interest in history had always been there. He had started his academic career by teaching American history for a year at Wheaton College before leaving for China. I once heard him explain this switch (which didn't last long) on the basis of the pre-war NCTS Church History professor not be returning to China. Whatever the reason, the next two years were dominated by historical research and then actually going on to teach as an interim at Gordon Divinity School in Boston.

"Alec is starting his fall work, preparing material for his church history class and working up some N[ew] T[estament] commentaries for translation into Chinese." My mother's letter of 22 September then went on to add a confidential item: " He is very nervous" and the word "nervous" is underlined four times. What she meant by the word "nervous" is unclear but it is certain that my father was coming into a new phase of his recovery from the psychological ravages of his war-time experiences. He dropped his detailed diary writing, his trips to Glenside and Westminster Seminary became a daily week-day routine. His note-taking there and at Temple University where his old church history professor at Princeton Seminary, Frederick Loetscher, was lecturing in retirement, became obsessive, almost manic. "Nervous" might meant that he was living on his nerves or anxious (when the invitation came) about the prospect of teaching in a new and challenging situation. The effect on his wife (never acknowledged) and his son were evident.

"Donald," my third grade teacher reported after the first quarter, "is especially interested in Social Studies and contributes along these lines to the class." And then she added in a telling aside: "We are trying to help him work a little more calmly." What Annie Morrell was trying to convey to my parents was that some of their intensity impacted their only child. Relief, however, came with the arrival of a new Principal. George Raab was everything my father was not: young, funny, confident, easy-going, athletic, blonde with a crew-cut and an ability to make you feel important. George Raab defined for me what it meant to be male. My parents would not let me have a crewcut but I tried anyway to get my hair to stand up. Months later, after we'd left Philadelphia, on a subway in Manhattan, I approached a stranger I thought was Mr. Raab but it turned out to be mistaken identity. I was crushed,

What was never discussed in front of me was my father's health. Aside from losing forty pounds (he was down to 130 when he was released) he had other unspecified health issues. On October 8, barely a year after the war ended, he was back in Presbyterian Hospital. The following summer Dad wrote to a cousin in Indiana: "We are delaying our return to China another year. Some weeks ago the doctor advised I was not yet in fit enough shape physically to go back this August." Meanwhile there was a restlessness, frequent inquiries to other schools, inspection of various alternative apartments in Philadelphia, and a yearning to resume the life he loved, that of an academic preparing Chinese pastors which had been ripped away from him by events beyond his control. By the end of 1946 he decided on a move. We were to go to New York City where he could study at Union Theological Seminary with the leading church historian of that generation, John T. MacNeill, who had the dual advantage to my father of being both Canadian and Presbyterian.

So on 24 January 1947 my third grade transcript was sent to Friends Academy in New York City. I had entered a whole new culture. Instead of a grotty turn-of-the century apartment we were now to be ensconced in Kennedy House, an eleven story apartment building overlooking Gramercy Park, arguably one of the most appealing locations in a city that had many. The property had been built by the Presbyterian Board of Foreign Missions for its staff and missionaries when on furlough back in 1911. Financed by a million and a quarter dollar bequest from the little known or honoured Scottish financier John Stewart Kennedy. Kennedy's largesse funded many community, cultural, and Presbyterian organizations in New York City. He had an eye for value. Those apartments, now a part of a condominium, each going for several millions. Twenty years later I was to marry the great-great granddaughter of Kennedy's Edinburgh business associate whose biography I would later write[22].

Because my mother's twin was in the city there are no letters from that period that can shed light on what the family was going through. We sublet our apartment in West Philadelphia, said good-bye to my Grandmother whom we had seen a lot of during the immediate previous month, perhaps in anticipation and preparation for our departure. Mother upgraded her musical qualifications at Julliard, not far from Union Seminary where my father was doing the same with Church History lectures. All these educational opportunities were paid for by the Mission Board, as was my schooling at an exclusive private school, Friends Seminary on East Sixteenth St.. It was originally a Quaker school, its reputation enhanced by alumnus Teddy Roosevelt. As its list of alumni/ae show, it always had a heavy commitment to the arts. I learned to play the recorder there (plastic because we couldn't afford the fancy German wood ones) and did a lot of water colour painting. I first learned to write script there though it did nothing for my penmanship, a

---

22   See my *A Kirk Disrupted: Charles Cowan and the Free Church of Scotland*. Fearn Scotland: Mentor, 2013. 319.

constant irritant for my father whose beautiful handwriting was held up to me as an unattainable model.

Living in New York was a heady experience for a nine-year old. There were other transitioning missionaries in the building and I was adopted as a kind of mascot. As I walked over to Third Ave., and then four blocks south to school, I passed endless fascinations. But it was that coveted key to the Park that was the *coup de grace*. Building snow forts in Gramercy Park might sometimes freeze me to the point almost of frostbite but it was wonderful, if rather solitary, given the exclusiveness of the privileged entrée. And there were church links too: the Board of Missions, at "156" or "Boardy," said by some missionaries with a wink or a nod became shorthand for bureaucracy, theological vagueness and institutional expediency.

156 Fifth Ave., Manhattan, headquarters 1893 - 1958
of the Presbyterian (USA) Board of Foreign Missions.

156 Fifth Ave., was awe-inspiring with its Art Deco entrance. New York Presbytery historically was in a different polarity theologically from Philadelphia Presbytery, so every Sunday we had to take the Broadway subway up to 120th St. where the only "sound" Presbyterian minister in Manhattan, John Hess McComb, held the fort at Broadway Presbyterian Church, across from Columbia University. Only later did I learn that the dispensational theology and strange ecclesiology (as it subsequently emerged) of Dad's Princeton Seminary classmate was held to be almost as toxic as the liberalism of Harry Emerson Fosdick, four blocks up on Riverside Drive. But McComb was exonerated as a potential promoter of NCTS. And when Bonhoeffer returned to Nazi Germany for eventual martyrdom it was the preaching of McComb, not Riverside, that gave him the courage to stay the course the Sunday before he left.

To me Muriel Fuller, the astrologer mentioned at the beginning of this book, epitomized the slightly risqué excitement of the city. As an editor and literary agent she always had extra books to share and give away. At the very time we were in New York, she scored a major literary coup. While it was not great classic literature, Frank Yerby's *The Foxes of Harrow*, with its moving dedication to Muriel Fuller, made hers a name to conjure with. It was the first book by a black writer to earn more than a million dollars for its author. Muriel Fuller's encouragement, as he noted in his tribute to her on the opening page, meant that his first novel (and there were many after), received the recognition it deserved. It was part of her quiet offensive against discrimination in the literary trade and her witness as a Christian, one who could not be categorised or pigeon-holed. Of course the sexually explicit contents of the book (tame by today's standards) were off-limits to me as a child, particularly when it became a motion picture the next year starring a scantily clad Maureen O'Hara. I felt great affection for Muriel Fuller, another of my courtesy aunts, as an encourager both of black authors and this marginalised missionary-kid.

This was the first time that I was introduced to *The New York Times*. It had a weekly philatelic column which I devoured but it was the day-to-day news bulletins from the Far East that drew the anxious attention of my parents over the breakfast table. Negotiations between the Kuomintang and the Communists, brokered by General Marshall, broke down that January. Full-scale civil war broke out, particularly in the northeast with Russia an active player. On 25 March my mother, in her role as secretary of the North China Theological Seminary, sent out an urgent summons to all supporters of the school to attend the annual meeting on 7 April at the law office of Charles Shinn on South 15ᵗʰ St in Philadelphia. She wrote: "There are some urgent matters requiring discussion, particularly in regards to future organization." Harry Romig, President of the American Council, had moved to Texas and a replacement was needed. "The Seminary needs our best thought and prayers at this critical time."

But there was a more immediate crisis in our family. Katherine Richer MacLeod was now herself ill. She was 74, of strong farm stock and had not been sick a day in her life. But recently she had been complaining of stomach pains and cramps. On 24 May she was diagnosed with what her death certificate described as "inoperable cancer of the intestinal tract." Unsuccessful surgery took place in Germantown Hospital but, as it was noted later that "the primary lesion was not determined." She remained for several weeks in hospital. The Gramercy Park idyll was over, the three of us moved into my Grandmother's now empty apartment, and I was sent off to camp. It was a strange experience for me and the family were not good explaining the reality of death. My two aunts came up from Washington where they were both now living, along with Cathie's husband Paul but without Mary's. John Addy was nowhere to be seen and I soon became aware that it was not just my grandmother that was dying but also Mary's marriage

Sending me off to camp seemed an easy solution. However, never having been away from a parent, and given our nomadic existence, it proved very threatening. The first camp I was sent to in June was a facility operated by my father's supporting church, First Presbyterian in Pittsburgh. My father accompanied me to the Latrobe station where we were met by an assistant minister and driven up the campsite. "I am sorry that when I took Donald out to the camp at Ligonier last

Wednesday I could not stay to meet you," my father wrote Clarence Edward Macartney, the doughty bachelor senior minister of First Church and new chair of the American Council of NCTS. He went on to explain that "My mother is critically ill in Germantown Hospital and I had to return immediately to Philadelphia." For the next fortnight I felt I was on display as "the son of the missionaries we support" and it was the worst experience so far of my childhood.

The camp drew from those who were a part of First Church's downtown ministry and included a more mixed group than I had ever encountered before. I was always the last chosen for any baseball game, sports never having been part of my childhood previously, and the counsellors did not strike me as particularly "spiritual." A vivid memory was the time when all adult supervisors had disappeared and a bunch of teenage boys, related to the "brass" of the church I was told, went wild with the camp's p. a. system, playing all sorts of popular music which I had never been allowed to listen to previously as being "worldly". By the time the associate minister took me, a few days early, to the station for a trip home on my own, I was completely traumatized. I had let the family down and what would the report be to my parents and would they continue to support us as a result? My mind raced with a vivid scenario of failure, disappointment, and financial ruin! I went back to a grandmother who was dying but no one had told me the full story; I was left in the dark.

But my parents had not given up on the camp idea. Mother found one that was more "spiritual" and emphasized Bible study and personal faith. Founded six years earlier by the remarkable former missionary Bessie Tracer and located between Reading and Philadelphia, Camp Santana was much more my sort of place – cerebral rather than sporting with an emphasis on skills such as I as a missionary-kid could connect with, handcrafts and instruction in how to be "born again" and what we would today call "discipleship." My young and earnest counsellor separated me from the other boys in my tent that last day before we broke up and, wisely or unwisely, made me solemnly swear that there would never be another day in my life that I would not have a personal devotional time.

In August my parents, exhausted by the emotional roller-coaster of Grandma MacLeod's illness, went up to our old haunt of Mountain Rest for two weeks of recuperation. Grandma actually was getting better when they returned and reports were mailed to her other daughter in Australia that there was an improvement in her condition. But the recovery was short-lived. She died on 3 September, the cause of death being "Inoperable lesion of the stomach."

I recall that my uncle Paul was telephoned by Cathie in Washington (where he had taken me to get me out of the house) with the news that Grandma had died. I was not supposed to be told until we arrived back in Philadelphia when my father would inform me himself. Unfortunately I heard something when I was presumably asleep. When he put the phone down I told him it was no longer a secret, Grandma was dead. At the end, missionaries had come from the nearby China Inland Mission home and sang her into heaven. Her choices were "When I survey the wondrous cross" and her favourite, "When we walk with the Lord." She was a remarkable woman who had more than her share of pain and sorrow. But she had an iron will. Pioneer missionaries were made of stern stuff.

One of the subplots of that momentous summer was the tension that grew between my mother and Dad's sister Mary, both of them competing for the attention of the same man. Mary took a leave of absence from her work in the Registrar's Office at George Washington University. At the same time her marriage had collapsed as her preacher husband had finally had enough. Their landlords, members of his church, had not made things easier. My mother's letters to her sister were full of angst, with frequent instructions to destroy her outpourings (which she never did). Things got worse, with my father caught in the middle. My mother, like many Christians, could not abide conflict of any kind and was completely unrealistic, to the point of dishonesty, whenever Christians clashed. As a missionary-kid I saw at close range conflicts and friction but was never provided with an example of how to handle them in a responsible and mature way.

Grandma's funeral at the First United Presbyterian Church (UPCNA) on Wayne Avenue in Germantown was the first I had ever attended. A triumphant affair with a ringing witness to the resurrection, it left a lasting impression. We then scattered quickly. Dad's one year appointment to Gordon Divinity School had begun, term was about to start and a faculty retreat had been scheduled. My mother was left with her two sisters-in-law not only to wind up Grandma's affairs but also to close out our apartment in West Philadelphia, which had been sublet to a medical student whose certification exams were being held at that time.

The distribution of Grandma's extensive collection of correspondence, curios, and furniture, was made quickly and somewhat arbitrarily. It was the destruction of old letters that represented a tragedy: thirty years of missionary correspondence from the time my grandparents came to China to her final departure. All I was allowed to do was to soak the stamps off the envelopes, all else was burned. When I see those hundreds of stamps today I rue the day the letters they represent were consigned to oblivion. My father, in defence of the decision, would recall a story of how a missionary, out on itineration in a rural village, had discovered his looted love letters being used as wallpaper. Preserving letters could raise the spectre, when read years later, of past hurts and shame.

Hard as it was to say "Good-bye" to Grandma, it was infinitely harder for her daughter out in Australia. The family had sent regular communications about Grandma's condition, all of which took a week to arrive in Australia. Just before the end, she rallied, and hope was rekindled. Encouraging words were posted but the end had come cruelly and finally. How should one let Annabella know? A cable? It was decided to give her a few more days of hope and mail the sad news of her death and funeral. International communication was difficult and dicey in 1947. Whether the right decision was made, who can say in this age of instantaneous internet communication. Our family, divided by the mishkid experience, was fragmented, having settled on different continents. I am not sure that any of her Indiana relatives attended the service either, including her two brothers in Ohio and Indiana. Her Highland Scottish in-laws got the news in ten days. The missionary experience had scattered a close knit family. But my Grandmother was at peace and her struggles with life and death were over.

CHAPTER 17:

Settled in Boston, 1947-8

I am not sure when the invitation for Dad to teach in Boston actually came. Presumably it arrived some time when we were in New York. As it became apparent that the doctors would not allow Dad to return to China immediately, he agreed to a year's appointment to Gordon Divinity School, a small seminary in the Boston suburb, to teach church history. The school, founded in 1889, was named after its founder, Adonirum Judson Gordon, pastor of Clarendon St. Baptist Church in Boston, an associate of Dwight L. Moody, and best known as author of the hymn "My Jesus I love Thee." The school provided a counterweight to the heavily institutionalized (and generally increasingly liberal) theological education offered by other local Protestant seminaries such as Andover Newton, Boston University and Harvard Divinity School, and emphasized from its inception foreign missions. There was a close link with Westminster Seminary and several of its professors were graduates. Gordon had a significant role in the growth of post-World War II evangelicalism. One of its adjunct professors was George Lewis Murray[23] from the Isle of Lewis whose picture appeared alongside Dad's in the 1947 catalogue. Going to Gordon, if he couldn't get to China to teach, was an ideal and congenial alternative.

Settling in Boston, given the circumstances of our summer, presented challenges. Trekking around the city we discovered a very tight real estate market. Veterans had priority (as well as money). From Revere to Roslindale we followed the ads for available rentals. Then something fortuitously opened up in Cambridge, just four blocks from Harvard Divinity School. My father became uncharacteristically aggressive in pursuing the Whitman's, owners of a typical turn-of-the- century three story house on Gorham St. They lived on the ground floor and rented the upper two stories as an apartment. The arrangement provided a separate bedroom for me, a study for my father and spooky closets under the eaves where my cousins and I could dare each other to proceed in the dark. In many ways it was the happiest and most settled place of my childhood – spacious, comfortable, and convenient, the closest to normalcy I would ever attain.

It was just as well that everything came together as I was, by the end of September 1947 a basket case. "All this unsettledness had made him extremely nervous, and flighty," Mother wrote her sister about me. "So Alec and I are going to try to make a quiet, happy atmosphere. We are nervous, too, so we mustn't be!!" Dad himself was under pressure. He had accepted a one year appointment to teach church history at Gordon Divinity School in Brookline across the Charles River from our new home. He had got the job on the basis of his Ph. D. from Edinburgh University but that was in philosophy. He had not previously taught church history, only that year twenty years previously at

---

23   George Lewis Murray (1896-1956) graduate of a special course to qualify for ordination, Presbyterian College, Montreal 1928-31, ordained PCC 1931. Scotstown, QC, 1931-5; First UPCNA of Boston, 1935-1956; Mayfair UPCNA Philadelphia 1956. See my *George Murray of "the U.P."* Boston: Newton Presbyterian Church, 1996.

Wheaton College. Preparation by necessity was from lecture to lecture and largely based on his recent note-taking. He was substituting for Paul King Jewett, a 1943 graduate of Westminster Seminary, allowing him to complete doctoral studies at Harvard.[24] In their lecturing, Jewett and Dad were presumably working the same material from Paul Wooley who taught church history at Westminster. Jewett, who was called to Fuller Seminary, Pasadena, California, on completion of his Harvard doctorate, switched from history to systematic theology there. Judging from his contribution to the sexuality debates now roiling mainline denominations, it might be argued he should have stayed with church history.

My father had made a diligent study of the best public schools in the Boston area and predictably Cambridge was high on that list. Louis Agassiz[25] Public school (now Maria Baldwin Public School), at the corner of Oxford and Sacramento Streets, was just an eight minute walk from our place. My fourth grade teacher, Rose M. Hill, was very much in the tradition of Maria L. Baldwin who seventy years earlier made history as one of the first Afro-American public school principals, starting a legacy of respectful tolerance, encouragement of unpopular opinions, stimulation of students' intellectual curiosity and a compassion for insecure children. Typically Rose Hill saw me messing with my old desk inkwell and gave me, at her expense, one of the earliest biro pens. She had students racing to the public library to research assigned projects. Years later, in her retirement when I was at Harvard Graduate School, I stopped by to see her in her apartment off Mass Ave not far from the school. I hope I encouraged her to know she had been a hero to one fortunate fourth-grader.

---

24   Paul King Jewett (1919-1991), a PC(USA) minister, wrote the seminal *Man as Male and Female: A Study in Sexual Relationships from a Theological Point of View.* Grand Rapids, MI: Eerdmans, 1975.

25   Named after a Nineteenth Century Swiss zoologist and Harvard professor, the school's name changed in 2002 to Maria L. Baldwin School. Agassiz, now regarded a racist bigot, is gone, thus "sanitising" history. Maria L. Baldwin, appointed Agassiz principal in 1889, was the first black woman to hold such a position.

My closest friend and academic rival at Agassiz School was Sam
Gorovitz who later went on to be one of America's leading medical
ethicists. After going to MIT and taking a doctorate in philosophy at
Stanford University he went on to teach philosophy and ethics first at
the University of Maryland and then, after 1986, at Syracuse University
where he was Dean of the Faculty of Arts and Sciences. One of his many
texts is *Doctor's Dilemmas: Moral Conflicts and Medical Care* (1985).
With his Jewish perspective, Sam often gets into biblical territory with
one title of a paper he delivered asking the question "Am I My Brother's
Keeper?" He is frequently consulted by the media on topics such as
assisted suicide. His home was *en route* to the Cambridge Public Library
which Miss Rose encouraged us to visit for further investigation about
a given subject. Sam and I would race along Irving St. to see who could
get there first, hurrying to borrow a book we both wanted. At the end of
that year he moved over to Brookline as I went to China. In old age we
have resumed our friendship.

Harold John Ockenga[26] was also a significant influence on me during
that Boston year. Ockenga was senior pastor at historic Park St. Church
on the Boston Common, an easy ride from Cambridge on public transportation. His time at Princeton Seminary had overlapped for a year
with my father's and they were acquainted. As a protégé of Macartney
for whom he had been an assistant, it was inevitable that Dad would try
to enlist him as a supporter of NCTS. Ockenga was one reason I was
set at an early age at becoming a minister. I preached my first sermon,
with his approval and encouragement, at a junior church service. I had
not been baptized so I joined a communicant's class for preparation. I
was required to memorise much of the Shorter Catechism and attended

---

26   Harold John Ockenga (1905-1985) attended Princeton Seminary (1927-1929)
      and graduated Westminster Seminary 1930. Ph.D. University of Pittsburgh.
      Minister Park St. Church, Boston (1937-1969). He was the first President of
      Fuller Seminary in 1947 and in 1969 became President of Gordon-Conwell
      Theological Seminary.

classes with an eager assistant pastor, Gleason Archer Jr.[27]. The others joining with me were all girls and much to my delight, when we were being catechized, one of them stumbled on her lines and I could not hide my pleasure at her discomfort. Gleason Archer dismissed all the others and then clobbered me, indicating that I might have attained the letter but certainly not the Spirit of the material. I was welcomed into membership at a memorable service on Maundy Thursday, 3 April, and received a beautiful leather-bound Thompson Chain Reference Bible, donated anonymously by Allan Comstock Emery Jr[28]., a Park St. deacon and prosperous wool merchant. His daughter was a sister-in-law of Muriel Fuller. In the tight circle I inhabited all things seem to interconnect.

It was the missionary emphasis of Park St. Church that helped me come to terms with the prospect of returning to war-torn China which I had been dreading (along with my mother on my behalf). Park St. Church had a yearly Missions Conference, borrowed from Oswald Smith and People's Church Toronto. The climax was a commitment service, dedicating both individuals and their money to the cause of world-wide missions. As the pledge money and life commitments were counted, there was a call for volunteers to come forward "to be obedient to the Great Commission, going into the entire world, in Jesus' words, to preach the gospel to the ends of the earth". With heads bowed in the congregation people started to walk to the front. Suddenly my mother was aware that her ten-year old son had gotten out of his seat and slowly walked down the carpeted (not saw dust) trail. She started to tear up because to her it was God's confirmation that it was all right to take him to China. An evening sermon by Dr. Ockenga spoke of the "imminent return of our Lord" based on Matthew 24:14 (KJV): "And this gospel

27   Gleason Archer, Jr. (1916-2004) Harvard College 1938 *Summa cum laude*; Ll.B. Suffolk Law School; Ph.D. Harvard 1944, Princeton Sem. 1945. Park St. Church 1945-8. taught Fuller Sem., 1948-65, TEDS, 1965-1986.

28   Allan C. Emery, Jr., (1919-2010) graduate of Wheaton College 1941, Ll.D.1986. Actively involved with the Billy Graham Evangelistic Association from 1950 and Gordon-Conwell Theological Seminary from 1969..

of the kingdom shall be preached in all the world for a witness unto all nations; and then shall the end come." As we turned off the radio (we listened but did not attend nights) I urged my parents to pray for Jesus' return to be hastened by the global proclamation of the gospel. Dad was unimpressed by this emphasis, concerned that the missionary call demanded a lifelong commitment based on realism, sacrifice and obedience.

Then it ended and life moved on. The happiest year of my childhood was over. As the summer of 1948 approached it was decided we were returning to China. My father had been given clearance by the doctors and his citizenship was scheduled for the end of the summer. In its usual efficient manner the Mission Board was arranging tickets and transportation. So we closed out the lovely apartment, said goodbye to my wonderful teacher and school and prepared to head for the Far East. The news from China was hardly reassuring: a bad situation had gotten worse. Inflation was rampant.

But before we left, there was the matter of my mother's parents' fiftieth wedding anniversary. Given their straitened circumstance it was not immediately clear how the event could be celebrated. Eventually it was decided to bring the whole family together to upper New York state at a campsite near Rome called Delta Lake owned and operated by the Christian and Missionary Alliance regional district, a denomination Marjorie was affiliated with in Brooklyn.

She had bought a modest cabin there. All five siblings and their families would attend, no small accomplishment. Grandmother's size and arthritis made it difficult for her to navigate in a campsite and so she had the best accommodation. The three sisters tried to feed the whole crowd. Uncle Carleton was notably absent though presumably it was his money that had originally bought the property. There were many truants from the daily program of inspirational services. Mother's brothers regularly disappeared for their smokes (not allowed on the site of a Christian camp) and heads huddled around a radio to listen to the Dodgers, who with the help of Jackie Robinson were soon to win what Americans modestly call baseball's "World Series". The old tensions in a religiously divided family prevailed: grace or no grace at meals, family daily Bible reading - should it be obligatory for all? And who was sneaking out for a beer or a movie in downtown Rome?

Delta Lake Conference Grounds, Miles grandparents' Golden Wedding, July 1948

When it was all over, I went to stay with my aunt Priscilla. I never knew whether my uncle Wesley really wanted me but I doubt it. A chubby child, I was sensitive about my weight and one day he drew attention to the size of my waistline, saying that at thirty-two inches it was larger than his had been when he went to college, For three weeks I stayed with them at their rented home in West Auburn, Maine. I did enjoy my uncle's library but apparently did not ingratiate myself with my cousins by not enlisting for chores. Instead, I read *Cry the Beloved Country*. Alan Paton's just published epic stirred me with its story of a wayward clergy child. My parents meanwhile were preparing for our departure in steamy New York City, packing, buying supplies unavailable in China, and counting the days until my father's naturalization papers would come through.

A letter to me from my father dated 12 July 1948 with its somewhat stilted expressions of love and the obligatory sermonette in the final paragraph, show neither awareness of my fearfulness at the future nor even of what would interest a ten year old child. In the past almost three years we had not really bonded or become a normal American family. When I re-joined my parents in August, in anticipation of a departure the first week of September, we were in a rented place near Wilton. My uncertainties became apparent when one night I kept myself awake, listening anxiously to a conversation between my parents and Dad's sister Cathie and husband Paul, trying to catch some information as to what the grownups were planning. Did they know how alone and scared I was as an only child about to set off on a strange adventure?

My father's preoccupations were typical. He spent time ransacking second hand bookstores for books that would be appropriate (from a guide he had bought) for children of a certain age. That summer he packed a whole library for me, with each of the next five years marked out with books suitable for someone of my age at that stage. Sadly by the time they had arrived in China and could eventually be unpacked, they were dated and inappropriate. I had moved on. He had tried, but my mother was no help, even though she understood me (and the culture) better. For our last night in the States the Board put us up in the Henry Hudson hotel where we could see the *Queen Elizabeth* berthed, ready to take us out the next day. I was excited and also scared.

As we were about to leave my parents sent a penny postcard to their supporters which has to me a distinctly anxious sound:

"We are sailing from New York on September 8, to return to our post in China, and the work of North China Theological Seminary. We have a tough assignment in a land of disorder and discomfort and greatly need your prayers on our behalf. Pray also for the Seminary that it may be largely used of God to build the Christian Church in China. We on our part will not forget to pray for you at home who support us."

CHAPTER 18:

Posh Travel, 1948

For the rest of my childhood, and ever after, the date "8 September 1948" had an almost mythical quality about it. Everything I had grown accustomed to, in spite of all our moves and dislocations had been predictable and stable in comparison to what was to follow. Or was it that way really? At ten years of age was it simply that I was now able to process the first ten years of our gyrations more seriously, the tensions developing between my parents. Mother, I suspect, did not want to go back to China given the chaos reported daily in the *New York Times* but accepted my father's concern about China and his need to be there at this moment in history. But noone really could grasp the situation in its entirety and complexity. At the age of 46 and with a strong commitment to his call to China, he was single-minded and nothing could have stopped him.

About one thing, however, my mother was definite. We would all travel as citizens of the same country. So on 31 August 1948 my father became an American citizen, having completed all the forms required and the two years of mandatory residency since his imbroglio at the border in Buffalo. His concession was reluctant: he still regarded himself as British. The late date of his swearing in meant that there was no way he could arrive in China for the beginning of the academic year. Further delaying our arrival was his desire to travel through Scotland so that he could reconnect with family who had been his most loyal supporters during the years of his imprisonment. And he was anxious to show off his son to a family noticeably sparse with representation in the next generation

In preparation for our arrival in Southampton a week later my father read me the classic that British schoolchildren discovered at an early age. *Our Island Story*, written by Henrietta Elizabeth Marshall at the height of the Edwardian Empire forty-three years earlier, had been his childhood staple at Chefoo and now it was my turn to be influenced. For the following two Christmases I was introduced to the sequels: first *Scotland's Story* followed in 1950, when appropriately we were in Hong Kong, *Our Empire Story*. Miss Marshall, a Scot with limited academic credentials, but with a knack (which owed much to William Shakespeare it later turned out) for making historical narrative (and legend) come alive. Miss Marshall (only later was her gender disclosed to me) instilled in me, as with so many others, an early fascination with history.

One passage stood out for me: her recreation of Jenny Geddes, the stool-thrower at St. Giles Cathedral Edinburgh. Her explanation for Jenny's rage struck a responsive chord: "Many of the people in Scotland had become Protestant. They were called Presbyterians, and like the Puritans, they chose to have a very simple form of worship, and very simple churches. This did not please Charles" (the King at the time). That story deeply resonated with me: while it was not *my* island story, I too was a Presbyterian, battling for the same faith. The story of "our island" followed by that of Scotland and "our empire," each with its allocation of heroes and villains, provided a very comfortable (and digestible) understanding of the complexities of the past. I was about to be introduced to many of the places she described (and explained) so dramatically. Henrietta Marshall made me an historian. Her interpretation was not only Whig, it was whimsy and I loved it.

My other introduction to things British was the *Queen Elizabeth* itself, named for the ever popular Scottish consort of George VI. The epitome of an old order now forever lost with its *art nouveau* decor, it was launched shortly after my birth date, pristine in its vaunted engineering excellence, when it was made into a troop ship almost immediately after launch. It introduced me to a whole new world. I was rushed by the bar, not allowed to go to any of the films on offer, and generally segregated from the other children, though we ate together as a group. Our first landfall was the Normandy coast as we sailed into Cherbourg harbour, still showing signs of the ravages of war with Juno Beach only an hour's drive away. On arrival in Southampton we were quickly cleared by customs and immigration as my father presented his shiny new American passport.

The boat train took us to Victoria station and from there a taxi brought us to Euston where we took the night train to Inverness. My father was like a homing pigeon with all his Scottish nativism surfacing. At Inverness we transferred the next morning to a train which brought us to Kyle of Locals, "a very beautiful ride through the highlands", as my mother later described it. "Streams were rushing down the mountain sides into the urns which sparkled along by the roadsides." Boarding the *Loch Seaforth* we took the four hour ride to Stornoway, arriving at dusk. We were greeted by a large number of assorted cousins as we docked, and then taken to "cousin" Joan's apartment across from the pier. In my first of a series of letters to my cousin Carleton I explained that although called cousin "she's over fifty". The aroma of fresh baked bread wafted up from the ground floor as I awoke the next morning. The view across to the Castle was spectacular with all the boats docked.

We had only twenty-four hours on the Isle of Lewis but the family ensured that we made the most of the limited time we had. My father as a minister and a missionary was highly respected. His reputation had been established as the son of Rev. Kenneth MacLeod, brother of two well-known clergy, three sons of a pious crofter with a Sabbath ferry. Everywhere we went I was handed folded up bills by relatives who were living, in those immediate post-war years, a subsistence existence. I was excited by my newfound wealth until I was subsequently told by my father that it was "for the ministry" and ordered to hand it all over to him. Fifty kinfolk saw us off at the airport, singing "God be with you till we meet again." This was my first awareness (which my parents had generally tried to keep from me) that returning to China was a serious, even dangerous, business. Before I could give it further thought, I was distracted by my first plane ride

The warm family fuzzies came to an abrupt end as we journeyed forty miles to Portmahomack a fishing village on the North Sea where Dad's uncle, after whom he was named, had been minister for over twenty years. I had been warned about Uncle Alex as stern and unforgiving. My father had been in college when his father died and Uncle Alex had sent his monthly donation for five pounds instead to him. Dad did not write a letter of thanks and after two months the cheques no longer appeared, a warning about failing to acknowledge gifts. Uncle Alex with his dark suits, his bowler hat, and his clerical collar, lived in a large manse cared for by his niece, cousin Chrissie who humanized him and snuck sugar for my porridge, something he strongly disapproved of. Uncle Alex took my measure and at one meal, as conversation got sticky, intoned to my mother "You have a most peculiar child," words never forgotten and often repeated.

Dad had allocated a generous four days for our time in Portmahomack but there were no hard feelings from the other relatives because Uncle Alex was the family's patriarch. The time was spent as Dad and he went through his Library and uncle Alex culled books from his collection, placing them in a tin trunk that would travel out to China separately, lovingly saying a lingering farewell to each treasure as he explained what that volume had meant to him, an old man (82 at the time) knowing his time had run out. It was a powerful demonstration of a bibliophile's obsessions. Two things stood out from our time there, as I reported to my cousin: Uncle Alex's stern sermon to his loving congregation and my escape to a ruined castle across the field, standing like a sentinel on a bluff overlooking the water. The ruins of the Sixteenth Century roofless Bellone Castle are now the residence of an Edinburgh fashion designer but to the eyes of a ten-year old the old wreck represented the beauty of ruins.

By Monday evening we were off on another night train to Glasgow but first made a flying trip to Edinburgh for a quick visit with the Torrance family, my parents' landlords while studying there a decade earlier, and to the Castle with its recreation of Scotland's past. In Glasgow we made a pilgrimage out to Blantyre, the birthplace of David Livingstone and my father recounted the stories of his father's (and his) missionary hero and the mill he had left at the age of fourteen to become a medical missionary in Africa. The circle was completed when, after taking the night train to London, awestruck I saw his grave on entering Westminster Abbey. Much of the following day in London was spent at the HMV Studio in Hayes, Middlesex, listening to 78 rpm records in a sound-proof studio. My mother, always with her pupils in mind, made her selections which were then to be boxed and shipped out on our passage to Hong Kong. Listening to record after record provided me an introduction to classical and even some popular music, from Alfred Cortot to Harry Lauder. We also purchased a wireless gramophone which it would be my task later to crank up for students at the seminary as they attended our musical soirées.

As the ship was about to sail, my mother reported that "Donald has been a brick about the high speed and very much interested in everything. He has seen a lot!" Our Foreign Mission Board had booked us First Class, with a family suite that gave me my own small room, on the *S. S. Canton* sailing from Southampton on 24 September 1948 just eleven days after we had arrived in Britain. "Posh" had been used by the British to describe luxury travel to India in Victorian times and ours fit the definition of "Port out, starboard home." The first night the printed menu featured an eight course meal with an Australian burgundy and a French sauterne. Our luxury accommodation was an embarrassment because a party from the China Inland Mission (CIM) was in steerage. We had met up with them while staying the days before we left at the CIM home in Newington Green in London and of course, as a CIM'er born and bred, my father quickly established many links. We joined them for prayer every morning at 7:30.

Say what you will, the so-called "liberal" mission boards looked after their members better than the "faith" missions. My father endeared himself to the children in the CIM party (their fathers having gone on ahead) by providing daily readings of *Swiss Family Robinson*, regarded as more suitable for impressionable children in its depiction of life on a desert island than *Robinson Crusoe*. And of course the relevance was immediate: we were all going to set up home in *terra incognita*. The whole implausible adventure, with its wildly incongruous collection of animals, and its moralisms, struck a responsive chord in all of the children seated respectfully around my father.

The Bay of Biscay kept its reputation for turbulence. "Donald loves the pool" my mother noted, but it was off limits when the sea turned choppy. I had done a water colour painting in Third Grade of the Rock of Gibraltar, based on an insurance company ad, and as we passed alongside it seemed just as reliable and strong. With my brownie box camera I tried to catch a picture of Pantalleria in the middle of the Mediterranean only to have it come out as a blurred line on the horizon. Docking at Port Said the Egyptian government was incredibly "fussy with regulations of all kinds, purses searched, cameras contrabanded" and all for a four hour stopover. I asked my father where all those people on the pier lived and was given my first reality check about conditions in other parts of the world when I was told that they were there because they had nowhere else to go. Sailing through the Suez Canal I eagerly looked for the place where the Israelites crossed the Red Sea. At the other end, amid scorching heat; we turned east to Aden where, in spite of what we were told, it rained for the first time in months. Mother wrote "I am still glad of this long journey and not weary of day after day at sea. " She was also grateful that Carleton Sr. had arranged for a parcel of medicines from the Lewis Drug Store in Brooklyn, including some new antibiotics, a lifesaver later in China.

On to Bombay with dhows everywhere as we crossed the Indian Ocean. A large number of passengers disembarked there. We went, a year and a half after independence and partition, to the Gate of India which commemorated the visit of George V as Emperor in 1911. At

Colombo I sent a post card to my cousin with the breathless note that "I am very thrilled at the thought of taking a rickshaw ride in Ceylon." At each stopover Dad and I would buy a collection of low value stamps and then, having affixed them with hinges, paste them in a book with careful parental instruction as to their significance in the country we'd visited. Landing at Penang on Sunday meant that we could visit a local congregation that evening, Dad chose the historic and imposing St George's Church. My first introduction to the beauty of an Anglican Evensong was memorable. I sang for the first time "The day Thou gavest Lord is ended" as in full view the sun set over the Bay of Bengal. Unforgettable.

In a three page double sided letter to my cousin from Singapore (where we lingered for two days) I described the welcome we had received from the Bible Society secretary. Ian Morrison. "Daddy knew Mr. Morrison in camp" I wrote, "and they have a seven-year old boy and a year and a half year old girl who frowns at everybody until she gets used to them. He has a very nice house (tall ceilings and lots of mosquito netting all around the beds)." Quite different accommodation from the time that our host and my father had been prison camp bunkmates. Ian Morrison took us everywhere. We called on the monkeys in the Botanical Garden and viewed the grotesquely garish Tiger Balm Garden. It would not be my last connection with the family: Ian's sister-in-law Cathie Nicoll was the senior staff member when I was appointed General Director of IVCF Canada in 1975.

It took us four days to travel from Singapore to Hong Kong across the South China Sea, arriving in Hong Kong early Monday morning, 25 October. We had been a month on board and the ship had become our home, our shelter. The news that greeted us that morning in the *South China Morning Post* was not good: The day we had left Singapore the key city of Changchun in Manchuria, capital of the old Japanese puppet state of Manchukuo, had fallen after one of Chiang Kai-shek's armies defected and the other surrendered. With the help of the Russians, Mao had achieved a major breakthrough and it was, as we now know, the beginning of the end of the Nationalist government. With the fall of Mukden the American consular staff would be held hostage and the breach between the Communists and the United States became explicit. Harry Truman had few options and being an American citizen in China was no longer an advantage for my father and his newly minted US passport. Sightseeing in Hong Kong, and the inevitable shopping, seemed almost an escapist anti-climax. We arranged for some of our freight to remain in a Hong Kong godown. "Alec said maybe we would be back home by Christmas," my mother wrote jauntily from Hong Kong, "but we decided that was a bad way to look at our arrival in China and wouldn't be a help to the best sort of work while we are here!" Then she added "I hope things will settle down and we can do a lasting job of work in the seminary."

It was in Hong Kong that I finished fractions. My home schooling had proceeded rather jerkily throughout the two months of travel. "We have been quite faithful about doing some lessons every day." My father's cousin Cathy MacKay, a Glasgow school teacher, had provided some school textbooks for me to use on my travels which were brought out as I sat down amid many distractions to complete my lessons. For creative writing I was to compose a so-called "travel letter" (which has not survived). Later I drew with black ink a series of pictures on open shells (which I had retrieved from a garbage tip) of scenes along the way, from Big Ben to the Peak tram to illustrate our journey. They were then hung and pinned to an open display case.

"Donald has been very adjustable, taking everything quite as a matter of course and balancing up the disagreeable with the novel in a very good spirit," my mother reassured our American partners from Hong Kong. "He is keenly interested in things. We are not certain where he will go to Wusih with us, or be left in Shanghai to go to school there – it is possible he could come home at least some weekends. Alex feels that would probably be better." The appearance of ignorance about what was really happening in China as we were about to arrive was perhaps feigned. As my mother privately reflected on what lay ahead she wrote from Port Said to her sister: "My heart almost paused when I think of his being away at school. And yet it seems almost inevitable. Because I know the Lord will *guide* clearly, I can trust the feelings … and the tears.

I am sure, are not 'the wrong kind' I want the best for him." Although, because of the chaos in China, I could not be sent away to boarding school as my father had been, this ten year old was about to experience the most terrifying year of his childhood. Within six months my mother and I would be back in Hong Kong, separated again, having experienced first-hand the Chinese revolution.

CHAPTER 19:
Arriving In Chaotic China, 1948

The last leg of our trip to China, Hong Kong to Shanghai, stood in marked contrast to the earlier part of the voyage. "The Pacific was anything but pacific," my mother reported. A tropical storm named Pat had confined passengers to their cabins. "Occasional doleful sounds" could be heard from behind closed doors. I, as a proud sailor, was one of the few who made it to meals. When our bedraggled party finally arrived on Monday evening 5 November there was no Presbyterian to meet us so we took the CIM lorry, shrouded in khaki tarpaulins, carrying only hand luggage, as fire trucks were summoned to our boat. We were unclear as to whether there would be anything to claim at customs the following day.

As my father returned to the customs jetty the next morning, Kay Kepler came to see us, travelling in from the China Bible Seminary where her husband Ken was teaching. Her update on conditions in China was sobering. I listened in on the grown-up conversation with rapt attention. This was not the old China, she told us, the China that we had known and loved. Instead everything that could go wrong had gone wrong. Up to now, a teacher was always honoured and respected. My father hoped that I could be sent to school at Kuling in the centre of the country, where his own boarding school at Chefoo had moved when its original site was deemed too vulnerable to a Communist takeover. Instead, I was registered at the Shanghai American School, a substantial 1920's era red brick edifice on Avenue Petain in the former French concession, now renamed Hengshan Lu. The fifth grade to which I was assigned had three teachers during my six months there, each leaving as the political situation worsened.

Four days after we arrived, ominously the American consul in Shanghai sent a notice to all American citizens in the eastern part of China to evacuate immediately while they still could leave. "If you read anything *very* bad, just remember that newspapers usually exaggerate," Mother advised her parents. My father asked the inevitable question: "Did we mistake the Lord's guidance that led us to give up our home and position in the U.S.A.?" Three years after the cessation of hostilities and the opening of the concentration camps, were we now facing further separation and dislocation? As we were about to despair there were two unusual signs of hope at the customs shed in regard to our baggage. It only took ten days to clear and it cost just fifty US dollars. Everyone we knew was amazed at these unexpected providences in such an unpredictable and toxic environment.

Customs cleared, their son registered for the Shanghai American School and parked with the Kepler's, my parents were now free to travel on to the new location of the seminary, Wusih, an industrial city 140 kilometres or two hours train travel from Shanghai on the main line to Nanking. Martin Hopkins and Professor Ting were at the railway station to greet them and help them navigate the crowds. The property which was for the next six months to be our family's home base (though I remained in Shanghai except for holidays) had been the compound of a wealthy individual who fortunately (for him) sold it to the seminary for the asking price as he left the country The main two storied house faced north at the compound's entrance. The five faculty members were scattered around the property in apartments. Classrooms were makeshift.

Surviving books and equipment had been loaded on a train and sent down from Hsuchow that summer. It was a matter of some amusement that all our furniture, retrieved from Shandong before the destruction of my childhood home, was now scattered around the property. Only the best could be shipped and, in a welcome burst of equality, for the first time fellow faculty could enjoy our sofas, beds, dining room suite, and kitchen equipment. The inequality between Western and Chinese staff had rankled me even as a child and now, as we visited fellow faculty members' apartments, we observed wryly and silently that justice had prevailed as our goods were now being shared. Only my Father's four boxes of books, left in the seminary library (and including our 78 rpm record collection) had been returned to us.

Hopkins and Ting drove them to the new site for the seminary, four miles out of town across from "Mei Yuan" (Plum Garden) a site noted for beauty and tranquillity. As they went through the large wrought-iron gates a crowd soon gathered: "we had barely got through the gates when faculty and students poured out to give us a welcome" my father remarked. That welcome was all the more intense because many realized how much our family had sacrificed to come to China at a time like that. We were loved and respected. My mother's first impressions were hardly cheerful. The cement calcimined walls and floor were bare, their room seemed "furniture-less and rug-less" though on closer inspection there was a bed, a bureau, and two folding chairs. There were no curtains but large shutters on the windows.

Dad soon established himself at Dr Hayes' historic desk. Though our situation was Spartan, Martin and Bessie Hopkins "did everything for the school and students first, and neglected themselves. They are eating better now that we have come, too." Mother used the word "heroic" to describe the Hopkins' self-sacrifice for the seminary community. She continued: "Food is difficult to obtain. Many schools are curtained or closed because of this and some of our students will likely be leaving soon. Dr. Hopkins feeds 159 in this courtyard. Our own diet is helped by remaining UNRRA supplies." UNRRA, the United Nations Relief and Rehabilitation Administration, was set up by the Allies (mostly American, some British and a little Canadian aid) in 1943 to help feed the victims of war. It was superseded by the Marshall Plan. UNRRA leftovers soon became a staple of the seminary diet as well as the black market.

And what did I make of this, safely ensconced in Shanghai with the Keplers? A verse I wrote my parents dated 14 November provides insight as to how I was coping with the changes and the stress:

"Hope to see you very soon
(Will next week do?)
Want talk all things,
Do you think Communist victory due?
Soldiers right outside our gates.
Hope they won't fall to Communist fate.
Misplaced Friday arithmetic
Hope to save face
Before Mrs. Scanland."

Mrs. Scanland, my Fifth Grade teacher, had quickly taken my measure. My 7 December report sheet showed A's in all subjects except spelling and arithmetic. Our class photo in the SAS yearbook shows a class of ten, four Chinese and six Caucasian. Half of us were mish-kids. The father of classmate Jacqueline Sprunt, my first love with whom I exchanged letters after evacuation, worked for the American President Lines.

The ten-day Thanksgiving 1948 school holiday was spread over two weekends to allow families in the interior to reconnect. Mother went to Shanghai with my winter clothing and to bring me back to Wusih. Her train trip in had been an adventure as was all rail travel throughout China at the time: only one train a day had reserved first class tickets (the only way to ensure you could go at the time stated) but the only seats available on that train turned out to be second class. As the train lurched toward Shanghai she wrote: "Around me people are lunching on a variety of things – round flat cakes filled with sesamum seeds, sugar sticks, candy, watermelon seeds, Mandarin oranges, Chinese powdery candy neatly packed in paper boxes. All the rinds, paper and sesamum seeds are dropped on the floor. It is really quite messy. Fortunately my sense of smell is quite affected by my cold, so I don't notice it much."

When settled in for the holiday in Wusih I realized that, for the first time in six months we were under the same roof as a family. "I wondered how Donald would react to this place" my mother anxiously confessed. Apparently I came across as "a good scout" and endeared myself to the students who asked me to provide a reading of a poem for their English club. I had never been so cold in my life – coal was no longer available as the coal fields had been occupied by the Communists. Instead we used kerosene, a coal derivative which still seemed available. I have always associated the holiday with the smell of kerosene coming from our portable heater. Thanksgiving dinner consisted of US Army surplus canned fried chicken and assorted local vegetables. For desert Mother produced canned Australian peaches and Dr Hopkins produced a box of army vintage (stale) chocolates. It was to have been a farewell for Bessie Hopkins but she had left suddenly when word arrived that she was booked for America the next Monday. Farewells and separations became a part of my life, saying good-bye to someone close to us.

Getting back to Shanghai was an adventure. With no vehicle to hail in sight we had to walk all the way into the city, with my father encouraging me as I grumbled over the next hill and later providing me with a mock certificate: "THIS IS TO CETIFY THAT ALISTAIR DONALD MACLEOD, AGE 10, DID ON THE 29TH DAY OF NOVEMBER DID WALK FROM NORTH CHINA THEOLOGICAL SEMINIARY, NEAR THE MEI YUAN, TO THE GRAND CANAL, NEAR THE TOWN OF WUSIH, KIANGSU, A DISTANCE OF SOME FIVE MILES IN TOKEN OF THIS FEAT THIS CERTIFICATE IS AWARDED HIM BY (signature) ALEX N. MacLEOD." A pedicab took us the last lap to a station packed with people sitting on suitcases only to learn we'd missed the one o'clock train because tickets were unobtainable. Miraculously some seminary students from Foochow surfaced and bought tickets for us for the four o'clock train. We passed the time during the three hour delay by having tea at the Southern Baptist mission. Adversity brought all foreigners and particularly all missionaries into close camaraderie and we had more in common theologically with Southern Baptists than some American Presbyterians.

Returning to the station we discovered that the students had already loaded our bags on the train . Forty minutes late, the train, by now in pitch darkness because its generator was no longer operational, took off. I was occupying a seat away from my mother. Both of us soon cramped up. There were people everywhere: riding on the roof, on the cow-catcher, out the doors and windows, standing over us. I let out a wail, audible to all but fortunately in English, piercing the darkness: "Mother this has been a **horrible** day!" The train inched ahead and we finally arrived in Shanghai at 9:30, three hours late. We went straight to the CIM home where Vivian Adolph had a hot meal ready for us. The next morning my mother (as she repeatedly did over the years subsequently with each crisis) landed in Hospital for two days. All she would say was that she had lost her voice. It was reported that Donald, "a good sport", "rather enjoys the memory of the day."

Our host Vivian Adolph was the wife of the CIM's medical health officer, Paul Adolph, who had been my father's college roommate. She had made the dining room of their apartment into a bedroom for me. They had two sons, Harold and Robert, who were by then rowdy teen-agers. Years later, before he died, Robert[29] would apologize for the ways in which they (or he) mercilessly teased me but I have no recollection of that at all. Here as previously in Kiangwan, transportation to school became a challenge. The Southern Baptist truck/bus was no longer sus-tainable because so many had departed. Without it I was faced with the alternative of either getting a pedicab or taking the municipal bus, a nightmare experience for a ten year old. I had lost my Chinese which would have been little help anyway because the five-tone Shanghai dialect, now little used, was then the vernacular.

---

29   Medical lab worker Robert (1936-2015) Bangla Desh with Association of Baptists
      for World Evangelism (1964-2004); surgeon Dr. Harold (1934-) Ethiopia with
      SIM (1966-1976 & 2000–2006) and in West Africa (1988-1996).

Hsuchow, the major rail hub in North Kiangsu where the seminary had relocated before the move to Wusih four months earlier, had now fallen. People were fleeing Nanking and the rumour was that the line to Shanghai had been cut. Indeed, there were rumours everywhere, among them that our NCTS President was closing the school down. My mother was urged not to return. But we had all been on a single passport and now she needed to get my father's new separate document to him because without it his situation was risky. "It is very urgent, I must go" she shouted at the ticket window and was told to come back early the next morning. She booked a taxi for 6:30 a.m. but it never showed and she finally nabbed a pedicab which took her to a crowded and chaotic North Station. She went from ticket window to ticket window banging on them in hopes of finding one open and a ticket for sale. She eventually did get through to Wusih only to return to Shanghai four days later. We would finally reunite as a family on Christmas Eve.

My father's state of mind at this point could only be imagined but it took its toll on all of us. The almost daily December letters he wrote my mother in Shanghai, none of which were preserved, were intense, judging from references to them elsewhere. My mother shared her deepest anxieties as prayer requests to her sister: "Pray that [Alex] will see things realistically and not avoid rapid decisions." And for me: "Pray that I will have peace about arrangements for Donald – and know what to do." For Dad it was the future that most exercised him. The Keplers' departure had been a wakeup call but also brought some criticism. But what were Dad's alternatives if he was to return to America? His superior at the Presbyterian office in Shanghai, Margaret Frame, was also raising questions about his future. She flagged his "theological position," his evident biases in his theological instruction, and his lack of support for the Church of Christ in China (CCC), as problems. Her questions came at the worst possible moment and betrayed a fundamental insensitivity. Supported by a strong faith, Dad also had influential backers. He wrote at length on 18 November to Clarence Edward Macartney: "Uppermost in all our minds is that we may have to flee at a moment's notice." Should that happen, it helped to have a loyal and sympathetic ally.

In his response to Miss Frame (with whom we always maintained a cordial personal relationship), Dad described his theological position as "orthodox Presbyterianism." He modestly listed his academic qualifications and experience. "I have twice given up good positions in America to come out to the East." As to his future outside China, he stated that "The thought of transferring to another mission field where another language must be learned leaves me quite cold. I have spent so many years in this short life trying to get some knowledge of English and Chinese that I do not feel any keenness for working outside these two languages." But he quietly wrote to friends about alternatives: Formosa (Taiwan), Korea and the Philippines. In each place he had contacts and some theological compatibility.

We returned to Wusih for a rather sombre Christmas. My mother had spent her three weeks in Shanghai acquiring seventy small gifts for the faculty children. I was assigned to wrap them but handicrafts have never been my thing so I got easily exasperated with wrapping paper and ribbons. One of the features of Christmas in Tenghsien had been a Messiah concert. The album of Handel's oratorio had fortunately been preserved and with our new wind-up gramophone I was tasked with changing the 78 rpm records and I cranking up the machine. The students and faculty gathered in the make-shift Chapel to hear the reassuring words that "unto us a child is born" and that his name was "Prince of Peace". We gathered as a family under a branch-substitute for a tree and exchanged gifts. On New Year's Day the faculty, staff and students, came round, wishing us a very happy (Western) New Year. "We shall return the calls on the Chinese New Year Day," my mother explained.

I returned to Shanghai alone, settling in to a third location in as many months, this time the dormitory behind the Shanghai American School. "I hope you are getting along nicely," my mother wrote anxiously. "I was feeling as though you had quite a lot of responsibility for your age, then I was sure you could take it, and really grow a lot in the experience." Dad's letters were filled with jolly adventures such as killing a nocturnal rat who had terrorized them, mother's had good advice: responding to a theological tussle I'd had with my Sunday School teacher (which she tried to dampen down), warning me not to skip piano lessons, and instructing me how to organize my day.

Their correspondence did little to alleviate my unhappiness and homesickness. Until I got to the States four years later those weeks boarding in the Shanghai American School dormitory were the unhappiest of my childhood. The older teenaged high school students in the dorm were typical adolescents exploring Shanghai by night with little restraint or control. My mother, on one of her anxious visits, brought some girls' only reading material for a slightly older mishkid who was having her first period and was in the infirmary. I asked for details about her and got only an embarrassed silence. It seemed I was always being left out of the loop. I had so many questions and there were so few answers.

In early February my mother moved into Shanghai and I settled into my fourth location in the city. I felt a deep sense of guilt that I had not been able to rise to the challenge and been a successful warrior in the Lord's Army. We took an apartment that the Presbyterian Church USA made available for us. Ten minutes' walk from the school at 19½ Tihwa Rd. we would walk together to "our" school. The other flat in the building was occupied by the West family who had a four or five year old son named Russell with whom I played the role of an older (and hopefully wiser) brother. Charles Converse West, later a distinguished professor of Christian Ethics at Princeton Seminary, had come to China in 1945 and was now assigned to Hangchow to which he commuted. Today it's an hour by bullet train but in 1949 it was three hours by rail. Theologically, West was as far from my father as he could be: passionately ecumenical, left-wing perhaps even pro-Communist at the time, and a graduate of Union Seminary, New York City.

Forty years later West would concede that among missionaries of his ilk "most did not grasp the enormity of events that overwhelmed us."[30] Among the liberal Protestant China establishment there was a great deal of naiveté about the prospect of a Communist takeover. "They thought

---

30   In Brown, G. Thompson. *Earthen Vessels and Transcendent Power*. (Maryknoll, NY: Orbis). 293.

they were 'agrarian reformers'" my father snorted. The most obvious example was the case of Methodist China Mishkid James Endicott who had retuned to China in 1925 as a missionary of the nascent United Church of Canada and became an apologist for left-wing causes, receiving the Stalin Peace Prize in 1952 at the height of the Cold War. Concern for social justice and Methodist primitivism had pushed him ever leftward[31].

And it was not just the liberals. Reuben A. Torrey Jr. (who had been in Shandong before the war) invited us over to his house on Rue Winling one evening and at one point, as we were having dinner, his adolescent son was summoned from the table to meet a caller. I was told subsequently that that visitor was a fifth column Communist spy receiving valuable information young Torrey had collected. It was all exciting cloak and dagger for an impressionable child but that a grandson of the great turn-of-the-century evangelist should be involved in espionage was unsettling. Why he was not sent home I still fail to understand.

Living in Shanghai made mother now a focus for all kinds of job opportunities as more and more fled from the city. A white Russian piano teacher, understandably concerned about the new regime, offered mother all his pupils as he was about to move to Brazil. The Principal at my School, Arthur Owen, lost his secretary and mother stepped in to assume that role. Gertrude Rinden, a Congregational missionary in Foochow since 1920, became our Fifth Grade teacher, the third in a row.

Dad joined us on 1 April and for the next three weeks went back and forth from Wusih to Shanghai, all the while carrying on his classes with his amazingly focussed concentration. While with us, he set an exam for his course on Galatians. He was in Wusih on 22 April when the Red Army entered the city. "They got here much faster than anyone expected but government troops had all been withdrawn," he reported. It was over, after only six months.

---

31   See Endicott, Stephen: *James D. Endicott: Rebel Out of China.* Toronto, Univ. of Toronto Press, 1980.

CHAPTER 20:

Life after Liberation, 1949

Once again war had divided our family. In Shanghai we waited eagerly for news of my father. He, in turn, tried to mail a reassuring letter to Mother, cycling over to the local post office at Runghsien the day after "liberation" "in hope that there might be one more outgoing mail to reach my family." He was soon surrounded by armed plainclothesmen. "I found myself looking down the wrong end of a gun barrel, fortunately they only fired questions and searched me, and then after a little conversation that was intended to be cheery on my part, they let me go my way." On return to the compound Dad made sure that the great gate on the main road was bolted shut. For the rest of the week they tried to be inconspicuous and stayed indoors.

May Day, that great Labour and Communist festival, started a busy week. At night our road, the main route between Nanking and Shanghai, just outside our compound, was clogged by well-disciplined soldiers marching towards the coast. Having already captured Nanking, they were proceeding with armoured vehicles. Their noise made sleep impossible. Cars would stop and demand entrance and Martin Hopkins, brave man that he was, would fearlessly come out and answer their questions as politely as possible. During the day, soldiers would visit and at night they would sleep on the porch, "borrow" the seminary car or bicycles. One pointed to the "Theological" in the sign and sneered "superstition". Nationalist planes were overhead but there was, surprisingly, no strafing of the marching Communist armies which provided a very visible target. Chiang's men had lost heart.

A brave student, Chang Chih-tao, set out early that Saturday, 7 May (the eve of my eleventh birthday), for Shanghai with letters to my mother and instructions to the Treasurer of the Mission. Only later that day did another student, named only as "Liu," return with upsetting news: he had gone to our duplex in Shanghai and found it deserted. He was told that my mother and I had left the country (actually we had gone ten days before). Dad entered that news in a poignant and despairing one liner: "Dorothy & Donald are in Hong kong."

We had indeed departed for Hong Kong. Taking advantage of an offer from the United States Navy, we had set sail on 27 April on the hospital ship USS *Repose*. On board there were 118 American passengers, all civilians, and 77 British military. The latter were casualties from the *Amethyst* incident the previous week. The *Amethyst* had been despatched from Shanghai to relieve the *Comet* which had been guarding the British Embassy in Nanking but came under heavy fire the morning of 20 April from the People's Liberation Army batteries on the north side of the river, killing the captain and disabling those on the bridge. The vessel was consequently beached. The HM *Comet* was sent down from Nanking to rescue the *Amethyst* as well as the cruiser *London* and the *Amethyst*'s sister vessel the RN *Black Swan* sailed upriver to join the rescue, all with loss of life.

Casualties' from the *Amethyst* were conveyed by sampan to the Nationalist side of the river, taken to a Mission Hospital at Kiangyin and sent on by train to Shanghai. Seventy-seven were three days later sent to Hong Kong on our boat, courtesy of the United States Navy. There is no memory of our mixing with these sailors but the impact of that so-called "Yangtse Incident" signalled a profound shift in the balance of power between the West and the new regime in China who refused to admit the legitimacy of any of the previous treaties (which had made the

Amethyst's guarding the British Embassy a legal right). It took almost forty years before the PLA battery commander admitted that his men had, indeed, fired the first shot. But by then the old political order, with its extraterritorial rights, that had both subjugated and even victimised the Chinese, but had also facilitated the missionary movement, was long gone. Missionaries could no longer be accused of being "running dogs of the imperialists" and the church, having had its links with the West abruptly severed, was now independent. Many have seen it as a providential assurance of spiritual vitality as the Western sending churches went into spiritual decline.

The *Amethyst* stirred in me some latent British chauvinism. As I followed developments in the *South China Morning Post* I thrilled when, at the end of July, the *Amethyst* made a run for the open sea and reported "Have re-joined the fleet south of Woosung. No damage. No casualties. God save the King." And then the epic response: "Please convey to the commanding officer and ship's company of HMS *Amethyst* my hearty congratulations on their daring exploit to rejoin the Fleet. The courage, skill and determination shown by all on board have my highest commendation. Splice the main brace." Being a mishkid with a multinational pedigree meant you were flexible in your patriotic loyalties.

Our journey was also not to be without its share of excitement. Missionary families gathered on the Shanghai wharf on 27 April. Each of us clutched the single suitcase we were allowed to bring with us. It was all so familiar: another evacuation, treasures left behind, fellow Christians abandoned, life's work once again disrupted if not terminated. But for my mother, it was a terrifying repetition of what had happened at the same pier less than eight years earlier. I watched as suddenly she collapsed, leaving me stranded as medical aid was summoned. She disappeared into one of the sheds along the wharf. I was now on my own. She never talked about it later (and there are no references in letters at the time, the preoccupation presumably being my father) but it was one of the unforgettable terrors of my childhood: who had my passport? Who had my ticket? Was I now to be an orphan before my eleventh birthday? Other adults rallied to me and tried to reassure me and I feigned bravery, but I was deeply shaken. I suppose, in retrospect it was another of her heart tremors which always seemed to happen in a time of crisis. Or perhaps it was a panic attack.

The other mishkids gathered around me and, after my mother rejoined us several hours later, we had a pleasant voyage to Hong Kong. One memory surfaces about the way in which we whiled away the time, when we weren't being coached with our SAS textbooks. The other mishkids introduced me to animal gin rummy, along with other board and card games. But mother expressly forbade me to play a game that she thought messaged playing cards and might pave the way to a life of gambling and sin! What is more I enjoyed it, it brought me into contact with the other children, and it was a tension-reliever. But mother was adamant and I "lost face," as the Chinese would say, with the others who found the prohibition incomprehensible, even absurd, as I do looking back. I also had a disillusioning experience when, having been told we were allowed a single suitcase, I discovered on the deck several trunks marked with the name of one of our China missionary of higher rank. Fortunately none of our belongings left behind were destroyed or vandalized (unlike the Japanese) but it left a sour taste. Rank, it seemed to an observant mishkid, trumped all else.

When we docked in Kowloon we were taken immediately to a guest hotel that the Presbyterian Church USA had recently purchased. Originally Philips House, we were told that a Mrs Philips, a Christian missionary and the owner, had changed the street number from unlucky 13 to 11A. A four story building, our rooms were on the second floor. Known as "the PMH" (Presbyterian Mission Home), it became my home for the longest period of uninterrupted time in my entire childhood. Ah Lee, a large avuncular Buddha-like man, ran the establishment from the registration desk to the right of the main door. On the left there was a homey sitting area dominated by a tasteful picture over a piano of a woman, hands clasped, bowing in front of a Temple, seeking (one assumes) answers, a powerful reminder of the missionary task. I was grateful to Ruth Hinshaw Walline, who had bought it from a white Russian artist in China, for sharing it with all of us. There was a profound love of beauty and the arts on the part of many of the Presbyterian (USA) missionary community and a rich cultural awareness.

It was in that same lounge that I had my first encounter with the so-called "facts of life." After Shanghai fell, sometime in June of 1949, the *South China Morning Post* had an article about the new occupiers of the city having closed all the brothels in the city. Picking up the paper on the coffee table there I asked mother in a loud voice easily heard by all the other guests waiting for their meal: "What's a brothel?" I can still remember her reply, responding without hesitation: "Where men and women do naughty things." The reaction of the other missionaries in the lounge could be imagined as an awkward silence followed an eleven year old's innocent question.

It did not take long for my mother to find work. She became missionary postmistress with her own office on the ground floor of the PMH. Up till now the postal system in China, true to Sir Robert Hart's vision seventy-five years previously, had held together through all the political turmoil but was now showing signs of strain as the Communist armies swept south. Mother's task was to receive and transfer all post so that missionaries could depend on hearing or being heard with despatch. To do this she had a whole collection of rubber stamps with the address in Chinese of every remaining missionary. Letters received from America would be sent to the addressee with the forwarding address stamped on the envelope or placed on a new one if there was no room. Letters were received by the missionary or sent on to the States to their designated recipient.

Postmistress Dorothy MacLeod reading letter outside
the PMH, 11A Carnarvon Rd., Kowloon, 1951

It was all hugely complicated but very important for those caught behind the Bamboo Curtain. In her two years of providing this service I never heard any complaints except that my philatelic buddies felt I had an unfair advantage in getting all the best stamps before they got a chance which was not true.

Our trips together to the Kowloon post office, next to the old railway station and not far from the Star Ferry, were the most revealing times I had with her. Somehow our walking together relaxed her and I was given entrée to the world of grownups. It was on one of those journeys that I was first told that my Aunt Mary was separated from Uncle John. "Why?" I inquired innocently about my initial encounter with marriage breakdown. It was a direct question and struggling for an honest reply to a searching inquiry, she described her as someone with a quick tongue who misused Scripture. To illustrate, she mentioned one incident which I found strangely unconvincing. When asked "Who will go for ice cream?" Mary had replied, "Here am I, send me" (a quote from the call of Isaiah).mother, who (as we have seen) always found relations with Mary challenging, appeared to make little allowance for an unhappy childhood as a China mishkid. John Addy paid a price for marital failure: he was defrocked as a minister in Carl McIntire's Bible Presbyterian Church, snuffing out a promising career.

Settling into Hong Kong life that summer we were painfully aware of the contrast between our ordered lives in the British crown colony and the collapse of the Kuomintang government in China. Refugees came streaming across the border as the relentless progress of the PLA proved unstoppable. Canton (or Guangzhou as it was now known), the short-lived capital of the Nationalist government after the fall of Nanjing, fell on 14 October. All summer missionaries arrived with stories of displacement and confusion. Particularly heart-rending were the accounts of Christians left behind to face the unknowns of a Communist takeover.

In this melee of emotions my mother and I sought shelter from the summer heat on Lantao Island, now the location of the Hong Kong International Airport and the ubiquitous Disneyland. There in the summer of 1949 we rented a cottage for a fortnight. A colony of twenty cabins built in the 1920s in the heyday of such missionary resorts, all very basic, nestled on Sunset Peak, 869 meters high. Mother and I took the ferry to Lantao, with groceries for the ten days we planned to stay. Other missionary families joined us as we arrived. I was embarrassed by my over-protective mother who insisted I have a sedan chair take me up.

"It is a gorgeous place", my mother wrote her sister, and "just a big misty cloud and you couldn't even see the mountain. The scenery was indescribable – all mountains and islands and blue sea and sky. And sometimes there *wasn't* any scenery – just a big white misty cloud so you couldn't see even to the next cottage. The cottages are all spread over the two peaks along the slope – not close together, but far enough away so you can feel private." There I, and the other mishkids enjoyed a moment of freedom as we put all the turmoil of the year past behind us. The swimming hole was marvellous: I cut myself on a rock leaving a battle scar on my foot which has ever since reminded me of that idyllic summer. At least one went skinny dipping. My friend got a suntan on his lower parts which we all found very risqué. His doctor father showed no sympathy at his discomfort, reminding him at the dinner table in front of all of us how he had acquired it.

Throughout the summer my mother felt I was somehow affected by all the emotional stress of our situation. Strange rashes appeared and frequent mild temperatures. There were at least three missionary doctor evacuees at the PMH and I could imagine that they ran for cover every time they saw my mother heading their way. It was humiliating enough to be the only kid who needed a sedan chair. Not only was I an only child but without my father around I now became the complete focus of my mother's attention. Letters home were filled with references to my every doing. Without my father around, she joined with the other parents of school-age children and disregarded his instructions of 20 August sent by cable, and enrolled me in Royden House in September. Located on Caine Road in the mid-levels on the island, it meant a steep walk up from the Star Ferry. The school featured so-called "progressive" pupil-centred education with three-week projects to be finished at one's own pace. My father was aghast when he arrived in Hong Kong on 27 September. By then I was already in classes at Royden House (such as they were) and the die was cast. It was an indication of more adjustments to come in their relationship and planning.

CHAPTER 21:

Readjusting To New Realities, 1949

For my father, who had remained behind the Bamboo Curtain, the summer of 1949 was a watershed. As with so many other missionaries who had felt God's call to China "liberation" was a game changer that completely altered the course of their lives. For a man who was China-born, had prepared himself for ministry there by earning five degrees, learned a language, and was completely committed to the cause of theological education in the Chinese church, the future seemed dark and uncertain. But it was nothing in comparison to what Chinese Christians were facing and, like any caring pastor, he shared their deep sense of bafflement and questioning. But there was also, honesty compels me to admit, an anger which sometimes surfaced as we waited for our future to unfold.

The conquerors had been renamed. They were no longer the dreaded Eighth Army ("Balu jwun") but had morphed into the People's Liberation Army ("Gie fang jwun") to make their presence more palatable. The young soldiers, weary from their exertions and heady with their victories, crowded into the seminary property. They were, for an invading army, generally well behaved. Some had never seen a white man before and the "big-nosed people" were an object of intense scrutiny. They were curious about everything, "wandered around everywhere at will or walked around you as you worked at your desk or sat down for a meal. They entered your classroom while you were lecturing, or stood in the aisles during a meeting. After we got used to them in a way, we decided that they must be told, it was disturbing and set one's nerves a-tingle." Frankness did not include politics. The church was not a political institution, Dad insisted.

But it was hard to stay aloof from what was happening. When Shanghai fell on 12 May the seminary students were required to take a day's holiday and go to town with paper lanterns and shout "Long life to Mao Zedong" and "Death to bandit Chiang." Soon after that the students took their final exams and graduation took place on 30 May, losing only two weeks in the academic year. "We said 'good-bye' with strong feelings, commending one another to God's care and promised to pray for each other in the uncertain and troubled days to come. There are times in China when it requires high courage and consecration to follow the call to service in the ministry of Christ's church," Dad wrote the American supporters of the seminary. The school was almost totally dependent now on foreign donations which rather compromised their independence in the eyes of the new government but was there was no alternative.

The first fortnight of June, Dad spent time packing and organizing his possessions. His work as registrar at the seminary was handed over to someone else. He closed out the relief money account, making a full and final accounting of how the money had been spent – a matter that got other missionaries elsewhere in trouble subsequently. Two of the seminary professors, traveling to Shanghai, mailed a letter (#7) to my mother who had been able the next day to get a reassuring cable back to him, the only method at the time of communication. Worried about what she had said about the possibility of evacuating from Hong Kong, he wired (#8) the next day "If possible stay Asia waiting developments."

On 17 June he left Wusih, cabling on arriving in Shanghai "Arrived Winling." (The Presbyterian compound was at 17 Rue Winling in the former French Concession.) Travel documents were required by the new authorities but he had rolled up his coat collar and, taking advantage of the general confusion, had managed to slip away and not be apprehended and sent home. Many other missionaries were not so fortunate: house arrests, imprisonment, demands for "confessions" and even martyrdom marked the demise of the Protestant missionary effort in China. When he arrived in Shanghai he found a city still under siege[32], blockaded by Nationalist ships. The Nationalists had scuttled many boats in the Whangpoo River which made navigation out of Shanghai impossible and caused deep resentment of the Kuomintang. Soldiers were posted at every corner, bayonets drawn. Friends of Americans were not only confused, they were objects of intense scrutiny. Americans were asking out.

Much of Dad's next few weeks in Shanghai were spent wrestling with his conscience (and in prayer, one assumes) about whether he should return to the seminary or re-join his family in Hong Kong. As so many clergy had already left the city, he was called on as a preacher for several Shanghai churches. A bulletin from an 11 September service that he conducted at the Shanghai Community Church (whose minister had left in May) survives and provides a fascinating insight into what the Western community in those immediate post-Liberation days was like. The Community Church had been built opposite the Shanghai American School in 1925 by the American community in Shanghai and the Rockefeller Foundation. Seating 1400, it was the centre of community life for US citizens as well as Americanized Chinese. Its musical programs were a focal point with choirs and soloists taking advantage of a massive organ and good acoustics. It was regarded by evangelicals as too liberal for their taste and I note in the bulletin that my father's master's degree and doctorate are both included perhaps to make allowance for his conservative theology. He used a well-worn sermon from Hebrews 11, "The Chief Hero of Faith." I am sure his honorarium was appreciated as times were tough.

---

32   See Wentworth & Mills, *Fair is the Name*. Los Angeles: Shanghai American School Association, 1997. 365-7.

They were indeed tough and getting worse. At some point during those post-Liberation months the previously tax-exempt Shanghai American School had been assessed a hefty land tax of US$76,000 (later reduced under appeal to US$12,500) and the Anglican Cathedral £24,000. Even before the outbreak of the Korean War the following June and the arrival of Chinese "volunteers" to bolster the flagging North Korean army, it was clear that foreigners were no longer welcome in the country by those in power. By August Dad had made his painful decision to leave China, the land of his birth, forever (as it turned out). He sweated over how he would convey this news to the NCTS faculty and particularly Martin Hopkins, the sole remaining Western faculty member (who would bravely stay on for another two and a half years amid great privation and sacrifice).

He had written, asking their advice. He started by contrasting the optimism of a few weeks earlier when he was about to ask my mother and me to return with the "dark" realities that now were becoming increasingly apparent. (There was as yet no censorship but he was being very careful.) It became apparent at the outset that my educational future weighed heavily on him, particularly the closing of Shanghai American School, owing to the exorbitant land tax, and the dangers attached to travelling to Kuling [boarding] School. "It is becoming abundantly plain now that Mrs. MacLeod and Donald cannot return for the present," he went on to say. He had gone down to the American President Lines to see if there was any possibility of a boat leaving and he was told that the "General Gordon" was due to depart for America on 17 September but it would not be disembarking passengers at Hong Kong. He was encouraged however to "begin the long process of obtaining permission from the authorities to leave Shanghai." It sounded ominous.

The political situation was a key concern with the Berlin airlift and Stalin's belligerence towards the other World War II Allies. "If I appraise the current 'cold' war between Russia and the West aright," he wrote[33] "I think that the coming 18 months will be most critical and may make

---

33   ANM to faculty, NCTS, 9 August 1949 in Appendix.

clear to us whether there is to be a shooting war or increasingly assured prospects of a truce." So he outlined the alternatives: staying on in Shanghai without any assurances that he would get travel permission to return to Wusih or perhaps find some other theological school where he could teach. The Canadian Presbyterians had a seminary in Taipei (so-called "Free China") where a classmate at Princeton, James Dickson[34], was Principal and which he was being told used an improved standard of Mandarin ("Kuo-yu"). Or there was Manila, which he misspelled and which had little appeal as his Board generally sent liberals there. So he threw himself on the advice and wisdom of his Chinese colleagues, two of whom had assisted him in the drafting of the letter.[35]

Five days later the faculty, with Martin Hopkins as scribe, sent back a response. "All represent the gravity of the present situation and though we plan to open on September 9th as announced, there is no guarantee that we can continue until the end of the fall term. We appreciate your willingness to return to Wusih and your loyalty to the seminary and to God's call to you." There was a genuine expression of appreciation for his work – "It will be a great loss to us not to have you here." But nevertheless it was up to him and "If you were outside China you would be free to present our needs." Hopkins added a personal request for Dad to take a bundle of letters with him if he was evacuated, still hoping that he could get a short pass to leave Wusih briefly. No mail had gone out for four months to his family.

Dad's penultimate letter to my mother (#16 as he numbered them) was sent on 24 August and he in turn got one from her dated 19 June that same day. The mails were erratic and unsure. Throughout September he was packing books and papers, frequently corresponding with Martin Hopkins (with a feeling of guilt?), and sailed from Shanghai on Sunday,

---

34 See my "Celebrating Our Cross-Cultural Evangelistic Missionary Heritage: The Centenary of James Ira Dickson" *Channels*. Vol. 16, No. 2. (Fall-Winter 1999/2000). 8-12.

35 Mr. Hu, who spoke English well, and translated for Pastor Ting who also met with him.

25 September, "at last" as he added in his diary. He arrived two days later and once again I was allowed to skip school for a family reunion, not that he valued my "education" at Royden House. We met outside the entrance to the Kowloon Wharf beside the Star Ferry as he and many other missionaries came off the boat. We proceeded along Salisbury Road to Nathan Road and then, turning right onto Carnarvon Road and the PMH at 11A, talking all the way and showing him our new neighbourhood. We were once again a united family.

CHAPTER 22:

A Last Goodbye to China, 1949

"I left China with regret," my father wrote his supporters in America. "But our family has had such prolonged separation – over 5 ½ years now – that it seemed the thing to do when the chance came." He went on to report on the leave of absence the faculty had given him, and his plans for the next few months: literary work and the preparation of the new curriculum approved in the spring and the textbooks that would be required for it. Before leaving Shanghai he had completed a small syllabus for one of his courses, "An Introduction to the Pauline Epistles." He would prepare material for a Christian Ethics course, a commentary on the Sermon on the Mount. "I have much to do, and much projected in mind for the future, and we want to stay close to China on this side of the Pacific where I can jump back in when the door opens a crack." How little he realized that an era had ended. 142 years after Robert Morrison, the first Protestant foreign missionary to China, had arrived in Canton, he had left mainland China for good. The great period of cross-cultural missionary activity in the Middle Kingdom was over,

My father's arrival in Hong Kong meant a change in my living arrangements. I was moved from the third floor to a tiny room on the fourth. No longer would I share a room with my mother. As a prepubescent boy that had been a questionable, particularly given the intense relationship that existed between my mother and me. "I think," she wrote, "it will be good for him to be out from under the inevitably constant supervision he has when he 'rooms' with me – and the extreme supervision when he 'rooms' with *both* of us!! He is pleased about it."

At the time, I was totally preoccupied with the 75th anniversary of the Universal Postal Union. My stamp-collecting buddies and I were excited by an announcement from the Hong Kong post office that, in concert with all the other colonies of the British Empire (and Britain itself), there would be a philatelic delight for passionate stamp collectors. In Hong Kong four values were to be issued on 10 October 1949. Fortunately for me that date, a Monday, was a holiday – the last time Hong Kong would celebrate the 1912 establishment of the Republic of China - it was replaced by a 1 October Communist alternative, the date when Mao declared the People's Republic in Tiananmen Square in Peking in 1949. So instead of taking the Star Ferry to what my father regarded as our academically dubious classes at Royden House School, we queued early outside the Kowloon post office, due to open at eight. We brought our pocket money and some specially printed envelopes, and eagerly went up to the counter and ordered what we could afford: 10 cent (local rate), 20 cent (doubled for air letters), 30 cent and, most expensive of all, the purple 80 cent variety, each with florid (and overblown) artwork. I was thrilled when the first day covers we had posted to ourselves arrived the next day. I was in philatelic heaven, heady stuff for an eleven year old and a good distraction from present realities.

My father's arrival had a mixed response from me. Apparently I was not all that eager to see him. "I am rather concerned about his attitude," Moher wrote about me at the time. "He seems a little discouraged … different from his ordinary cheerful casualness." And she went on to confide in her sister: "Alec is so eager for him not to be ill, that he unconsciously is a little 'harder' on him than at any other time." I was fighting a cold at the time and the doctors had, at least by my mother's account, forbidden me to have "any physical training." The only exercise I got was playing soccer or "Kick the Can" along Carnarvon Road. Swimming at the Y would come later.

So we three were briefly cooped up in one room, even though I was soon to move into my own tiny chamber. With the arrival of more "stuff" with my father, our quarters were very crowded and messy. Books were everywhere: my father's papers lay out on his desk ("which is larger than mine" she wrote). Records were stashed away in a trunk and the windup gramophone was out on a table. For the next two years that would be our base, emphasising the reality that, as Dad would say, we were "pilgrims and sojourners." It was none too soon that I was moved.

The contrast with the Changs could not have been greater. Somehow during that summer mother had become the musical tutor for a well-connected family of political exiles with three daughters, originally from Shandong, who had a beautiful spread in Kowloon Tong, at the time a leafy suburb north of Boundary Road much favoured by wealthy colonists and affluent Chinese émigrés. The Changs would send their chauffeur to pick up my mother once a week for piano lessons for the three girls to whom she became attached. Mr. Chang made no Christian profession but mother was constantly vexed about the state of Mrs. Chang's soul. She also found it difficult, owing to social and cultural norms unfamiliar to her, to relate to Mrs. Chang, a *grand dame*. She committed what she called a *faux pas*, unspecified. "I have felt dreadfully about it, especially since the time is passing, and there is so little of a spiritual opening." As for me, I was dazzled by the sumptuous gifts we received from them: ornate embroidered bedspreads and a Chinese ivory puzzle ball and stand, with delicate carving requiring great skill by the carver.

The PMH was constantly receiving people from the interior and their reports about the new regime's attitude toward foreigners, particularly missionaries, were not encouraging. I was surrounded by some of the most interesting people that any child could want for stimulation. One of the more unusual was Barbara Kelman Hayes whose room was directly above ours. One time absentmindedly she burst into our bedroom, mumbled an apology, and disappeared. Like many other fractured families at the time, her husband John was stranded in China. There was something strangely attractive (and innocent) about this tall angular and brilliant woman which I found hugely compelling. As the daughter-in-law of Watson Hayes, the founder of NCTS, we would have been expected to have much in common but how little I knew the back story.

Barbara Hayes was the daughter of John Kelman who had occupied prestigious pulpits in Manhattan and Edinburgh. She and John met as students at Oxford, where he was a Rhodes Scholar. His father warned him about the spiritual peril of such an honour, compounded by his marriage to someone whose own father, for all his fame and piety, was not of the same theological persuasion. The final breach came when John chose Union Seminary, New York, over Princeton. When he and Barbara returned to China to work with students in Peiping as members of the Presbyterian Mission, his presence was an embarrassment to Dr. Hayes and to NCTS. All this could later be forgiven because, having sent his wife and family home, he accompanied his parents to prisoner of war camp, declining repatriation so he could stay with them. They had been finally and forcibly taken from their home in Tenghsien, the last to leave, and interned in Weihsien prison camp. There his 86 year old father died. After the war John Haves accompanied his mother, now senile and mercifully unaware of her situation, back to America where she soon passed away.

John and Barbara Hayes returned to China in 1947 but by now their marriage was in name only. He was assigned to serve in south China where he was to be later brutalized by the new regime. For a while Barbara stayed on in Hong Kong, working for the Church of Christ in China, which seemed almost an act of defiance against all her father-in-law had stood for. She started to befriend British military personnel, mothering some of the young men away from home on their compulsory military service. She asked my mother if one of them, who had children in England and said he was missing them, could establish a friendship with me, taking me out for treats and movies. My mother might have appeared naive but she was quite knowledgeable about the risk of paedophilia and insisted, much to my embarrassment but also for my safety, that she would accompany me whenever I was with him. Needless to say, the relationship did not last beyond two visits.

Dad's 48th birthday fell on a Saturday in 1949 and mother arranged a party for "all under twenty" at PMH. It was not the sort of occasion that my father enjoyed but mother thought that by limiting it to that group she avoided grownups feeling "left out". Fourteen gathered for cake and ice cream and I was in charge of the games. I think that mother was trying to compensate for my isolation socially. The party, held in the front lobby of PMH, ended with singing around the piano. It provided some release from the tension of crumbling Nationalist fortunes in China. Four days later Chiang Kai-shek left for exile in Taiwan, his support on what we now called "the Mainland" having collapsed. Three days later Chengdu in Sichuan, the last major city still in the hands of the Kuomintang fell. Only fortress Taiwan would remain in their possession.

The preparation committee for Yuletide 1949 was determined to make the holiday a special event. Christmas that year fell on a Sunday and the Wednesday before the young people had arranged a special program with music and readings. The highlight was Janet Stewart recounting the Christmas story from *Ben Hur*. Janet was a hugely popular young woman who took on the role of a youth worker with all of us mishkids. She seemed to understand teenagers. Her 45 rpm record player was always playing the latest pop music and musicals from the States, Frank Sinatra being a favourite. Janet's courtship with a handsome bearded YMCA worker named Shepherd (ex-Royal Navy) was the stuff of fairy-tale romances, though my mother disapproved, not being sure of his state of grace. I was sure, however, that Janet Stewart was everything I wanted to see in the opposite gender: accepting, fun, modern, and understanding. Her wedding and subsequent disappearance brought sadness to all of us but she had made a significant impact on many bewildered mishkids.

Christmas Eve, Saturday, was a time for shopping – fortunately most had already made their choices. Dad took mother to the Moutrie Piano Company in the old Prince's Building where she made several selections of 78 rpm records: César Franck's *Variations* and a favourite pianist, Myra Hess. In the afternoon it was my time to go shopping with my father. Earlier I had taken the #5 bus out to Fu Shan where workmen were pruning trees and I had collected what was described as a very reputable tree, probably a pruning, which we then set up and decorated. In the evening, there was a house party with singing and games. Sunday we were not allowed to open our gifts, being very strict Sabbatarians, but went to church and Dad led a Bible Study group for some military people. We provided a special meal for the wife and son of one of the NCTS students who was presently in California. I remember my gift as a set of Reeves watercolours as I was starting to enjoy painting as a hobby. But my main thrill was presenting to my parents the gift of a collection of shells describing our trip to China and the inked in pictures of the sites along the way with the multicolours of the shells providing contrast. It had all been prepared behind closed doors which my parents wisely respected.

So the year, and the decade, ended. Dad was called in by Ed Walline, his immediate superior, to discuss his future and whether the American Presbyterian Mission should continue to support him, Dad's response was that he was not intimidated by recent events in China: there was no sign of closure rather an almost naïve confidence that things would be righted and their work would continue. In his little study at the back of the fourth floor, Dad worked feverishly on his literary projects, a commentary on I Peter which he found highly relevant for a church undergoing persecution. He was also developing his course notes on Christian ethics which he felt the Chinese church needed in the light of the unfolding political and economic drama and which became his commentary on the Sermon on the Mount. There was no question about his hard work – his hours showed an almost obsessive intensity which left little or no time for family. But how did this fit into the overall strategy for the future of the church in China (if there was one)? "We are ready to go back to China" Mother wrote at the time, "but so far no passes are allowed to return. I am going to sell my piano in Philadelphia and Alec wants to get rid of all superfluous goods, especially the easy chair we brought out."

Indeed, easy chairs were no longer required for China missionaries. An era had ended. But for me a whole new life was about to begin. I was going to be privileged to attend one of the best schools the British colonial service could provide, and receive an education that would shape the rest of my life.

CHAPTER 23:
Half-Century Hong Kong Hiatus, 1950

King George V School – "KG-5" as it was affectionately known – provided the families of the British colonizers of Hong Kong some compensation for their Empire building. It provided an education that, on the "A" level was equal to anything available in the English public school system. Its educational staff were generally First Class graduates of Oxbridge and its academic standards were demanding and of the highest order. My three years there were intellectually stimulating and mentally demanding, requiring discipline and hard work but personally very rewarding.

According to a front page picture on the 6 February 1937 edition of the *Hongkong Telegraph,* the site of a new Central British School was being levelled and prepared for construction. The RAF photograph conveyed something of the size of the property and in marked contrast to the original school, built next to St. Andrew's Church on Nathan Rd. and built at the end of the Nineteenth Century (and now an historical site). Architecturally the building, shaped as an "E", was very 1930's. The main entrance (which students entered only on rare occasions) led you to the Principal's Office. Outside there was "The Square" so called, the place where hapless students were required to stand for misdemeanours, shamed as a public spectacle. The wing to your right had classrooms for the lower forms, and also upstairs, the art and geography rooms. On your immediate left was the prefects' office.

The war intervened three years after the building was erected. The experiences of surrender and incarceration dominated the psyche of all of us, so I was much at home. Experiences at Stanley Camp, where many of my classmates as very young children, had spent the war, were dominant. So was the feeling of British invincibility under terrible privation and sequestration. Carved in stone over the entry to the Assembly Hall for all to see, were the words of Winston Churchill: "Never in the field of human conflict was so much owed by so many to so few." British heroism and British superiority, so much a part of the imperial order, were always assumed. There was rumoured to be a 10% ceiling on the number of non-Caucasians admitted. One of my buddies was Freer, his father a Cardiff stevedore who had taken a Chinese wife. The protrusions on his shoulders were called "coolie bumps" which I regarded as racist. In fact most of the Chinese did better academically than the Caucasians. The girl I competed with for first place was Helen Huang, the granddaughter of Huang Fu, Chiang Kai-shek's comrade in arms who had died prematurely in 1936. I only came first when she went to America my final year. We became friends when I tried to rescue her from the Seventh-day Adventists who were making a dead set for her. Our long conversations during lunch hour, pouring over our Bibles together, became the subject of gossip. Trans-racial relationship of any depth were not tolerated.

On 12 December 1949 I had taken my entrance qualification exam for King George V School. My mother had wound me up with preparatory tutoring: "We're doing some arithmetic and English review" she wrote, noting that I had had no previous French or physics or chemistry. Sequestering me away for several days prior to exams for intense revision took a terrible toll on my psyche and for the next thirteen years I seemed to crash before and during exams to the detriment of my academic career. I passed the entrance exam with flying colours in spite of my che-quered previous schooling and was placed in Form 2A. The streaming of students was particularly unfortunate. My friend Harold was placed in Form 2C or more ominously, "2 remove". My buddy qualified for Form 3B which put him among the average students without guarantee of post-secondary education. The other mishkids were all over the map, breaking up our cohesiveness as a group.

To lessen the anxiety over what awaited us, a distracting day-long family excursion to Junk Bay was arranged by parents at PMH for the New Year's holiday Monday, one week prior to the new educational challenge. "We had an all-day junk trip," I later reported. "It started off in a fog in the morning, with four oarsmen (two men, two women) as our navigators. Then when the fog lifted a breeze came up, and we had a picnic lunch on a beach, basked in the sun, and then walked all afternoon. It was really gorgeous." At the end of that week, not to be outdone, my parents and I had our own private excursion. Equipped with sandwiches and a full thermos flask, we took the train to Shatin station in the New Territories to visit the beautiful grounds of the Lutheran Theological Seminary in Fanling. "We have enjoyed our fre-quent little trips to the hills these weeks in Hong Kong," my mother wrote a friend in Philadelphia. "We are squeezed in at the Home here so that it is a joy to be able to take a bus and very quickly reach the foot of hills where we can climb and be alone and have a feeling of space."

So on 9 January 1950 a new chapter in my life began. There were eight of us China mishkids waiting for the bus that morning. I recall the pride that I felt with my new uniform: grey slacks, brown jacket (a colour combination that always bothered me), and school tie (brown and blue stripes, horrors!) and that all important badge which identified us as students at KG-5, a shield with yellow and blue and a rampant lion. Forget your badge and you had to go home and get it immediately, we were warned. I carried my rattan wicker case with brand new note-books (each with that rampant lion and the school motto *Honestas ante honores*) and the textbooks we had already been able to purchase. It was very exciting and very different from anything I had known previously.

Leaving 149 Waterloo Rd. Kowloon Tong in KG-5 uniform and rattan briefcase

On arrival we were disgorged to the Assembly Room and given our instructions. Mrs. Lawrence (of whom I have few memories) was my homeroom teacher. She was responsible for "General English (Writing, Spelling, Literature, Composition and Grammar)". I started languages: French and Latin being the options, and took maths with the redoubtable Mrs. Hill, very old school, with whom I had little empathy. Art was my delight and the school studio a joy. History, with the text *From Ur to Rome* (which I almost memorized), was the high point of my courses. "Donald finds the school very British" it was reported. Of course I did and I loved it.

My father continued his almost manic work schedule, self-discipline honed during his years as a POW. He seemed to be obsessed with the need to justify his existence by working twelve hours a day on composition and translation of his commentaries, drafts of which he would send, as they were being prepared, chapter by chapter to NCTS. He was determined that his colleagues would know that, though exiled, he was still very much engaged as their partner in theological education and in the life and ministry of the Chinese church. He kept a careful record of the hours of each literary assistant, recording them in his diary. He required them because, unlike Martin Hopkins, he could not write the characters himself, nor was he a natural linguist. One of those working with him had said that his work should be considered volunteering without pay. Later one of them reneged and demanded full salary, far in excess of the time actually worked. Father produced a full record of the hours spent with the correct amount of money earned, leaving the vengeful amanuensis speechless.

Twelve hour days, six day a week, proved difficult for my mother to cope with. Fortunately her music provided an "out" and her friendship with Caroline Braga brought considerable release. Caroline was her piano instructor, her sister Mary mine. Initially mother found Caroline's insistence on certain hand gestures at the keyboard artificial and inhibiting – she complained that she had ruined Liszt's *Leibestraum*, a favourite of hers, by insisting that her hands at the keyboard be artificially arched. Over time they grew close and Caroline Braga opened doors for her, giving her entrée to playing the piano on Hong Kong Rediffusion. That hugely popular service, which started in 1949, provided piped-in music, BBC news, and entertainment to suit all tastes in English and Cantonese.

Church life during our years in Hong Kong was very complicated. There was no Presbyterian congregation. The 1930 Union Church on Jordan Road, east of Nathan Road was regarded by most of the Presbyterians at the PMH as the nearest alternative. Originally founded by the London Missionary Society, it represented a bland mix of English Free Church traditions. Theologically it was a hybrid and we went for more robust alternatives parting company with the other missionaries. We lighted on the Emmanuel Church affiliated with the Bible Institute of Los Angeles where Caroline Braga was the musician and Mother became a backup. She went on to accept an invitation to be the regular musician at the Kowloon Tong Christian and Missionary Alliance Church, then meeting in a primary school. It has since become one of the largest congregations in Hong Kong, with an imposing sanctuary on Waterloo Rd, and has seeded many others, both there and among the Hong Kong *diaspora* in North America. A sermon preached by visiting evangelist, R. R. Brown of Omaha[36], was significant for me in my spiritual experience.

My father favoured St. Andrew's Anglican (within walking distance of the PMH) and going there taught me to love the 1662 Prayer Book. He preached some times at Christ Church, a daughter congregation. I was a member of the Fourth Hong Kong Boy Scout Troop, sponsored by St. John's Anglican Cathedral on the island. And there were various youth groups I attended: the Southern Baptist "GARA" (combining their male and female pre-teenage groups "Girls in Action" and "Royal Ambassadors") and led by Mrs. Eloise Cauthen at their compound on Boundary Rd. There was also a Christian Endeavor chapter to which I was admitted when I turned 12 and which met at the PMH. It was led by David Dilworth, later a much loved Presbyterian pastor and professor at Whitworth College in Spokane, a pastor who had a commitment to us mishkids. My first or second meeting he threw out a theological question and in a nervous response I cited a text wrongly. His graciousness in correcting me I have always remembered. Lacking in all our church tramping was any link to a Chinese-speaking congregation, the excuse being that churches used the local language, Cantonese, rather than our Mandarin. That of course no longer holds true.

"A very good start" was the comment by Principal Mr. Mulcahy at the end of my first term at KG-5. My grades were modest: all B's and C's. Mrs. Hill wrote: "Has done quite good work, but entry needs much more care." She would hound me for neatness for the next two years. "Keen" was the word that most teachers used to describe me. I got a C in history and a C+ in science. With an average age of 11 years and 5 months (5 months younger than I was) we were all products of World War II. As the school was about to reconvene for the second term on 24 April 1950, we were not far from another conflagration that would deeply affect both Hong Kong and relations between China and the

---

36   Robert Roger Brown (1885-1964) founder and pastor for 41 years of Omaha's Gospel Tabernacle (now Christ Community Church) Named "Dean of Broadcasting" his weekly broadcast was heard by half a million people.

West, overshadowing the next three years I would spend in the Far East. The invasion of South Korea by the North on 25 June 1950 changed the whole dynamic of international relations in a volatile and combustible area. The United States and Russia played out their proxy war at the expense of those closest to the action and who were most affected by shifts in the balance of power.

CHAPTER 24:
Rheumatic Ruminations? 1950

The day before I was to return to KG-5 for the second term my mother wrote a long reply to her sister in response to a frank letter informing her that her hunch was right: their 72 year-old mother was indeed slowly dying of heart disease and there was nothing that could be done medically to prolong her life. This was the dread of every missionary isolated on a distant field. If there was a family member in need of care there was little that could be done – letters were slow, cables short and unreliable, and quick and cheap transportation home not available. Indeed my mother had gone to Edwin Walline as head of the Mission, asking if they could fund her trip back to America for the summer. He was not encouraging because we had been on the field for too short a time and mission funds for travel were stretched already. Too many of our Presbyterian Mission in both Korea and China were returning home after the Communist takeovers.

Her mother's situation dominated my mother's waking moments at that time. Overweight, arthritic, and depressive, it was probably a merciful ending though brutally hard on her oldest child. Since my grandfather's business had failed over a decade earlier he and my grandmother, as we have seen, seemed dependent on the generous hospitality of Marjorie and her husband, living for part of the year on his family's second property in Wilton Connecticut. Grandma returned home to Massachusetts as the end approached, and died there on 16 June 1950. It had been a long and painful exit and my mother felt helpless. "Sometimes I feel a wave of desire to be there, carrying the burden," she wrote six weeks before the end finally came. Well-meaning family originally tried to shield her from the developing crisis by providing half- truths until the gravity of the situation could no longer be hidden. Belle Miles, brother Bob's wife, pleasantly surprised mother as the one who gave her sensitive comfort and solace with a welcome description of her final days and the funeral. On hearing the news, my father instructed me to tell my mother that I was deeply sorry for her loss. I was troubled in conscience about such an implicit dishonesty.

In the midst of all this turmoil, Mother continued with her postal work, a major and welcome distraction. The whole mailing room was now given to her: a weighty responsibility as direct mail between the United States and Communist China had ceased. Hong Kong was now the transfer destination with post addressed to 11A Carnarvon Rd from America and readdressed and sent on to missionaries caught behind the Bamboo Curtain. The volume was considerable. The American Presbyterian Mission in China, at one time had been the largest foreign denominational agency in the country. Exiting and expelled missionaries required, and were dependent on, reliable postal communication. "I have been <u>over</u> busy" she admitted, "organizing things. Organizing was much needed and I can't help admitting I am doing a fair job. Hundreds of dollars' worth of Postal business goes through our office and we really have a sub-station. I thought 'I can't' but I like it." At the same time she was typing the English manuscript of Dad's 1 Peter commentary. By mid-May she was at page 39 "and have learned a great deal. I notice greater fluency and ease as he writes more and more. Also greater length!"

"Exams in a British school are a very exciting event" my mother explained to our American family, "No little test sort of thing" she added. We both went off to Cheung Chau for three days of revision in preparation. My first set of serious exams took place the first week of July, one of them scheduled for the Fourth conflicting with a picnic arranged for patriotic Americans at PMH, The discussion in our family was intense: skip the exam, reschedule it or tough it out and miss the firecrackers, Needless to say, scholarship trumped nationality. Mother felt that I could either skip it altogether or have it scheduled for another time with a specially set exam paper. My father was appalled. At his insistence I took the exam and missed the picnic, Brits trumped Yanks, in our family at least.

"Very good" was the Principal's summary of my report for the end of the year, Even Mrs. Hill, my nemesis, noted that there had been "considerable improvement" and that I had risen from 21st in the class to third place. Though I was more settled, everything around me seemed to be in flux. Rumours abounded that the PMH was to be sold, and the twenty who lived there housed elsewhere. We were a diverse group, theologically and vocationally. As our Christmas letter explained: "some handling executive and financial affairs, some teaching in Mission schools, some doing Bible teaching and preaching among the Chinese, in the local churches and work among the British soldiers, of whom there are about thirty thousand." But it was not sustainable. Hong Kong had never been a Presbyterian center and some of the work assignments seemed almost artificial. And my father's literary work, had it not been supported independently by the NCTS American Council, would have been one of the first to go. Biblical commentaries with a high view of the inspired text were little appreciated. The collapse of the foreign missionary effort in China had left a vacuum.

The immediate and more pressing concern during the summer of 1950 was my health. Swelling knees had landed me in bed and a final diagnosis, after a jurisdictional conflict between the Mission Dr. Everett Murray (unlicensed in the colony to practise) and Oxford-trained physician Dr. Antony Warren Dawson-Groves (licensed in Hong Kong since 1938), led the latter to conclude that I had rheumatic fever. "He says Hongkong is an ideal climate for him – it is wonderful in all the changes and apparently mixed-up sequence of events in his life there are evidences all the way that 'all things *do* work together for good'" (quoting

Romans 8:28). "He apparently has no evidence of heart strain, and that is the thing to watch ... He is of course limited in physical sports and exercise." Apparently the phys. ed. instructor at KG-5 had taken a special interest in me and felt that my attitude was right: "He thinks of it more as an inconvenience." And my mother added: "Alec, of course, does not want to feel it is more than just a thing he will outgrow if we do not pay too much attention to it."

On Cheung Chau Island 1951

That summer we spent several idyllic weeks on Cheung Chau (also called "Dumbbell" from the shape of the topography of the Island). Because of my joint swelling I was not allowed to climb up Lantau Island which would have been my first choice. Mother was the agent for two spaces on the island that the Mission had rented: we had the cottage and the Ruch's had a second floor flat in a place with a gorgeous view. Harold Ruch, my age, and I had a great time together. I continued my water-colours, getting ready for a hobby exhibit at KG-5 in October. Mother kept up a dizzying round of entertaining at our place. One day five people from CNEC (the Chinese Native Evangelisation Crusade) including the founder Fred Savage and his wife Geraldine came for a day's excursion, a relief from the heat of the city. The group had close links with NCTS and one of the party, David Chen, had been a student of Dad's. Excitement came from a Communist battery on nearby Lintin Island where "vigorous artillery fire" started when a Royal Navy vessel got closer than they liked. Onlookers from Cheung Chau crowded to a hill for a view of the firing. We regarded it as a lark.

We came home to celebrate the season. I described it as "the best holiday I ever had". With money from my affluent aunt and uncle in America I was given a Japanese camera with the latest high-powered lens. Fred Savage had made the selection and he was very knowledgeable about such matters. He was another of my heroes. Though my father was distant, preoccupied, and did not have any practical or athletic interests, someone else was always there to help me with a tennis racket or a dark-room. Most adult friends of my parents were either "aunt" or "uncle", a designation that rapidly ended when at boarding school chapel speakers and missionary guests resumed their formal names after ridicule by classmates who asked if my family was endless. I was teased mercilessly about having so many notable "close friends of the family". Looking back, being mentored by so many exceptional and gifted individuals was one of the great advantages of being a mishkid.

One of those notables was William Treman Blackstone, "Uncle Bill" as we called him. He was the grandson of the author of the classic *Jesus Is Coming*. My mother was his accompanist throughout the 1950 holidays. With his rich tenor voice, he was magnificent. And seemed wealthy to us impoverished MKs. Scion of a prominent Southern California fundamentalist family, he was generously supported by First Presbyterian Church in Hollywood, at the time the largest in the denomination. They were the only people in PMH with a car. Mother found Betty, his wife, with her West Coast style (form-fitting dresses and lots of nail polish) a stretch to reconcile with her strong convictions but Mother was once a Baptist! Their oldest, son Bob, collected Chinese antiques which could be purchased for a song at that time. They also had two daughters but Margaret was too old for me and the other, Jeanette, too young. Uncle Bill had style as he walked down the PMH corridors, chest expanded, singing with panache at full volume. I loved it.

CHAPTER 25:

Maternal Meltdown, 1951

1951 at the Presbyterian Mission Home in Kowloon started off with "a beautiful wedding" (my mother's description) when PC(USA) missionary Janet Stewart married her heartthrob. There was a memorable moment when, coming down the stairs to get into the waiting car, she paused in front of a mirror and said to no one in particular as everyone was watching, "Why, I am terrific!" "If you put charm and modesty and candour and sweetness into it, you have the idea," my usually critical mother stated. It was typical of Janet's uninhibited *joie de vivre* for which all of us smitten males loved her. Going off with a sailor who had gone to Oxford seemed so romantic, even if he was now employed by the YMCA.All of us China mishkids felt the loss: Janet had unusual pastoral skills with teenagers.

Her wedding was a welcome reprise from a time of darkness and fear. There was an effort to convey those feelings in a letter home: "We are so near stark reality. There are so many things that don't get into letters at all and I realize that you don't have a real picture and words can't do justice to it." She continued: "We see people still living normally, a steady stream of refugees from the other side of 'The Curtain' – penniless, homeless – people from the higher classes as well as fakers. *Now* they are people who have fled from death, not just inconvenience and uncertainty. There are thousands of refugees in Hongkong who have fled from interior China afraid to go back and afraid of what may happen in Hongkong."

The Korean War was going badly for the United States and their allies in the United Nations. We were thirty miles away from a country that had changed the whole course of the conflict. I followed the ebb and flow of the battle with pins on a large map of Korea with utter fascination as we found ourselves in the cockpit of history: the Pusan perimeter, followed by the Inchon landing, the march into North Korea, the crossing of the Yalu River by Chinese "volunteers" and then, by January 1951, the stalemate. With the US Fleet in the Taiwan straits, sent at the outbreak of the war, the possibility of a conflagration sparked by a hot-headed General Douglas MacArthur (a hero to my faraway grandfather), was always a possibility. One had to be grateful to American President Harry Truman for his cool head.

The plight of missionaries caught in China was an increasing worry. "Since these latest developments," mother wrote in mid-January, "the freezing of USA funds, etc., those who have applied to come out seem to be all held up in their permits to leave and some of them are ill and there are children there." Their plight prompted serious questions about God's goodness. Her faith was being challenged. "It is not necessary to describe what they went through in the way of accusations, and questioning and appropriation of their possessions, and finally, a 'trial'." Hardest of all, were the betrayals of colleagues one of whom, to secure their freedom, said hatefully, "Push them out" to their tormentors as the only way for them to be freed. It was heart-rending, particularly as my mother became deeply involved in pastoral care for Christians under siege to help them deal with their experiences. Even the much loved Janet Stewart, now Mrs. Jack Shepherd, came for counsel.

Then there was silence. Mother appeared to have had a complete breakdown. No one seemed to be able to understand what was happening to her. For two months there was little or no communication with family in America. Twin sister Marjorie finally cabled asking for an explanation as to why her weekly and sometimes twice weekly letters had come to such an abrupt end. A disjointed and incoherent half letter on 3 April which mother gave me to mail (presumably so Dad would not edit or destroy it) was full of denial. She explained her silence as the result of "a little germ of some kind, not very severe" which she dismissed as a peptic ulcer. My father replied six days later: "Dorothy has asked me to cable you in fulfilment of a promise she made & not be alarming to you. But I can't figure out anything to say that would be truthful & not alarming & at the same time mean something definite. So I tell her to wait for the blood tests." By early May she was more coherent. "I had a cold and a digestive upset and my heart was misbehaving, and I had to give up and was very ill." But she went on to reveal her state of mind and her depression: "I felt I was not going to get well. I rested on the promise 'In my father's house are many mansions.'" She was quite delusional: "The doctors decided to give me these injections supposed to give my brains a jouncing" she wrote and digitalis was prescribed, indicating the possibility of heart disease. But for six weeks she was isolated with only my father and a nurse to respond to her needs. The Changs, whose daughters she had tutored at the piano, also made regular visits with expensive and thoughtful gifts.

For me the whole sequence of events with my mother was deeply disturbing. Like my father, it was hard to know what to say about it that made much sense. Suddenly their room was "off limits", quietness was demanded, and for some weeks I was only allowed short visits with my mother. Because their room was just across the hall from mine, I could see doctors, a nurse, invited guests, coming and going with no explanation as to what was going on. My father was distracted, anxious to complete his commentary on I Peter. In that letter to his sister-in-law about mother he quickly reverted to his own commentary: "I regret that, in spite of driving at it for many months, I am not getting it out before China is almost completely vacated by missionaries." Mother's illness was a setback for his work.

On 16 April Carolyn, daughter of Baker James Cauthen who would in the 1970s make a name for himself as head of the largest and best-financed denominational missionary organization in the world, turned 14. Her mother, gifted in Southern U. S. hospitality, arranged a wonderful birthday party for her at the Southern Baptist compound on Boundary Road where they lived. I was excited to be invited and set out for the event by bus. Midway there I remembered that I did not have a gift. So I panicked, turned round, went back to mother and with her help located both gift wrapping paper and a gift and was ready to return, late, to the party. As I was about to leave my father turned up. Choked with a rage that I had never previously witnessed, he berated me for disturbing mother and disobeying instructions. He then ordered me into his office, closed the door, made me drop my trousers and then beat me with his razor strap. I went on, very late, to the party, almost in tears, trying to keep my composure. My father was obviously under great strain but that unforgettable incident forever altered our relationship.

It was fortuitous at that point that we could put much that had happened behind us and make a fresh start by being required to move and so leave painful memories associated with our location behind. During the six weeks of mother's confinement the Presbyterian Church (USA) was negotiating the sale of 11A Carnarvon Road to a group of investors headed by our avuncular man at the front desk, Ah Lee. The rationale behind this transaction was the reality that the usefulness of such a facility was disappearing as now many, if not most, of the denomination's missionaries had left China. But there was also a financial and business imperative. During its 113 years in China the Presbyterian mission, one of the largest in the country, had acquired a lot of valuable real estate for its schools, hospitals, housing, and churches and that equity had provided a basis for further investment and even speculation. With the confiscation of most foreign-owned religious properties, that was gone. The Kowloon property, had it been retained, would have soared in value. But at the time many investors regarded Hong Kong as a risky place and were anxious to jump ship. So with the transfer of the title deed missionaries were given a few weeks' notice to either leave the city or find alternative accommodation.

It was left to my father to find a new home for us and for our freight, much of which had never been opened since we arrived in China three years previously. On 20 April he relocated our possessions to a place the Mission had set up. I would finally have the stapler I had wanted, as well as my stamp collection and books, the lack of which had created a sense of impermanence and rootlessness. Then he went on to inspecy a two-bedroom apartment in Kowloon Tong at 149 Waterloo Road, at the end of the 7 and 8 bus lines, at the base of Lion Rock Mountain. The place turned out to be ideal, all I ever wanted in the first permanent dwelling place I'd had since leaving Boston three years earlier. It was on the second floor of an orphanage run by a California-based agency called the Peniel Mission. It had a yard and was patrolled by a police dog instead of the menacing cut glass on wall tops. It looked out over a garden, with nothing then on the other side of Waterloo Road. There I found happiness.

We moved in the day before my thirteenth birthday. The next day Dad was back at work, translating, proofreading, and checking language for accuracy. He also went and paid HK$4575 to the printer as his Chinese I Peter commentary came off the press. Mother was negotiating for a piano at Moutrie's with an uncooperative salesman. "I have been enjoying an experiment in spiritual chemistry. All possible anxieties or problems or distress even over the ghastly suffering in China or Korea – seeing them sublimated and dissolved in the 'all things' verses in the Bible." I was exploring the best route to KG-5, discovered that my new location had halved the time required as I took the #7 bus and walked up past the Jr. School the back way to KG-5. It was a relief to be out of the claustrophobia of the PMH and have a life of my own, even if it was lonelier and more isolated.

As the PMH crowd was breaking up, my closest friend was returning with his family to Kansas for his final year of high school. He came to inspect our new quarters after church the last Sunday of May and we had a final opportunity to share our common faith. He had been a member of a so-called cell group of five high schoolers that had been engaged in intense Bible Study and prayer with a strong influence from the Navigators. Cornelius Cowles, son of a Pentecostal missionary and a brilliant pianist, took the lead and Eric Webster, the head prefect at KG-5, was one of the members. All were "on fire for Jesus". As he and I said good-bye, we committed ourselves to pray for each other and stay in touch. I have a pile of his letters, sharing his experiences as he travelled through Europe sight-seeing (as we would two years later). One of them was signed off with "God bless you and the others in Hong Kong and may you learn to know Jesus and God more and more."

He arrived in early September in the small prairie town where his family had farmed for generations. High school was a shock: "We call all the men teachers by their first names," he noted. Academically the place was very weak compared to KG-5. "The United States isn't the best place to try to be a Christian," he wrote. "I haven't gotten too far but I always keep trying. It's really tough with nobody else to talk to about Christian things and problems. Is Taft [a military member of the cell group] still there or has he gone to Korea? The director of religious education is just like Janet. She just got married a couple of weeks ago. Is Mr. Blackstone leaving or not?" He was evidently missing the PMH crowd. By the New Year (his final letter) he wrote: "I have done more Bible study than I was doing before but it is only in spells and is not regular. I think I finished all the Navigator's Bible verses so that I will only have to review them."

Then I heard no more until years later I tracked him down. He graduated from high school and as the son of missionaries qualified for aid, chose a Presbyterian USA college, Buena Vista, in Kansas for his first year. There his faith was challenged in the compulsory Bible class. Disillusioned, he went on the next year to the College of Wooster in Ohio, another PCUSA school, where his senior thesis (majoring in Bible) was an analysis of the Synoptic Gospels which his instructor convinced him were inconsistent, unreliable and probably fabricated. Having lost his faith he maintained the missionary impulse of his parents by going out to Uganda to teach in an Islamic school. Dante should have included educators like those my fellow China mishkid encountered in two Presbyterian colleges in his description of The Inferno.

As tests for the second, or summer, semester were being held my mother wrote: "I think the exams are a bit on the stiff side. Now comes the waiting for grades and <u>placing</u> in every subject and generating averages. Keen competition. I don't altogether like it." When the results were posted I placed second in a class of 26 with an average of 75.6%. Never a linguist, I had flubbed the Latin exam but otherwise the grades were reassuring. Miss Carcary, my much appreciated Glaswegian geography teacher, summarized the impression I was making: "A most interested and & intelligent boy." I had weathered the trauma of my mother's unexplained illness, and had been relocated, losing friends as the Far East was in turbulence. At 13 I was about to feel the unsettling effects of puberty and adolescence. Naturally high-strung, my temperament would bring challenges as my preoccupied parents dealt with their own future. I was increasingly on my own.

CHAPTER 26:

Magnificent Macao, 1951

"**R**ight now our magazine rack is littered with folders on Macao from my music teacher," I wrote family gathered in Connecticut for a reunion. "She's a member of the famous Braga family," I continued. Summer 1951 was dominated for me by a visit to the Portuguese colony of Macao which I had spent weeks researching. Mary Braga, my music teacher and her sister Caroline lived in an old house on Chatham Rd. which I would visit every week. I actually had more interest in the research than the piano playing. The Roman Catholic patriarch of the Braga family, José Pedro Braga, was married to Australian Evangelical Protestant Olive Pauline Pollard. Together they produced thirteen children all of whom she raised as Evangelicals. Associations with the Braga family provided me an entrée into regional history. Two grandchildren, Stuart and Fran Braga, were in my class at KG-5.

I don't know how much my fascination with the saga of the Braga clan resonated with my American family but, with the help of Mary Braga, I researched their history as a preparation for visiting Macao. "Formerly Portuguese, the family moved over here in 1841 when Hong Kong was founded," I enthused in my letter. I had been trusted with some quasi-historical documents from the extensive Braga collection.

Unfortunately the young daughter in our neighbouring apartment took one of them off the phone table we shared and vandalized it, devastating me but providing a valuable lesson about keeping historical documents safe. My father was most interested in my seeing the grave of Robert Morrison in the Protestant Cemetery in Macao. Robert Morrison was the first Protestant missionary to China and died in 1837. I was most interested in acquiring some mint Macao stamps at the Macao philatelic bureau to bring my collection up to date.

So we set out for a three hour ride on the ferry *Hu-man*, leaving Friday morning 24 August. As we docked, the façade of the ruined St. Paul's Church, the inspiration for the hymn "In the cross of Christ I glory", was in full view. Mother wrote later that "We stayed at a hotel overlooking the sea, on the point almost next door to the Governor's House. Donald studied maps and history and planned a good deal for our stay, so we really saw just about everything that was interesting. He and Alec are excellent guides, though sometimes a shade too zealous for a less energetic lady. We viewed the colony from every high spot." I went off on my own with my sketch book and watercolours and painted some local beauty spots. The low point was an angry exchange between my parents at the Macao main post office, which unsettled me.

We returned to our apartment after "a real vacation" though it had lasted only three days. Our move to Kowloon Tong had been providential. Here we had privacy and were not all the time "on public display" with shared meals, common washroom, and laundry facilities, and efforts to avoid controversy – theological or political – with people with whom we often had basic differences. You learned to keep your mouth shut, a challenge for a voluble preteen but good practice for later in life. The food had been remarkably good but some culinary items, such as canned Australian rabbit meat, I found disgusting. One resident had found my father's constant clacking away at his manual typewriter irritating. And above all, there was the uncertainty of our common future looming over all of us. It was surprising that there was not more conflict.

Another advantage of our new housing, now that we had a full-time amah, was the opportunity for my mother to resume her favoured role as hostess. A two week break in Cheung Chau in September just before school, meant that our unoccupied apartment could be used by three single women who had just escaped out of China, badly roughed up, and who needed domestic tranquillity. Meanwhile we, in our holiday cottage, were welcoming co-workers who were glad to escape the heat of the city. "All our guests have been Chinese and we are glad. We do not have the close contacts here that we used to have in the Seminary – and we do like to feel that they can count on our being 'open house' to them – does them good and us."

The time away gave Dad a second chance to reflect on a year's work and catch up on correspondence. "For well over a year," he wrote a college classmate in New Jersey, "I have been working up a Commentary on the First Epistle of Peter, I finished the English mss last December, & since then have been working with the help of Chinese assistants at putting it into Chinese. It will be nearly 350 pages. Just at present it is about half printed, I get a bundle of proof sheets to read each week, & make corrections & alterations & get them back to the printer. The first proofs are the ones that take the most time & require most care. The second & third just require checking to see that all corrections have been attended to by the typesetter. At least that's all I have time for (it's my 4th reading of the Commentary) but I have a Chinese read it again. It is being printed by the Chung Hwa Book Company, one of the biggest Chinese publishing houses. It is coming out under the auspices of the Christian Witness Press of the China Inland Mission." I am sure my mother was grateful the to see Dad huddled up with young Chinese secretaries hour after hour in a very small room. One of them, "Ellen", had become almost a member of our family.

We returned to a busy social life. One evening in October all eleven Presbyterians from our Mission still left in Hong Kong turned up at our house for a prayer meeting and supper provided by my mother. The celebrity culture of American evangelicalism in the mid-twentieth century was now developing and a string of international notables, each doing the Pacific circuit visited us, including Ravensbrück concentration camp survivor Corrie Ten Boom. In mid-November 1951, Beth

Jaderquist Paddon, Wheaton class of 1926, head of the Women's Union Missionary Society, came for dinner. That evening I caught the wrong bus back from school, tried to take a short cut through a building site, and arrived covered in mud. Embarrassment all round. Making an impression, so important to my mother, was not my thing. She and I missed the visit of the greatest celebrity of all in the evangelical stratosphere: Dad was in Taiwan on 29 December 1952 when he met Billy Graham at the Grand Hotel in Taipei. We missed him by a week. Graham's in-laws, Dr. Nelson and Virginia Bell[37], had been Southern Presbyterian medical missionaries near Hsuchow. Billy and Ruth Graham were both 1943 Wheaton College graduates which brought them into my parents' orbit.

With the completion of his commentary on I Peter and the military stalemate in the Far East in the final months of 1951, our family was at an impasse. It was clear that we would not be returning to China, so a decision as to our future had to be made. I was now a teenager and any decisions made by my parents would impact me and my future. Our lives could not stay on hold indefinitely.

---

37   Lemuel Nelson Bell (1894-1973) went to China in 1916 to serve the Love & Mercy Hospital Qingjangpu, Jiangsu, leaving China in 1941, going on to create in 1942 the *Southern Presbyterian Journal* and in 1957 join *Christianity Today* staff when founded in 1957. He had a profound influence on his son-in-law Billy Graham.

CHAPTER 27:
Intellectual Challenges at KG-5, 1951

That autumn of 1951 we had a new history teacher at KG-5. The name "Conrad W. Watson" in a bold pen can be seen on KG-5 memorabilia and on my report book at the end of term: "Excellent – always" as I placed first in the class. Mr. Watson made at least two in his class – I and Stuart Braga – life-long historians. As Stuart wrote me fifty years later: Mr. Watson "had a great deal to do with my life-long commitment to History and History teaching," a tribute with which I can concur.

Not that he was without blemishes. He had a problem with alcohol and would sometimes appear hung over with dark glasses to lessen the effect of his indulgence, something that only made sense later. He would give out lines – 500 to be handed in the next day - if we couldn't answer one of his questions (fortunately I could) and then he would return to class the next morning to say that we could forget the assigned punishment. Unfortunately some of the more conscientious girls in the class had already completed their quota. Our text was the excellent History Series for Grammar Schools published by Ginn & Co. in the 1930s and written by a group of women historians.

Watson held our interest in class and inspired you to write history essays with panache. He was not squeamish: Mrs. Lawrence, who preceded him, had objected when I described the Pope declaring Elizabeth a "bastard" because of the illegitimacy of her parents' union. One of the American agencies in Hong Kong offered a prize for the best historical essay in our class and I received a book for my effort on Cardinal Wolsey. I still remember whole chunks out of *The Days of the Tudors and Stuarts*, the third in the series which had begun with *From Ur to Rome*. After Mr. Watson I could not countenance anyone calling history "dull." It seemed totally inconceivable.

Throughout this time Mother was still struggling with the prospect of a second breakdown. The news from the mainland was increasingly dour. "I am beginning to see that there is a difference between prayer which is earnest and intense, for those suffering people in China – and carrying a burden of anxiety for them which drains one's own strength and the ability to carry on efficiently." She itemized all the cruelties being perpetrated on Christians, and especially the few remaining missionaries. She had given her life to spread the Word in the Middle Kingdom, so was she now culpable in their suffering? One did not even dare to go down that self-destructive path.

Mother's own activities were not going that well either. She had been asked to teach at the True Light Middle School, a girls' high school, founded by Presbyterian missionaries in 1872 in Canton and now affiliated with the Church of Christ in China (CCC). The School had relocated to Hong Kong two years earlier and was housed at 115 Waterloo Road, an easy distance from our home. Her assignment there legitimized her ministry in the denomination as a missionary of the denomination. It seemed an ideal solution given the ambiguity of her situation. Ma Yi Yang was the formidable Principal who had led them out of Communist China. Mother was approached to teach Bible but now her classes were not going well. On 12 October mother met with Dr. Ma who informed her that there were complaints from her students. She told mother that "the study is too hard for the girls; they do not want to buy Bibles." (a Christian school?) "And she is thinking of changing the class into a

Chinese-language class. I told her frankly that I hoped she would talk directly to the girls. Mother had given them too much Bible and had attempted to respond to their personal problems.

Once again, theological differences within the Presbyterian mission had created difficulties. Mother, however, had support from many quarters. Her musical giftedness also provided a bridge across ideological divides .Working closely with Caroline Braga, she had never lacked piano students. And she also received support from Rev. and Mrs. Roberts, independent Presbyterians connected with the ministry of the Bible Institute of Los Angeles. In addition to pastoring the Emmanuel Church he ran a Christian bookstore on the premises, and taught at the relocated Hunan Bible Institute. Mrs. Roberts told mother not to quit her Bible class. Edwin Walline[38], the one to whom she was accountable in the Presbyterian mission, affirmed her teaching. And eventually she sorted things out with Dr. Ma with whom she developed a growing mutual respect.

My father was also being challenged in his work. He had already started on his second literary project, a commentary (which he had begun while in China) on the Sermon on the Mount. The printer, with whom he had signed a contract for his commentary on I Peter, claimed to have run out of type for Dad's theological language. There was no let-up as he raced to finish the book: Christmas Eve he took the second proofs of pages 331-356 to the printer of. That day he was working on the Preface and the Table of Contents. And three days later he provided the calligraphy for the title page, artistically done by Professor Weng who was well-known in China for the beauty of his brushed characters.

---

38   Edwin E. Walline (1890-1965) was appointed to the PC(USA) China mission in
      1917 after graduation from Park College and McCormick Seminary from which
      in 1929 he received a DD. He served in rural Kwantung but was almost immedi-
      ately placed in administration. Briefly interned in Pootung, he had a strategic role
      after the War in Shanghai ("years of great strain") as chair of the China Council
      which soon ceased to exist. Moving to Hong Kong he helped found Chung Chi
      College in 1951. A true liberal he served the PCUSA & CCC for 47 years.

Our Christmas 1951 was on hold. The annual Christmas letter had to be delayed to give our supporters the reassurance of a published book. Mother spent her time practicing as accompanist for the True Light College Girls Choir's Christmas concert. A month to the day our postponed Christmas celebration was held. Dad finally had the finished book in his hands on 25 January 1952. His excitement knew no bounds. Copies were sent out to many of his seminary classmates, colleagues and supporters, few of whom could actually read Chinese. More significantly, he developed a system of sending one or two copies a day in brown paper wrappers to pastors across China without a forwarding address so that there would be no incrimination. There was a print run of two thousand, some with a blue cover and white paper, and others with a green cover and newsprint. The total cost was HK$10,603 which came from the American Council of NCTS. By the autumn of 1952 he had mailed 216 copies to pastors in China. It was his way of opening one door when all portals seemed tightly shut. Unfortunately a later generation wanted an exposition that was not quite so basic and addressed critical issues. With sermon suggestions and study questions his book targeted a less sophisticated audience. But at a time when there was growing persecution and the threat of extinction, Dad's exposition of I Peter with its encouragement for challenged believers met a real need.

At school we had a new math teacher that term. Mr. Gamble was young, brash, and very bright. The contrast with his predecessor, Mrs. Hill, could not have been more striking. He singled me out almost from the start as someone who would profit from a lot of attention. Mathematics was supposed to be his subject but that did not in any way inhibit him from introducing the class to all kinds of other material. The Third Programme of the BBC was one of his delights and facilitated interesting discussions of why elitism was a good thing in a democracy and how repulsive he found people who tried to eliminate it. Gambell was a big fan of James Thurber, the *New Yorker* cartoonist. Thurber's embattled male provided him an opportunity to digress onto social causes. He championed Dostoevsky and by the following term this fourteen year old was earnestly engrossed in *Crime and Punishment.*

He, even more than my own mother, introduced me to the delights of classical music and especially opera: Beniamino Gigli, the Italian tenor, was a favourite and he brought a portable record player to class one day to ensure that we understood the score.

Then I let him down. Fran Braga's mother complained about some off-colour story that he had entertained the class with. The report went to the top and he was called into the headmaster's office, along with the offended parent. In his defence he said "Donald MacLeod doesn't seem to mind my humour." Whereupon Mr. Potter leaned over and said, "As a matter of fact the MacLeod's are one of the families complaining." When I heard about that exchange I felt I had betrayed him, I was Judas.

At the end of 1952, I won the Middle Form Mathematics Prize. By then I was in Taiwan, but Mr. Gamble wrote me a personal letter saying that he had chosen for my award the classic 1935 *Mathematics for the Millions* by Lancelot Hogben[39]. He suggested I read it carefully. Hogben had renounced his Plymouth Brethren heritage and was virulently anti-Christian. This choice of reading material with its high recommendation has often made me wonder whether Mr. Gamble as my favourite KG-5 teacher also wanted to divest me of my religious hang-up. He had already had no small part in my rebellion that first term in 1952.

---

39   Lancelot Hogben (1895-1975) educated Trinity College, Cambridge, he had wide scientific interests. His academic career included a spell at McGill in the 1920s, as well as Cape Town. He went on to LSE in 1936 when he became a Fellow of the Royal Society. Famed for work on eugenics, endocrinology and social biology.

CHAPTER 28:

Conflicted Identities, 1952

"King Georgy had a date
King Georgy stayed out late,
He was the King.
King George stayed out 'til four
Queen Mary met him at the door,
God save the King."

This iconoclastic rhyme, sung to the tune of "God Save the King", became a handy way of Yanks annoying Brits at KG-5. Behind the shock and insult of the verse there was a real problem for some of us. We had grown up not sure which of three national identities we should claim as our own: our mother's, our father's or our country of residence, the only one we had really experienced growing up. Our ambivalence could be disconcerting if not downright dangerous. Surrounded by a hostile power, we also carried the weight of the past. Seven years after the war, with many former internees among us, loyalty to the British crown was a serious matter. That was soon to be powerfully demonstrated to me.

On 6 February 1952, a Wednesday morning, King George VI was found dead in his bed after suffering a coronary thrombosis. The ripple effects of that event radiated from Sandringham to the ends of his rapidly shrinking Empire. Four days later, to ensure that I would never forget the drama of the event, my father took me that Saturday on the Star Ferry to the Cenotaph to hear the proclamation of the accession of a new head of state. The change of monarch marked not only a new era for the crown colony of Hong Kong but also a year of turmoil for this teenaged mishkid seeking to find his identity in an adult world.

My Diary entry for Saturday, 9 February, put it all in the perspective of an almost fourteen year old: "Worked on my exercise book. At 10:00 A.M. went with Dad to Statue Square to hear Elizabeth II proclaimed. Homework - afternoon." My Christmas present that neglected holiday was a *Letts School-Boys Diary* for 1952. Letts had been producing diaries for the Empire since 1810, and by the time I started mine they were an integral part of British identity. It came replete with French and Latin verbs, logarithms and anti-logarithms, school and university sports statistics, cricket teams, countries of the world with particular reference to members of the Empire, important books one should read, etc. etc. This list of useful information was all contained in a slim pocket edition 3 ½ by 6 inches that seemed endless though compact. My diary always started well each 1 January but flickered and faded usually by February or, in the case of my first effort, to the end of April.

Not only were individuals encouraged to keep a diary, KG-5 classes were as well. One friend kept a diary for his class which apparently was too racy for his teacher and he ended up in the headmaster's office and was caned. I can recall my awe at the welts on his rear as he dropped his trousers to show off his war wounds. Mr. O'Hanrahan started daily class journaling in Fourth Form and I and some luckless girl were co-editors. Inevitably the writing became competitive: "Can you top this?" seemed to be the challenge. But in early 1952 I was experimenting with how far I could go.

The view of KG-5 clock tower from Classroom 4A.

Several influences encouraged this pushback, unthinkable to either of my parents from their experience growing up. Mother should have learned something from her brothers but they were much younger and she was away from home when their rebellion started. Several factors contributed to my angst. Eddy Blight joined our class and his name appears regularly in my diary. Eddy was American; his father an American army officer attached to a Hong Kong listening post. When he joined us in the KG-5 dining hall for lunch I was teased because, it was claimed, I had now reverted to the American way of holding a knife and fork! Knowing an American my own age who was not a mishkid was a new and exciting experience. And his family's lifestyle seemed to be the height of luxury.

I was at Eddy's when the riots broke out on Saturday 1 March 1952. Incited by agitators sympathetic to Peking, demonstrators wanting so-called "comfort stations" for Communists being mistreated, it was claimed, by the Hong Kong government. A procession of ten thousand, waving banners stating that "Hong Kong is China" started at the Kowloon rail station, making its way up Nathan Road singing Communist songs and roughing up a so-called "European" police inspector and throwing stones at two "Europeans" emerging from a taxi. Mother had a hysterical call from a friend in an apartment right on Nathan Road, a ringside seat. She then called me – "I tried to head him off and tell him to stay there until we could find out more, but his friend said he had already gone ... I was glad when Donald came in calmly about two hours later, after the worst was over. He had only been delayed and kept waiting for the bus and didn't know much about the rioting – Alec was so calm that it just wouldn't have been worthwhile to get excited." Radio reports sensationalized the riots, greatly upsetting my Red scare McCarthyite grandfather as he heard (and read) wildly exaggerated reports. But the situation quickly quieted down and we were safe.

My friend Eddy, Edward M. Blight Jr., was highly intelligent, and an all-rounder. As an Eagle Scout in the Staes he knew all about knots and semaphore signalling and had accumulated, it seemed, endless Merit Badges. He was eight months older at a stage of life when that gap makes a big difference. He brought out my adolescent insecurities. I craved his friendship as the brother I lacked. I never regarded Eddy as a committed Christian, a concern of my mother's. In April that year he joined me after Scouts for a weekend at our place. I was petrified that my mother would be too religious and gave her strict instructions about praying and Scripture reading. When I thought she was too preachy I would kick her under the table. Mother was worried that I was compromising. Eddy and I gradually drifted apart.

In later life Ed Blight had a distinguished career as a physician. After matriculating at KG-5 he went on to The Citadel, the top-ranked

Military College of South Carolina, where he was the first to get a 4.0 GPA average for the four years, a tribute to the education he had received in Hong Kong. After taking his MD at UCSF Medical School (where he met his wife, a fellow student), he spent twenty years in the military as a battle group surgeon and urologist and rose to the rank of Colonel. His 2015 obituary, proudly citing his KG-5 experience, stated that "Blight loved the Citadel, loved to read, loved the San Francisco Giants, and loved his family. But most of all, he loved God and lived his entire life from a Christian world view." Whether my reluctant and stumbling witness had anything to do with that faith I somewhat doubt. Ironic that one of the strongest Christians from my time as a Mishkid came not from the missionary community but from an army brat. My regret is that I only rediscovered Eddy after he died.

We also had a new home room teacher assigned to us in January 1952. Mr. O'Halloran, again a memorable educator, taught us English. Aggressively Irish, on St. Patrick's Day he showed up with a blazer adorned with a badge picturing an Irish harp. On one occasion he got carried away with a poetic description of his final breakup with his girl-friend in Dublin as night fell. She was unwilling to travel to the Far East. O'Halloran was fixated on sonnets and had us memorize many of the best: Shakespeare particularly, but also Milton and Wordsworth, lines that still haunt me to this day. Unfortunately when I returned to the States and my less than adequate English teacher would start a sonnet I would complete it by heart which did nothing for my reputation. O'Halloran also coached us in recitation of poetry and Hillarie Belloc's "Tarantella" with those mnemonic lines "the fleas that tease in the High Pyrenees" always remind me of the cadence of language. His parting words as I left KG-5 at the end of the year were: "Donald has intel-ligence, works conscientiously and reaps his due success."

He had not always been that positive about me. 27 March 1952 was Parents' Day at KG-5, an opportunity for mothers and fathers to discover how their offspring were being educated, teachers to show off their skills, and compliant students to shine as examples of respectful behaviour. All went well for me until the final class, 3:00 to 4:00, English taught by

Mr. O'Halloran. I was not paying attention and somehow was caught twenty-five minutes before the final bell, passing a note and/or creating a disturbance. Exasperated O'Halloran sent me (for the first time since I had come to KG-5) to "The Square" - the space in the front hall as guests entered the building, just outside the headmaster's office – where I would be very visible to all visitors but particularly to the Headmaster who could mete out whatever punishment he deemed appropriate. I suddenly realised, having forgotten what day it was, that parents, some of them my parents' friends and colleagues, might see me. I was both mortified and fearful. Through those anxious minutes until the bell rang I did some soul-searching. There is a reference, illegible, to Mr. Potter the Headmaster in my Diary entry for the day. But his summary of my Easter term debacle could not have been clearer. Writing in my report book he penned these stinging words. "Although still good, I have noticed some falling off in his work & conduct. I want to see him do much better next term."

Neither parent showed much awareness of that stage of adolescence but what parent does? My father never had "the talk" that every growing young man expects but dreads. Instead, my mother's attention was more directed to my reading material: "Donald is reading juvenile stuff – Biggles of the air force, or something like that." She explained that "Biggles is a whole series – I don't know what it's like, but it's certainly not very profound." The Biggles series, written by First World War RAF pilot W. E. Johns, was the choice of most early-teen British schoolboys at the time. Starting in 1932, the scenario always seemed to be variations on the theme of Biggles rescuing someone in peril with supporting females, his upper crust cousin Algernon Lacey ("Algy"), and working class Ginger Hebblethwaite. The books were an introduction to the British class system, racist, but otherwise morally circumspect, except for the occasional swearword. And they provided a bond with my contemporaries at KG-5.

My parents' major preoccupation at the time was their professional future. Our friends, the Lewis family, had gone back to what was now renamed Peking in 1950 (later Beijing) only to try a year later to leave. It took them a further year but eventually they got an exit permit. Charles, their son who was my age, had eaten a popsicle from a roadside stand, something I would have thought he would have been warned against, and came down with typhoid which nearly cost him his life. The incident made us think about our own family's future. On 19 May 1951 Mother reported "Alec has been invited to teach in the Presbyterian Seminary (Canadian) in Formosa. They are very eager for us to go there, and of course it would be a very challenging work." She sounded relieved: uncertainty was over.

Negotiations took over a year. Dad's classmate from Princeton Seminary, Principal James Dickson, came for an interview on behalf of the Taiwan Theological College in March 1952, and it was finally agreed that Dad would start teaching there that September. The slow pace of negotiations was caused by many concerns: my father's literary work, the fact that he spoke only Mandarin and the Formosan Church was fiercely Taiwanese in language and culture, and inter-board relationships. Since there was no English language secondary school on the island at the time, my schooling made a quick move challenging. Alternatives for me were discussed: boarding school in the Philippines or at the Canadian Academy in Kobe Japan, sending me home a year before they were due to leave on furlough or even Calvert home schooling. It was unsettling that the onus fell on me. It was finally decided that Dad would go ahead of us for four months and that I would see out the school year.

CHAPTER 29:

Adolescent Angst, 1952

"**N**ow Alex is at work on his next project, a Commentary on the Sermon on the Mount and the first instalment has been published in Chen Kuang magazine," my mother explained to her sister. There had been no lull in his literary work. Before he arrived in Hong Kong, the NCTS faculty had requested a text book that could be used for teaching Christian ethics, a vital need in a country in convulsion. By the beginning of the summer of 1952 he was half way through, completing the English manuscript on which he would base the Chinese translation. He worked with the actual text (from the gospel of Matthew chapters 5 through 7) and he was now almost through his exposition of chapter 6 in English but only at the conclusion of the Beatitudes, at the beginning of chapter 5 in Chinese. As his time in Hong Kong was rapidly drawing to an end, how would he be able to complete the project? "I should like very much to have it published before the opening of the second term of most Christian schools next January-February, certainly before next June, when we are due to return home." Time was running out.

Exams at KG-5 began with Latin on 4 July, an ultimate affront to an American! "The exams were particularly difficult," my anxious mother explained to her sister, "apparently because the school year is being changed, and *this* year ends in December as usual. and then the next 'year' ends the following June. So courses are being speeded up, and exams seemed to aim at pushing *down* as many people as possible early in the game so that the change would not completely swamp them." I was pushed down by Mr. Gamble, described as "our-fresh-from-Oxford Maths professor" (for whom my mother had no truck anyway) with a 49 in arithmetic, though all in all I didn't fare too badly, placing third in the class.

After all the drama of the previous months, two weeks in Cheung Chau, which had become a refuge for us, were welcome. The unusually hot summer had been particularly unhealthy for my father, unusual because he had been remarkably strong after recovering from his prisoner of war experience. On 14 August, the seventh anniversary of V-J Day, the family celebrated with Mother the completion of the typed manuscript Dad had given her, the first stage of his second commentary now finished. Four days later we set off for Cheung Chau, My father was anxious for time by ourselves but we kept having visitors: the Chang family came out the day after we arrived, John[40] and Mary Su and their family the next day. Of all the NCTS students we associated with in those years in Hong Kong, John was probably the closest to us, working with Dad on the language of his commentaries. Mother tried to help him with his musical composition without much success. He was an original. John was himself going out that same year in what turned out to be a seven year travelling evangelistic ministry which took him to all the countries of the Far East. Meanwhile, as Dad was preparing to leave, there were visas to clear, farewells for my father to make, including an NCTS graduates final get together. On 13 September, a Saturday, my mother and I saw him off on the steamship *Wingsang* for Keelung, north Taiwan. Two days later, a new stage in his life began. Mother and I would remain at 149 Waterloo Road until the New Year

---

40   John Su (Su Zuoyang) (1916-2007) born in Kowloon, Hong Kong. Graduate NCTS (1934-7), worked on Hebrew lexicon there (1940-1) Ordained Gansu 1947. Authored hundreds of hymns, founded *Voice of the Heavenly People*.

For the next two and a half months, Mother went through her usual routines, involved in the lives of many. Mrs. Pao, who had hovered between life and death, was a constant concern. Mrs. Chiu (or Chew), married to an Ipoh Malaya rubber planter, was helped by her friendship when he took another wife and she escaped briefly to Hong Kong. In preparation for potential opportunities in Taiwan, mother was coached by Caroline Braga, spending a whole week with her observing, as a silent presence in her piano classes, her pedagogical methodology. Dad wrote warning over her recommendation of a new edition of Hannah Whittall Smith's *The Christian's Secret of a Happy Life* which he regarded, because of its Quaker quietism, introspection and perfectionism, as a potentially dangerous book

There was now huge pressure on me academically at KG-5. Helen Huang had gone to America and I was no longer competing with her for the top place in our class. It turned out that I ended the academic year with my best grades ever. I placed first in the class with an 82.8 average. Mr Potter, my earlier nemesis, signed me out of KG-5 with the comment "Work & conduct excellent, I am sorry he is leaving the school." I had come a long way in 1952. The faculty loaded me down with textbooks and materials for the next four months of self-tutoring. I was sorry to leave but excited with that concept of self-tutoring. Anticipating further isolation, and with most of my friends already having left Hong Kong, I was going to be very much on my own. But the challenge of integrating into a Chinese environment, with Chinese language and art tutoring arranged, would open many new doors. As a China mishkids I was finally going to be introduced to the real culture of the Middle Kingdom. My father, born and raised in China for the first eighteen years of his life, cossetted in the British bubble that was Chefoo boarding schools, only learned about China when he returned twelve years later. I was going to be integrated, given a Chinese name, able to read and speak the language. It was totally unrealistic, idealism out of control, but at least I could dream of the promise of the future.

CHAPTER 30:

Chinese Immersion, Taiwan, 1953

Our time in Taiwan was to be brief as my parents were due for furlough. In spite of that, it was important for them to settle and set down roots there, even though for only a short time. We rented a house – Japanese style with tatami floor and slim sliding panels. Mrs. Dickson called it "Four Bananas" because of the trees in our front yard. Located on a laneway off North Chung Shan Road, second section, its modest size contrasted with the imposing missionary "bungalows" of an earlier era - both on the island and in the NCTS compound in Shandong where, pre-war, foreigners had lived in comparative splendour unlike their Chinese faculty colleagues. All our belongings were brought out of storage, things we hadn't seen for almost five years suddenly appeared and our library re-established itself on new book shelves delivered from a carpenter. It struck me that my parents were saying "Finally we have a home for you. This will be your base. In all your travels this should be in your mind's eye the place where our family finds coherence and order." The trouble with being a China mishkid during that period was that you had no sense of permanence or stability. Now "New Village, Number 2, Lane 39, North Chung Shan Road, Second Section" would be our identity. Just over four months later our possessions would be placed back in boxes, furniture left with other missionaries, and we'd be on the road again. "Everything flows" as Heraclitus once affirmed.

On firm land after a delayed and tempestuous journey, the first thing we saw as we arrived in Keelung that Saturday, 3 January 1953, was the flag that we had known so well in the old days in China. It was flying in full view on the pier. Coming to Taiwan after three and a half years in Hong Kong was like re-entering our past. Americans were number one among aliens allowed into the country as protectors of Taiwanese independence, on which the island relied. We were welcome. Eisenhower, not Elizabeth II, was deferred to. On the island the use of Mandarin, with the inference that we were supporters of Chiang Kai-shek, was more problematic. Six years earlier the island, only just returned to China after fifty years of Japanese occupation, was the scene of a bloody insurrection as Taiwanese sought greater autonomy. Missionaries would describe in hushed tones (the mention of the tragedy was forbidden for forty years) how soldiers stationed on Chung Shan Road, near the Presbyterian compound, fired indiscriminately on any and all passers-by that 28 February 1949, ever after known as the 228 Massacre.

Missionaries, expelled from China, had flooded into Taiwan in the hundreds. James Dickson who had invited Dad had also welcomed all evangelical Protestants to share in what was regarded as a particularly promising and potentially fruitful time for the expansion of Christianity on the island in the light of what was happening on the Mainland. Two million refugees had fled to Taiwan, creating chaos in housing and accommodation, as well as social tensions and general dislocation. The Mainland government vowed to claim the island as its legitimate spoil because of their triumph in the island's civil war, thus bringing constant fear and concern. Reports of shelling from the mainland onto Quemoy, the island across the strait, still occupied by the Nationalists, sent ripples of anxiety among the exiles. Separation and dislocation had created much psychic turmoil. As refugees everywhere they were tired, scared, disoriented and heart-broken.

Presbyterians on the island had ambivalent loyalties. They were identified with the Taiwanese and were champions of their identity as separate from their new Han Chinese rulers. After Dutch attempts at colonization in the Seventeenth Century and some Reformed missionary efforts, the island had been reached in 1865 by English Presbyterian missionaries in the South and in the North by the intrepid George Leslie MacKay for the Canadian Presbyterians. MacKay had so identified with the Taiwanese that he took one (the remarkable Tiu Chang-miâ or Minnie MacKay) as his bride, defying the contemporary strictures against biracial marriages. During the Second World War many of the aboriginal mountain tribespeople became Christians and today 30% of them are Presbyterian. At the time of church union in Canada in 1925, George Leslie MacKay's son, George William, successfully kept the Taiwan mission out of the United Church of Canada (though Unionist Hugh MacMillan stayed on as an advocate for theological inclusivism). As a result the northern synod has generally been more conservative in theology than its southern neighbour which, though founded by an evangelical Scot (James Laidlaw Maxwell), generally reflected the theological flexibility of the founding denomination. So we again found ourselves in·a mixed theological situation. Though initially warmly welcomed that was not to last. Six years after arrival my father was told he was no longer welcome, thanks to the machinations of Ted Johnson, the Canadian Presbyterian Foreign Missions Secretary. That recall was eventually rescinded but it was very painful for father. Not only was Johnson's theology different from Dad's he was another of those who in the 1930s had found Communism very attractive[41].

At first all seemed well. "The missionary community is more harmonious and more spiritually minded than any other group since Tenghsien days, that we have been in, and I wish you could have been at

---

41   Johnson's uncle was the "Red Dean" Hewlett Johnson who first visited China in 1931 and was awarded the Stalin Peace Prize in 1951. As an undergraduate, Johnson joined the Student Volunteer Movement which in Canada in the 1930s was pro-communist. See my "The Missionary Who Wasn't: The Centenary of Wilfred Cantwell Smith (1916-2000)" to be found on my website (adonaldmacleod.com) Smith, appointed a PCC missionary to India in 1939, founded the Communist Party of the Punjab ins 1942, returning to Canada 1946.

the prayer meeting last evening," my mother wrote her sister. The night before, at a business meeting prior to a time of prayer, a controversial item had been settled amicably and without division or acrimony. As a visiting missionary from Japan stated "I hardly thought it could happen, but it did." Mother was assigned a Bible Class as well as the ubiquitous English classes, always in high demand. Dad was teaching two classes at the Taiwan Theological College – one on I Peter with his commentary as the text, and another on Paul's letter to the Colossians. At the same time he was racing to complete for publication his commentary on The Sermon On The Mount before leaving on furlough. He was fortunate to find more secretarial assistance. NCTS American Council again footed the bill.

I had my own instructors: a tutor in the Chinese language as well as someone who could help me with writing characters in the notebook provided grade school students, with ink and brush, inscribing them over the square provided with a faint outline of what was required. I had freedom and with a bicycle I ventured all over Taipei, visiting temples, churches, museums and other places of interest and using my recently acquired Chinese. I also had tutors: Father Weingarten taught me advanced Latin and Dr Crowell (a Ph.D. in chemistry) set me loose in the chemistry laboratory of Tam Kang College in Tamsui where there was a large quantity of left-over elements for cataloguing and organizing, untouched since the Japanese departure had left them in chaos. And there was my own eclectic reading: a three volume set of Scott's semi-historical Scottish poetry and the complete works of Nathaniel Hawthorne. I worked through two centuries of British history from the Stuarts to the Hanoverians, having only previously gotten up to the Seventeenth Century. Mr. Watson had provided me with the texts I needed and I made meticulous notes on my readings.

My greatest educational experience in Taiwan was due to a remarkable couple, Donald Dale (not yet 30) and his wife Penny Dale. A serious asthmatic, I identified with him in so many ways beyond the name we shared. He was also a China mishkid, born in Szechuan to a missionary doctor in a Presbyterian hospital. At one time Donald had reacted violently against his Christian Brethren heritage, slamming a Bible to the floor during family devotions. He had met Penny while she was training as a nurse. Both loved China and Jesus. They travelled out to a posting at a municipal hospital in West China with a promised salary of "ten sacks of rice" a month. At the very same time we were also travelling to China. Like us, political conflict drove them out. They arrived in Taiwan in April 1949, one of the earliest evacuated missionaries to arrive there. He was hired by the MacKay Hospital, then in a woeful state. Donald Dale was a very perceptive diagnostician, seeing right through my mother's doctor fixations, and particularly empathetic with China mishkids, having been one himself. I joined a group of young men at his home for a weekday evening Bible study. He was funny, quick, and inspirational and understood teenagers.

Some time on the weekend of 18 – 20 March I happened to be in downtown Taipei at the newsstand that sold the *South China Morning Post,* straight from Hong Kong. I knew that Prize Day at KG-5 was sometime that week but, picking up the paper, I had the surprise of my life. Leafing through to page 5 I saw the headline "Annual Prize-Giving – Hundreds Attend Function at King George V School – Progress in Many Branches". After an account of the speech delivered by the chairman of the Board of Governors, the prize list appeared. To my elation my name occurred four times. For the class prize, the math prize (thank you Mr. Gamble), the History Prize, and a special commendation for Geography. I walked home on air that afternoon.

I did a lot of travelling around the island during those five months. One trip involved covering the various "Tais" – Taitung "East Tai" on the southeast coast, Tainan, "south Tai" at the lower end of the island and "Central Tai" – Taichung. I went up into the mountains with Lillian Dickson, founder of Mustard Seed Mission and a phenomenon. She was married to the Jim Dickson who had brought us to the Island, and had been our hostess before we settled into our own home, as with countless others. I travelled on a water buffalo and worshipped with aboriginals in a simple bamboo chapel, unforgettable. There was a family weekend in

Sun Moon Lake, a beauty spot in the mountains, which provided some respite from the city.

All the time I was being introduced to extraordinary people: Hildur Hermanson[42] ("Miss Clean"), a Canadian Prairie public health nurse who gave her name to the "Hermie-tage", a large turn of the century missionary "bungalow" in the Canadian compound, close by the MacKay Hospital where all the single lady missionaries associated with the Canadian Presbyterian Women's Missionary Society lived. The Southern Presbyterians (many of whom we knew from the mainland) were particularly congenial, warmly outgoing, and excellent cooks. They made the best peanut butter you could get anywhere. George Hudson, their tent evangelist, had a unique ministry, and "Ham", E. H. Hamilton, Dad's 1941 travelling companion was there. That ever ebullient China Mishkid James R. Graham III was supported by friends of Billy Graham (no relation) and was busy developing plans for Christ's College. Dad claimed his pulpit Mandarin was impeccable and his spirit unquenchable.

Then on 4 June my Taiwan interlude was over. Mother and I flew to Hong Kong and then she put me on a flight through to Geneva. Dad, in his methodical way, had planned my life for years ahead with letters (as noted in his Diary in early 1953) going out to Stony Brook School, Stanford Reid at McGill University and particularly at this point to Charles Arbuthnot, a representative from our PC(USA) Mission Board to the World Council of Church's headquarter in Geneva. "Do you know of a farm where my son can spend the summer and learn to speak French?" So I was being sent on ahead, half way across the globe, just having turned 15, to spend two months with strangers. Elie Pradervand and his wife would be my guardians for the summer. I was being pushed out of the nest and I was brimming with confidence and enthusiasm. My Taiwan experience had given me wings.

---

42   See my "Hildur Kristine Hermanson (Miss Wash)" in John Moir, Ed., *Gifts and Graces*, vol. 2. PCC Committee on History, Don Mills, ON. 37-41.

Chapter 31:

Swiss Summer, 1953

Mother saw me off from Kai Tak Airport, Hong Kong, on Wednesday evening 10 June 1953. The six days in Hong Kong were supposed to provide me with an opportunity to reconnect with the three and a half years I had spent there, renewing friendships and reestablishing relationships. Instead I had a distinct unwillingness to open up the past. Fran Braga had invited me to a beach party but I showed no desire to host a party which my mother had agreed to arrange. I did go briefly to KG-5, looked around the building but my class was involved in preparation for "O" level exams. As a mishkid I could not afford to be sentimental. As a mishkid I could not afford to be sentimental. Relationships were transient; life seemed constantly disrupted, so why take up the past? I did not continue to follow up any of my Hong Kong friendships and never heard from them until years later when the Internet reconnected us. At that point I had moved on. As with many mishkids I was queasy about more good-byes and separations.

Mother felt that I seemed much more mature than most fifteen-year-olds. She thought the airline considered me older than my actual age and fretted that they would not look after me as a minor. Allowing for some maternal prideful exaggeration, she had a point. Increasingly all my interactions had been with adults – as an only child there were no alternatives in an alien culture. It was good preparation for a round-the-world flight but not for life. I sent long letters from each of our stopovers travelling west. In my father's diary there is no record of my travel so completely was he absorbed in completing his commentary on the Sermon on the Mount. "We're now flying over Siam. After an hour or so [in flight], we could see Hainan for about thirty minutes. At about eleven we went back on to land – Indo-China coast just above Hanoi. At 11:45 you could see a large river which I guess was the Mekong. We are due to arrive in about ½ hour at Rangoon. I looked everywhere to see you after getting on board but the steward bawled me out." My last views of Southeast Asia were historic. Shortly names, many of them vestiges of a colonial past, changed and with it political stability and predictability. I had a lot to learn. For instance, whenever I saw an Asian I started to speak Chinese, not always appreciated by total strangers.

"We keep changing our clocks back - 3 ½ hours difference between Hong Kong and Calcutta," I wrote from the Indian metropolis. The excitement of the flight was wearing off. "Suppose you will be eating supper now but it's only 3:45." At Karachi a man who spoke only broken English and was "not too immaculate (I mean filthy)" needed help to make himself understood. There was engine trouble leaving Bahrain and we turned back but there was a bonus arriving at the dawn: "back again and can see the town by daylight. At 6:00 the sun rose over the desert and it was beautiful." I continued: "Bahrain uses Indian rupees but there is nothing much to see or buy. We could detect the minarets and mud houses of Manama and Martafarata [presumably Muharraq], where the planes land. Quite a sight. It's too bad we weren't delayed at Cairo, which is so much more interesting than this place." How life – and Bahrain - have changed.

It was at Bahrain that a young man, probably no more than five or six years my senior but very worldly-wise, boarded and sat near me. We were both heading to Europe and I found his stories of selling contraband alcohol to Arabs (very profitable) quite, should I say, intoxicating. Cairo was next on our flight plan and memorable views of the desert, the Suez

Canal and the pyramids. My letter from Egypt had stamps with blocked out images of King Farouk, the revolution having only taken place less than a year previously. We flew out across the Mediterranean to Rome, the last stop before we were to arrive in Zurich. But by that time the plane's pressurization equipment was giving trouble and it was obvious we could not fly the Alps. Three of us destined for Zurich deplaned and were put up at a five-star hotel, the elegant Qurinale, in Rome. My booze friend and I shared a room, my first experience of such luxury.

We came down in the morning to catch our TWA flight to Zurich. First however we were treated to a three course gourmet breakfast. As the waiter took the napkin and placed it on my lap I was attempting to be blasé and sophisticated. But the egg course undid me: somehow as I was cutting into the sausage I managed to have the whole plate with a full cooked breakfast with eggs sunny-side up slip into my lap and create a mess. I was so mortified I never saw my friend again – someone later said I was protected by divine intervention. Going outside, I fell in love with Rome as most visitors do, excited and overwhelmed. There had been an election the previous Sunday and posters were everywhere. In the few minutes I had J did a quick tour of the aqueduct and Rome's legendary cobblestoned streets. I was quite fearless on this, my first visit to Rome.

Then on to Switzerland, first to Zurich with TWA, and a short run to Geneva by a Swissair puddle-jumper. "The Swissair plane was small and flew low so I saw a lot – so clean in comparison with China with no pigs in the street", I marvelled. As I got off the plane in Geneva, tired and anxious about where I was headed, Charles Arbuthnot, the Board representative, was waiting for me, much to my relief. It was ironic that my guardian would be a man who served the World Council of Churches (WCC) for our Presbyterian mission, presumably the sort of bureaucrat that I had been brought up to dismiss as an "ecumaniac". He would have been aware of Dad's reputation from his colleague John Hamlin, formerly of our Mission in Shandong. My father had inquired the previous December asking about the feasibility of my mother and me staying in Switzerland the next summer so that I could learn French. Unknown to me, it was all part of my father's well-thought-out vision for my future. He had decided that I was going to college in Montreal's McGill University, to study under his friend Stanford Reid. Speaking French would be an asset in Québec. He already had it all worked out.

Charles Arbuthnot had replied positively almost immediately. "This is not exactly a new type of request. It happens that two small sons, aged 10 and 11, of Mrs. Arbuthnot's brother are in the vicinity at a very attractive place right now doing the sort of thing that you hope for Donald. They are staying with Monsieur and Madame Elie Pradervand of Crête Vandoeuvres, Geneva. M. Pradervand is a farmer and the uncle of my friend and colleague Pastor Marcel Pradervand the General Secretary of the World Presbyterian Alliance. He and his wife are fine Christian folk who have taken an interest in my nephews far beyond any *pension*. The boys follow Mr. Pradervand around in his work, have the company of the Pradervand daughter aged 13 and of the older twin- sons about 19 or 18." It sounded an ideal arrangement. Arbuthnot wisely recommended my mother not coming with me as it would limit my use of the French language while there. That nephew, Marcel Pradervand, was a figure of some significance, a Swiss Reformed pastor in London during the war who had valiantly served as an emissary for stranded Christians.

Arbuthnot arranged for a cable from the Geneva airport to confirm to my parents that I'd arrived safely. After taking me home for lunch, I was driven to the farm and introduced to Madame Pradervand. Soon, as if from nowhere, the whole family came out and introduced themselves to me. I later provided individual profiles of each for my parents, the operative word for each being "nice". "Milo – aged 29 – rather burly and doesn't talk much; Irène aged 25 nice quite a Christian who teaches Sunday School at the Vandeouvres Church; Pierre 19 rather brusque but very nice; and Elias [one of] twins 17 and my favourite in the family, he is an apprentice." The family patriarch I described as "tough" but I went on to qualify it by saying that he had "a heart as wide as the Pacific Ocean." His wife, whom I always called "Madame" was "a nice lady fat and jovial who calls herself a *paysan suisse*. She is like Grandmother MacLeod, of German Swiss extraction." Fat and jovial she might be but she found it understandably difficult when I would retire to my room to read a book when the rest of the family were in the orchard or the hay fields. I was definitely no farmer. There were also two resident hired helpers: a *berger* who looked after the cows and an Italian labourer. Quite an establishment – I'd never seen anything like it in China where non-Chinese were not expected to do this kind of work. It was an eye-opener for me.

Agriculturally the Pradervand farm was mixed. There was a large orchard with what I described as "tons of cherries" hanging from the trees, all of which had to be picked as the summer progressed and they ripened. Out in the fields there were the *Betterave* – the lowly sugar beet. The cows were sent over the border for summer grazing and I followed them there as they were put out to summer pasture. Farm machinery was both a mystery and a fascination – someone else did maintenance for them. I was tasked with collecting eggs, which I rather enjoyed. I also learned to dig up the sugar beets without damaging them and was taught how to pick cherries correctly. These were then put in large vats for cherry wine. At that point I approached Charles Arbuthnot asking him, in all innocence, whether I was compromising my total abstinence family's scruples. He took my inquiry seriously, though it must have caused some incredulity. He reassured me, giving me clergy exoneration for my question of conscience.

There were occasional trips into Geneva when someone was heading into town. Geneva was a city of endless fascination and history. I became expert in the sights of the city including the Reformation monument, the St. Pierre cathedral, the Oratory where Calvin taught. I went to bookstores and asked if they had anything about or by "Jean Calvin" only to have the name corrected after several rebuffs – "Jean *Cauvin*" Pierre and I would bike down to the Lake and swim there. I was envious of his continental *costume de bain* having been compelled by my mother to wear short pants for swimming in the interests of modesty. That insistence had ended my swimming career at the Kowloon Y, my only athletic interest.

Mme. Pradervand had me write my parents in French so that they would know they were getting good value for their nine francs a day.

"Madam Pradervand lave aujourd'hui les vêtements et le linge de la famille. Sa fille lui aide et aussi une autre dame. C'est la deuxième fois depuis mon arrivée."[43] I am sure that Madame was anxious to impress my parents with both my language and my laundry. Unfortunately neither parent could read French, so it was wasted on them. But the French spoken in Switzerland was much easier to grasp and copy than anything in France, slower, somehow more articulate, and predictable. When I erred into slang I was rebuked. "Un bat galurin" I picked up as Genevan slang for a stylish hat. A shocked Irène told me never to speak such *argot* again.

Eating together as a large family was another new experience. Though I was never served wine, there was an aura of warmth and acceptance. I loved the big wheels of Emmentaler cheese that were put out on the table for us to cut into. Madame had all sorts of confectionaries made with Swiss chocolate. And there was music and dancing. One of the Pradervand boys, I don't remember which one, brought out his accordion and the tunes he played still ring in my ear. The popular song "Mocking Bird Hill" had a French version which I memorized: "Qu'il fait bon sur ma colline/Dormir tout là-haut/Là-haut sur ma colline/La colline aux oiseaux" with its lilting melody never fails to bring back the summer of 1953 to me, hackneyed as its words may be, it is still deeply emotional.

No one worked on Sunday, other than the *berger* with the cows and other necessary farm chores. Sundays Milo went out on his motor-cycle and Pierre attended to his horses. Monsieur would drive whoever wanted a ride to the church in the village, affiliated with the state Reformed Church that dated back to John Calvin and the Reformation. I always took my Louis Segond Bible. The local Pasteur was Révérend Paul Dunant.

---

43 "Today Madame Pradervand washed clothing and family (bed) linen. Her daughter helped her and also another lady. It is the second time since my arrival."

Révérend Paul Dunant

He had previously served in the Ardèche area of France, southwest of Lyon, rugged hill country that the revocation of the Edict of Nantes in 1685 had affected, but still remained mostly Protestant. In the 1930s it was the scene of a charismatic renewal which touched Paul Dunant who went from Geneva to minister to Reformed churches in that remote area. His time in Ardèche had influenced his subsequent ministry which was spiritual, personal, and evangelistic in contrast to some other clergy of the Genevan churches.

I was amazed to discover, as we were talking after church, that the minister had a son, Jean-Jacques, who had just graduated from Emmaus Bible School in Lausanne. His fiancée Georgette, was in church that Sunday. They planned to go out under the Overseas Missionary Fellowship (OMF/CIM) to Singapore. The society had been renamed, following the expulsion of Christian missionaries from China, but it was originally the China Inland Mission that our family had been a part of since my grandparents had gone to China in the 1890s. I was awestruck at the coincidence that had brought us together. I suddenly had someone who had some understanding of my unique background and heritage. My unusual identity as a China mishkid was known and respected. It was a great gift as I was reorienting myself to life after China. Fifty years later I would reconnect with their daughter Suzanne who is presently, as I write, married to a home missionary in Saint-Jérôme, Québec, only ten miles from where I began my ministry as a student pastor aged 19 in a small Anglophone enclave.

Then it was all over. On 22 July my father sent a cable from Hong Kong to Charles Arbuthnot: "MacLeods enroute Donald proceed Thursday Rome," followed by a second cable when their plane turned back because of engine trouble: "MacLeods delayed one day." That amazingly flexible man arranged (and rearranged) my rail ticket to Rome. I took a sleeper on Saturday night, arriving Rome at 6:30 in the morning of 26 July 1953. For the next three and a half weeks the three of us travelled at a dizzying pace. As my mother later explained it to her sister: "Alec's zeal to finish his book and proof reading carries over into the sightseeing, and of course it means we shall have more to remember, though it is pretty strenuous."

We "did Rome" in less than two days, took an early morning train through the St. Gothard tunnel to the idyllic Alpine village of Göschenen on a Tuesday evening, giving us a night to explore its waterfall, valley and bridges. The next morning we left for Flüelen where we caught a steamer on the Lake of Four Cantons and went from Lucerne to Berne with its marvellous clocks and on to Geneva where I proudly showed them the sights.

Father and son at the Reformation Monument, Geneva, 30 July 1953

We journeyed out to the Pradervands where my parents received a not altogether positive report of my doings from Madame and mother distributed her gifts from China, one of which was still, sixty years later, in the proud possession of the family. Immediately afterwards we jumped on the night train to Paris, my father economizing on time available by travelling at night. We stopped off at Paris, covering most of the tourist-y sights. My best memory is the hotel clerk who spoke to me in her Parisian French as I more slowly showed off my newly acquired *français de Suisse*. How many languages do you speak, she asked me? I proudly replied "Three: English, French and Chinese." She was the first (and last) ever to congratulate me on my linguistic skills, which held me back in Graduate School, where German was more useful.

We crossed the Channel at Dieppe and once again found ourselves in London staying at the Ivanhoe Hotel in Bloomsbury. Our pace was almost feverish, leaving my 52 year old mother far behind. We reconnected with friends of my father's from prison camp days, the George Scott's, and moved at their invitation to the less expensive CIM home on Newington Green. There the excitement caused by viewing the Coronation on a twelve inch television screen was still palpable. A tour bus ride to Eton College and Hampton Court Palace, and another to Oxford and Blenheim, made the most of the limited time we had. By the end of that week we took the night train to Edinburgh and a visit to the home where my parents had boarded sixteen years earlier, 12 Chalmers Crescent, the residence of Thomas and Annie Torrance. Mr. Torrance, who had gone out to China with my grandfather in 1897 under the CIM, was then 82 but still remarkably quick of mind and told us reassuring stories of how Evangelicals were on the ascendency in the Church of Scotland, a sad delusion.

Slipping over to Glasgow two days later Dad discovered that he had run out of money, which I found unsettling. Fortunately the Board came to our rescue with a cable transfer. We made the mandatory trip to Blantyre, genuflected before David Livingstone, and then again a night train to Inverness and on to Portmahomack. There I developed a more positive impression of Dad's uncle Alex than on our previous visit. Cousin Chrissie, his niece and housekeeper, enveloped me with love and scones. Dad gave him two whole days knowing that he would never see him again. An early morning bus took us to Inverness ans connected us to an excursion to Culloden in the interest of consolidating my knowledge of Scottish history. We then flew to Stornoway to be welcomed by many members of our extended family. Not only the living members but the dead were also included with mandatory visits to family gravesites. including a recognition of my frandfather's death and busial in China which was just as well as his actual grave would later be destroyed by Red Guards.. At the family croft I met Cousin Alex MacLeod (names ran out quickly in our family) and his Canadian wife Doris, home from Nova Scotia. They would later be an important part of my life. Though mocked (and now vanishing) a Sabbath on the Isle of Lewis I always found a restful experience, and the next day we were off to Inverness by plane and then train to Glasgow. We stayed with family there as my parents shopped and a cousin almost blew me out of their apartment with a bagpipe concert. Bagpipes are great but only out of doors, I discovered.

We sailed from Greenock to Canada on the *Empress of Scotland* on Wednesday, 20 August, in a state of utter exhaustion. My father had scripted everything. Before he sailed he posted a letter to Stanford Reid in Montreal, hoping to connect with him when we arrived. I never knew whether my mother's fall down stairs early Sunday morning, 23 August, was a result of her overdoing the frantic itinerary that we had just gone through. With a broken wrist, she was placed in the ship's infirmary but soon recovered. We were met by my father's sister Cathie and her husband Paul Ruby who had driven up from Philadelphia to welcome us to North America. My aunt Cathie had just changed citizenship after living in the States 27 years as a British subject (and never been to the UK). The immigration official, when she handed him her new passport at the Canadian border, said, "That's very recent." She smiled back thinking he was referring to her date of birth, not the passport itself. My uncle, with his marvellous sense of humour, a novelty in our family, found it hysterically funny. Dad spent the next two days taking us around Montreal, focussing on McGill University and doing a sales promotional job. We then drove through Vermont, visited Middlebury, mother's "heathen college" before she transferred to the safety of Wheaton. We stopped overnight at Danbury, avoided Wilton (no one was there), and arrived on August 28 in New York, where the temperature was in the 90° range. We had booked at the Kennedy apartments. No longer at Gramercy Park, they had moved to a location opposite Barnard College near Columbia University and Riverside Church.

It was all familiar turf. I was "home." Or was it home? I was not really sure where I fitted in. 1953 had been a tumultuous and challenging year which I had thoroughly enjoyed and I had adapted well to all the changes. I was now about to be shipped off to boarding school not altogether sure of my identity. There I would be challenged as I had never been before.

CHAPTER 32:

Crash Landing in America, 1953

On Friday morning, 10 September 1953, the 8:39 train out of Penn Station Manhattan took me to the next stage of my life. Like most milestones I approached it with a mixture of dread, anticipation, and excitement. The Stony Brook School for Boys had been a part of our family's story for a generation. Dad had gone there in 1923 to teach. following graduation from Wheaton College, as a 22 year old China mishkid needing some cash and direction. Frank Gaebelein, the Headmaster, himself only two years older than my father, had set up (with the help of some wealthy Brooklyn businessmen) a new secondary school for boys on the grounds of the Stony Brook Assembly, a fundamentalist summer conference ministry that needed an occupant the rest of the year for its extensive (and expensive) facilities. Mother was one of hundreds of young people who had travelled there, starting in 1919, in search of inspiration and faith. The place reeked with memories as the three of us walked up Chapman Parkway from the station. Chapman

Parkway was named after Wilbur Chapman[44], one of the founders of the Assembly and a spellbinding Second Advent speaker whose dynamic pulpit presence had sent hundreds overseas as missionaries at the high noon of missionary advance.

We walked past Frank Gaebelein's home on our right. It was an unpretentious house erected by the Grosvenor family (Mrs. Grosvenor was Alexander Graham Bell's daughter) shortly after Frank, who was a bachelor when the School was established, took a wife from the local gentry. It was a boarding school which provided a Christian environment for parents concerned about their children's grounding in the faith. Among the items entering students were asked to include in their kit was the *Pilgrim Study Bible* (1952 edition), a scaled down version of the Scofield Bible which Frank's father, Arno, had helped to edit back in 1909. According to this teaching, history was divided into seven *dispensations*, marking periods of time when God dealt with humankind in different ways. Thus one could not say the Lord's Prayer today as that was for a future *kingdom* dispensation. It taught a future return of Jesus *prior* to a millennium of peace and justice *and then shall the End come*, quoting Jesus. A litmus test of orthodoxy was whether you were *premillennial* or not. For people who prided themselves on being in the mainstream of orthodox Christianity it was, to say the least, creative and innovative. It was also highly divisive among Christians. Dad told me to forget the *Pilgrim Bible* as he didn't think it important for me to acquire a copy when I went to "the Brook", as it was called affectionately.

Proceeding past Grosvenor House our next stop would have been Memorial Hall, a building recently erected for classrooms, offices, and a library as a Memorial to Stony Brook students who had been killed in the Second World War. That conflict dominated post-war America and the school was no exception. Eight of the twelve faculty members (as opposed to administrative and support staff) were veterans. Most had

---

44   (John) Wilbur Chapman (1859-1918) Presbyterian minister and Moderator of the 1917 General Assembly. Graduate of Lake Forest College & Lane Seminary. Chair, Committee on Evangelism PC(USA) 1902-1918.

their teaching qualifications with degrees paid for through the 1944 Servicemen's Readjustment Act (the so-called GI Bill of Rights). Like most of their contemporaries they were all fiercely patriotic and yet also curiously insular, in spite of having served overseas and rubbed shoulders with many nationalities and cultural identities. This was the 1950s and though the Korean War had left America less confident than the Second World War, there was still a lot of American particularism and triumphalism. Service in the military had inspired a no-nonsense disciplinary rigidity which did not allow any softness or malfeasance. It was fiercely male; athletics were an important aspect of every part of the life of the school as was (and is) common with all American secondary schools. The contrast with KG-5 was great. Gone for me was the easy cosmopolitanism, the flexibility of cultures, the variety of races and nationalities, the delight in academic inquiry and excellence. Without girls and with few ethnic minorities, I would find the school frighteningly insular and provincial. The faculty seemed to come from the fundamentalist subculture with most of the younger faculty being graduates of Christian colleges, some of dubious academic value.

So I mounted the steps of Memorial Hall with both curiosity and apprehension. We had an appointment to meet with Marvin W. Goldberg, Director of Studies. Marvin Goldberg was a Stony Brook institution. For forty years he shaped the school. Alumni/ae still say he was the most significant teacher or coach they ever had. Belonging to a family converted to Christianity from Judaism, he had attended a small upstate New York Wesleyan Methodist school, Houghton College, graduating in 1936 (as did two other faculty members) and later taking a Master's in Education at Harvard. When we met with him on that day, he was 39 and had been at Stony Brook for eight years. He had done all his homework in preparation for our visit. It was clear to him that British and American secondary educational systems did not mesh easily. Dad suggested subsequently, in a letter to him, that he read a recent article in *Time* magazine about the differences between the two. As with many mishkids, the discontinuities in educational systems could present a challenge. Bible, of course, was easy as I'd not had much more than basic Scripture knowledge at KG-5; in English we were way ahead in Hong Kong, particularly with Warren Hershey teaching. It was hard to peg my Latin and French. Science and Math seem to be universal in education.

To me, Marvin Goldberg came across as a martinet, in spite of the almost universal praise alumni heaped upon him. Demanding, uncompromising, he was totally unbending in his relationships. I always felt that silence about his Jewish heritage meant that there was a certain disconnectedness with his past. Dorothie, his meek and patient wife, was once driving their car to a cross country meet (I was manager of the team) when she discovered she had left the emergency brake on. "Don't tell Marvin I did that" with a look of terror in her eyes as she turned to me. I never heard him laugh, nor do I remember many, if any, lighter moments with him, though he had a wonderful smile. He was not good with insecure people, myself included, though on occasion he could show real compassion. One time when I was the only one in the class who had passed a physics test and he had allowed a re-testing, several of the re-takers received higher grades than mine, he showed some understanding when I said that wasn't fair to me. "You could have taken the exam again with the others," he retorted. "Do you really think I could have – what would the others have said?" I plaintively responded. He said simply "Oh yes." and gave me a higher grade. He knew how tenuous my position was, how great my unpopularity as "a brain," and reached out to me on that occasion.

It was my misfortunate that Frank Gaebelein was on leave my first semester at Stony Brook. Pierson Curtis (known affectionately as "PC") was in charge. He had come to the school in 1924, the year my father had left. Five years later my uncle Wesley Ingles came to join him in the English department. Pierson Curtis was the only one on the faculty who had an undergraduate degree from an Ivy League school (Princeton). He was a grandson of Arthur Tappan Pierson, "Father of Fundamentalism," promoter of missions and contributor of five articles for the Scofield Bible. There is a 1910 picture of a twelve year old "PC" on the grass at a family get-together at Northfield conference grounds, so different from the image of the man I disliked. "PC" was probably the most respected teacher at the Brook. A veritable "Mr. Chips", he remained there for forty-four years. Pierson Curtis took my measure early on, and in spite of being at one time a mishkid himself, gave every evidence he despised me. One incident stands out. Early on in my time there, somebody had taken a special delivery letter from my mailbox, sent from my anxious mother, and had torn it into fragments that still had my name and address visible. Destroying a letter like this was a criminal offence and very serious. I took the fragments, when I had recovered them, and showed them to "PC" because he was acting Headmaster. "What am I supposed to do?" he asked. "I want you to be cognizant of it," I replied. He shot back at me in what I took to be a sarcastic voice: "I will be *cognizant*" said with what I thought was a sneer. Needless to say, nothing happened.

My parents and I went over to Johnston Hall for a lunch provided for incoming students and their parents. To get there one had to pass Hopkins Hall and Dad pointed out the room that he had as dorm supervisor during his brief (and challenging) year as a 22 year-old China Mishkid supervising, he claimed, a group of spoiled rich kids sent to the school as a kind of reformatory. The building, intended originally as a summer dormitory for the Assembly, was now rather ramshackle, clearly showing its age. Opposite Hopkins Hall was Hageman dormitory which was to be my home for the next two years. My room was at the top of the stairs on the second floor, second on the left. As my parents deposited my luggage there, I was introduced to my roommate. He was heavyset, bigger than I was, with coiffed hair and a distinct air of upper middle class West Coast moneyed sophistication. I was already intimidated. He introduced himself and immediately Dad started to make a connection with an aunt who had served with our Mission in the 1930's in Canton; then another link, an older brother, a recent SBS graduate, whose engagement was about to be announced to a woman whose parents were CIM'ers. Dad, ever innocent, thought there were secure bonds forged through evangelical China Mishkid connections that would stand the test of time. On return to Princeton he wrote a chatty letter to my new roommate's parents. It was never answered.

Four or five days later I returned to my room to find a group of students standing around. There was no place to sit on my side of the room because my bed had been taken out and placed on the roof of the front porch. My roommate had made his position clear: he was not going to live with me and I would have to move. I asked what the problem was and he said that we were incompatible. When my own son was in a similar situation as a frosh in a student dorm at Rensselaer Tech, he stood his ground and his roommate had to go. But I lacked self-confidence and I crumpled. Something died in me that afternoon which I never completely regained. Fifty-nine years later, I had lunch with the man who took my bed and wanted to ask why, as a fellow mishkid, he would have done that to another one. But my nerve failed me. He had obviously forgotten all about it. But I never could. Richard Purchase, a preachers-kid from South Jersey, came to my rescue and took me in. I was very (shall always be) grateful to him and to his family.

"We got Donald set down in SB" Mother wrote her sister three days later from Princeton "and came back feeling rather hollow yesterday." My mother had never had a boarding school experience but for my father it was *deja-vu* all over again. I didn't keep many of their letters to me during the time they were in Princeton, but I see one written later that school year which began, as they all did, "My dear laddie" (I was 16 at the time) and went on: "Thanks for your letter, which came today. It had no date, and the writing was atrocious, but I suppose all that must be overlooked, on account of your busyness, In any case, thanks a lot. We're glad to know that you are still in the land of the living."

Registration included getting lined up with sports participation. Athletics typically were a big part of school life and I signed up for cross-country running. I had just been to see a New York cardiologist the day before we arrived. His conclusion was that my heart, in spite of my earlier rheumatic fever, was now clear of any lingering complications. I don't think anything was shared with the school about my physical limitations. Jim Boice,[45] later a preacher, expositor and writer, got an exemption from athletics for one year (but he had connections). I had not been allowed any exercise and few games at KG-5. I struggled with cross-country running for a few days but ended up being disqualified. What I would have been able to participate in was swimming, my basic athletic activity growing up, but there was, at the time, no pool nor any arrangement for students to get to one.

This was fine with my father, who had no interest in athletic success for me. On 15 April 1954, as I was thinking of trying out for tennis with my aunt Cathie's hand-me-down battered racquet, he wrote, "It's good to be enthusiastic about tennis but don't let it encroach on thorough preparation for classes. That's a problem all students have, & it becomes 'more big' in University. There are so many calls, so much to do, so many extra-curricular (outside of classes & studies for them) activities. How much time should I give to this or that? For a student in school classes & prep work must have priority." The end result was a consensus among my classmates that I was, in the slang of the time, a co-ordo as in "uncoordinated". It did not help me integrate into American teenage culture nor win me friends.

What I also didn't grasp at the time was the wider picture: winning at athletics was vital for the reputation of a prep school. Fall was the season for football: Stony Brook had a terrible year in 1954, losing six of the seven scheduled games, winning only the first against Concordia, Bronxville, a Lutheran Missouri Synod German style *gymnasium*. Basketball in the winter wasn't much better: 17 losses, 3 wins (one of which was against the alumni). Varsity baseball didn't do well either. What Stony Brook did excel in were individual sports such as cross country running, wrestling and track, all of which depended on an athlete's personal dedication and discipline and inspired coaching. Here of course Marvin Goldberg excelled.

---

45   James Montgomery Boice (1938-2000) graduated SBS 1956, Harvard College 1960; Princeton Seminary, 1963, Univ. of Basle PhD 1966; *Christian Today* 1966-8; Tenth Presbyterian Church, Philadelphia, 1968-2000.

My first report card, after a month, showed that I had placed fourth in a class of 34. I got high honours in Bible and Physics, my poorest grade ("Good") in English and Algebra. The results were posted on the bulletin board; honours and high honours students were publicised. My classmates were aghast: I was a brain, given unwanted nicknames like "Donald Dictionary" and "Ellsworth Encyclopaedia". There was wry amusement about the Bible grade, my memorizing of the seven dispensations had brought me to the top of the class. Our instructor, Robert Ward, had just graduated from Dallas Seminary. It took me two months but by December, some of the emotional trauma behind me, I was at the top of my class, a position which I maintained for much of the time I was at the Brook except when personal issues distracted me. But I was dissatisfied; I missed the intellectual excitement of KG-5, and felt adrift.

Trips back to Princeton for Columbus Day weekend and Thanksgiving gave a welcome break in my routine. But they were also a reminder that soon there would be no place to enjoy a break with family and I would be on my own. Mother reflected after my October visit that "We felt a little lonely this weekend after having Don last week. And it came over me sweepingly, what going back to Formosa would be like. However many people had done it, and the Lord has given them the grace and even added a portion of joy." And after Thanksgiving she wrote: "I always feel lonely when he goes back to school –it is a continual adjustment."

The Christmas holiday started on 17 December, a Thursday. I met up with my parents in New York. My presence seems to have reminded my father's about his programme for my future and I see from his diary that on 18 December he wrote Professor Stanford Reid at McGill University, presumably to inquire about my being his charge when I went to McGill in a year and half's time, something he did not share with me. Without a car and limited finances, we were totally dependent on family members, particularly my aunt Cathie and her husband Paul, to ferry us around. Everyone seemed eager to drive us. This chauffeuring provided a warm sense of family togetherness which I assumed would continue to be the case when my parents returned to Taiwan, which was scheduled (depending on the doctor's prognosis of Dad's incipient diabetes) for the end of the summer. It was not, however, I discovered to last past their departure. I would soon be on my own.

That Christmas I was particularly looking forward to connecting again with the friend from Hong Kong days I mentioned previously whose letters had dried up. He had come east from the College of Wooster to be with his parents who were also on furlough. He wrote that he would travel to Princeton to see me on the Monday after Christmas. I was excited at renewing the friendship of someone with whom I had shared so much in the past. When he arrived, it soon became clear that we had nothing in common anymore and that faith no longer resonated with him as it had so powerfully in the past. I was deeply disappointed at this loss, something seemed to have died. It would be over fifty years later that I would contact him again. He had completely slipped out of my orbit. I can't imagine what his parents thought of this *volte face* but I do know that the dread that this might also happen to me, as it had with so many other mishkids, was part of my own parents' overprotectiveness.

Nothing could have prepared any of us for the fact that shortly after their return to Taiwan, both caring aunts, father's sister Cathie and mother's sister Priscilla, each of whom lived in Philadelphia, would be diagnosed with terminal breast cancer. Cathie died in early 1957 and Priscilla two years later in 1959. My father's plan to send me to Canada where we had no links other than a tenuous one with the childless Reids, meant that I was soon to be very much on my own. One of my childhood favourite stories was Hector Malot's 1878 *Sans Famille*, an account of the foundling Rémi's unsuccessful attempts to find a home with repeated disappointments. In a moment of high drama he cries after being once again cast out, "Alone! I should always be alone." As a China mishkid at times I identified with Rémi.

CHAPTER 33:
Goodbye to All That, 1954-5

Frank E. Gaebelein at the 1959 SBS graduation, casting an eagle eye on me Students called him affectionately LitDit after his honourary Ll. D.

In late January of 1954 Frank Gaebelein returned from his sabbatical to take up once again the leadership of Stony Brook School. Only occasionally in life is one permitted to witness greatness and my debt to Frank Gaebelein is incalculable. For me life at the School, and my whole educational experience, now brightened substantially. He was, as the Scots say, "a man of parts" or in the often overworked expression which appeared in one of his obituaries, "a man of Renaissance interests"[46].He had, while still in his teens, been an Army officer in the First World War. He had trained to be a concert pianist, showing early talent. As a member of the Alpine Clubs of both the United States and Canada, he had an athleticism that drove him to climb mountains in North America and Europe. Socially he could mix with all classes and was comfortable with every strata of society. In retirement he was an active member of the prestigious Cosmos Club of Washington. He was a man of great self-discipline and during his life he published twenty books and edited many others. A master stylist, he guided the language of the New International Version of the Bible. His final project, editing a twelve volume *Expositor's Bible Commentary,* was half done at his death. Without formal theological training, his biblical exposition was practical and accessible. In so many ways he was a seminal figure in twentieth century evangelicalism in America.

"Donald is among the boys we would like to have back at Stony Brook," Gaebelein wrote my father in early April 1954. It had been announced that I was one of two early inductees into the school's *Cum Laude Society* so it was all *pro forma.* However, it meant a lot to my father who wrote me at school: "We have received a letter from your Headmaster which makes us very happy. We look forward to your taking another year and graduating there." I was surprised at the gratuitous comments from both Dad and Gaebelein as I'd not thought (nor had Dad) about doing anything else.

The school's proximity to Manhattan had great cultural advantages. On a Saturday in mid-February, my roommate Dick Purchase, my ex-roommate, and I went to the Metropolitan Opera's production of Wagner's *Die Walküre*. Margaret Harshaw, then in her 40's, was at the

---

46   "Memorials: Frank E, Gaebelein" *Journal of the Evangelical Theological Society.* Vol. 27.1(March 1984) 127-8.

peak of her form as Brünnhilde and the incomparable bass baritone, Hans Hotter, also in his 40's, was Hunding. We had excellent seats. My roommate remembers the experience: "We followed the horseshoe curve of the hallway for a few minutes, when a little man jumped out of a side door and said, 'You want seats I presume!' We all said, 'Yes!' Instructing us to wait there, he disappeared and presently returned and said, 'Follow me.' He found us a row with 3 or 4 empty seats, no doubt from season ticket holders who were not present. I was the last one in and the usher shocked me by whispering, 'I get paid for this!' 'How much, I asked.' 'Two dollars' he replied. I paid him from our funds."[47] On hearing of our intended adventure, Mother had sent a stern warning. "I have never been to the opera, and probably never shall. If this comes before you go, if you do, consider and look around to see how you feel about it – if it is the most worthwhile form of musical enjoyment and what the atmosphere of it all is. I am glad to hear that you are going to Jack Wyrtzen's meeting as well." Wyrtzen was a youth evangelist who had Saturday night rallies at the Gospel Tabernacle in Times Square.

So the year wore on. One late winter day Mr. Bisgrove came over to me after a meal and informed me that I had placed among the highest in the country in an American history exam, of all things for a China Mishkid who had gone to a British school. My achievement was due to a 1912 textbook which had come out with us to China and that I read over and over for lack of an alternative. At the end of the year I stood at the head of the class, though chemistry was my weak point. When my parents came for closing exercises and prize-giving, Mother complained that I seemed angry as I went up to the podium. I guess there was residual anger after a difficult year. But Frank Gaebelein's return midyear had made a big difference.

I returned "home" to Princeton for the summer. Those three months were surreal. Instead of preparing me for life on my own, with driving lessons and a part-time job, my parents' priority was to see as many family and friends as possible before they returned to Asia in the autumn. First

---

47   Email from Rev. Richard T. Purchase to me, dated 15 February 2017.

(24-30 June) there was a trip to Indiana and my paternal grandmother's family. Mary and Cathie, her daughters, accompanied us with husband Paul as chauffeur. My parents' twenty-fifth wedding anniversary, 26 June 1954, was celebrated in Plymouth, Ohio, at the home of Grandpa's half-uncle/brother, George Searle, a country doctor noted for his outspokenness. When told about the occasion, he turned to my father and said, memorably, "Good God, man, how have you managed to live with *that* woman for twenty-five years?" When we reached my Hoosier grandmother's farm, three of her four children visited the site and chose her gravestone seven years after she died. Lawrence Miller, Dad's Indiana first cousin, "hired" me to cut grass providing me a first paycheque.

On 19 August we left Princeton, driving to Wilton, Connecticut, in pouring rain. We subsequently journeyed up to Schenectady, upstate New York, where Dad preached at First Presbyterian Church. Herbert Mekeel[48], minister there for the previous seventeen years (twenty more to go) had a reputation for "muscular discipleship.". Over two hundred young men went into the ministry under his tutelage. Mekeel had close ties with Montreal and the Canadian Church and Dad hoped I could connect with him. I was impressed that Mekeel immediately singled me out for a personal conversation. He would reappear in my life later, not always helpfully. From Schenectady we drove around New England saying final farewells to mother's aging relatives. Finally on 17 September I was deposited back at Stony Brook School. It was a good way to be grateful for boarding school and the breakup of family.

As they prepared to return to Taiwan, the end of October, Dad was anxious to settle my future. Without much reference to me, he sent the application forms to McGill. Bruce Ross, the Associate Registrar, replied immediately. "It is true that the College Board tests are more particularly suitable to people who are conversant with American History and American life in general, but we shall bear in mind the fact that your

---

48   See my "'The Dominie': Herbert S. Mekeel, His Clergy Conscripts, and Their Impact on the Presbyterian Church in Canada, 1935-1979." *Papers of the Canadian Society of Presbyterian History* 32 (2007): 49-67.

son has spent only a part of his education in the United States when we judge them." Apparently Dr. Gaebelein had also sent a letter of recommendation at Dad's request. The name of Stanford Reid had surfaced in Ross' letter to Dad. "I shall ask Dr. Reid to keep in mind" my application. He concluded "Donald has done well at the Stony Brook School, and I expect that he will do equally well in the College Board tests which he will write in January or March 1955."

Ross' letter reflected the insularity of Canadian universities in the early 1950's, coming across as patronizing and condescending. A further letter a week later acknowledged receipt of my transcripts from Hong Kong and provided banking information for Dad at his request. Bruce Ross was courteous and tireless. But Dad was not through yet with his research into my future. A final letter from McGill, this time from the Dean of the Divinity Faculty, James S. Thomson[49], responded to Dad's concern as to what undergraduate courses a pre-theological student should take. He wrote: "I was interested to receive your letter, and I am glad to note that your son intends to study here at McGill University." Did I? It was only later on that I found this correspondence. My father had rushed into committing me to a future in which I had no immediate emotional investment. And he wrote to people on my behalf that I had not authorized. In his defence I can only say that my parents were leaving and he wanted to sew up my future securely, a future that included (it would appear in hindsight) becoming a Canadian and being directed and guided by Stanford Reid. It was the unavoidable result of separation and of his years as a China mishkid. In theology and fathering he had definite and unshakeable convictionscerns and ideals.

I came in from Stony Brook to spend a final weekend with my parents before their departure. There had been the usual flurry of circular letters, informing all their supporters of their departure to Taiwan. Halloween 1954 was a busy day: Dad and I went up to the First Presbyterian

---

49 James S. Thomson (1872-1972) graduate Trinity College, Glasgow; came to Pine Hill Divinity, Halifax 1930, 2nd Pres. Univ of SK, 1937-1949; Founding Dean Faculty of Divinity, McGill 1949-1957. Moderator, UCC, 1956-8.

Church of Williamsbridge, 225th St., the Bronx, where he was preaching for his friend Albert Gantz. Aunt Marjorie arrived from Wilton. I was packed off back to school on the 8:12 a.m. train. I can still see them, on the platform in Pennsylvania Station in the dark, waving me off a final time. "Our boy, Donald, will be remaining behind. He is now 16," their circular stated, "He is enjoying Stony Brook, and profiting by an excellent Christian education. We feel we have left him in good hands."

That autumn was a fulfilling time for me academically and intellectually. There were two highlights. One was a specially guided study of Blaise Pascal's *Pensées* by Lawrence Farr, a luckless wanderer who only lasted a year on faculty and knew less French than I, but the material was enlightening. Emile Caillet, a professor at Princeton Seminary and a close friend of Gaebelein's, had brought Pascal to the attention of evangelicals. Farr tutored me in "French 3," probably the first and last time it was part of the curriculum. This specially created course capitalized on my Swiss linguistic experience. The other highlight was Gaebelein's Senior Class on Romans, the high watermark of my Stony Brook career as it was for many others.[50] I did an assignment for him on the inspiration of the Scriptures, using Francis Landed Paton's book which proved very helpful subsequently.

"How thankful I am for him" Mother wrote of me from Pasadena on 11 November as she was about to sail to Taiwan. "When it sweeps over me, as it does still acutely, that we are really away from him, and for how long, I just turn it into prayer for him, and am thankful that there is special promise toward him, while we are so far away – I shall like to think of him being with you at Thanksgiving," she wrote her sister. Thanksgiving in Wilton was different. A cable from my parents arrived on the day: "Greetings from near Wake Island." They seemed a long ways and there was no family warmth at Wilton.

50　He taught the "parenthesis" interpretation of Romans chapters 9 to 11, and provided a moderate interpretation about the future of the Jewish people, insisting that the kingdom would be restored to Israel, an interpretation inherited from his father and typical of dispensational premillennial fundamentalists then.

My uncle's testiness was confirmed two weeks later when I went into New York for a heart checkup arranged by the Board. I was late for my appointment, went galloping up the subway stairs, and tore into the cardiologist's office. He took my blood pressure and determined that I was in serious danger and ordered complete rest. Then the question arose: Where could I stay? I suggested my uncle's place, since he was a doctor. The cardiologist called Carleton at his Brooklyn office and asked if he would take me in. The phone crackled as he shouted so I could hear: "Absolutely not! He's not coming here. We don't want him." I was devastated. Looking back I have some sympathy for him. He'd taken on a lifetime project when his father-in- law never left them and enough was enough.

So for my first Christmas on my own, with Cathie not able to have me because of her cancer surgery, I accepted an invitation to spend the holiday at my roommate's home in Woodbury, New Jersey. I had met his whole family in the summer when we made the hour's drive to meet them. She had taken another mishkid into their parsonage previously and knew more than most about the challenges involved. Her brother, Gerald Snell, who had been killed in a car accident,,was a Westminster Seminary graduate. She had gone to Providence Bible Institute where she met a Baptist student for the ministry. Their marriage was a mutu- ally supportive one and he was now pastoring the First Baptist Church of Woodbury, known as "the Church of the Royal Welcome". We even- tually agreed, at her suggestion, that I could call her my "Temporary Stepmother" abbreviated to "TSM" and she provided a welcome refuge.

I got a clerical job that holiday at the Witherspoon Building with Westminster Press, the publishing arm of the Presbyterian Church (USA), organizing lists of addresses. I would take the bus from Woodbury into Philadelphia each morning and return at night. I earned a modest amount, on an hourly basis. I think that being a Presbyterian mishkid they gave me preference. It was my first experience with women who had to go back to work because, as one said, she needed a new living room carpet. My uncle Paul, who was at the time concerned about my aunt Cathie's recent cancer diagnosis, had a sales office in Camden,

New Jersey, with the Reynolds Metals Co. He picked me up and drove me out to their home in Drexel Hill where I spent Christmas Day. They treated me with warm affection and respect, making the holiday a very pleasant time..

In spite of my father's expressed wishes for my future and his application on my behalf to McGill, and my mother's keen desire for me to pursue my application to Wheaton, I now applied to Harvard. With grades all "High honours" (with the exception of chemistry) I knew I had a chance to get into America's most prestigious university and thus "guarantee my future" as one of their promotional materials promised. Harvard set me up with an alumnus interviewing me at the prestigious Union Club on South Broad St. and the interview went well. The choices were there and the future was before me. Wheaton represented the past, McGill moving to Canada and Harvard remaining Stateside.

CHAPTER 34:

Valedictory Anticlimax, 1955

"**B**ut why are they going back to such an apparently fruitless task? When crowded out of China proper they labored in Hong Kong. Now it's Formosa. You simply *cannot* keep them out of God's work!"[51] Dad's Princeton Seminary classmate Bill Jones asked the same questions I was asking at the time. Editor of the magazine *Christian Youth,* his description of my father's single-minded commitment concluded, after reminiscing about their life as students: "*I* did not go to China. He did. And he suffered greatly." Jones highlighted a quality of my father's that he admired but that also deeply affected my life: his single-minded determination which would shape my life as he thought best for me. That stubborn tenacity was to lead to the worst summer I ever remember and redirected my whole life. I was at a crossroads: become a Canadian as he wished, secure my faith by studying under his friend Stanford Reid, and possibly spend the rest of my life serving in a denomination about which

---

51   Jones, "Is God In China?" *Christian Youth* (30 January 1955), 55. William James
Jones (1901-1975) was a graduate of Wheaton College class of 1925 and PTS
1928. He served as secretary of the League of Evangelical Students (1929-32) and
was then publications secretary of the American Sunday School Union (1942-66).

I knew nothing but had happy memories for him. For a sixteen-year old, separated from his parents, struggling to make his way, and without many other resources, it was a real crossroads. Meanwhile my parents' trip on the proverbial "slow boat to China" had been circuitous and rambling, putting them out of reach. Several stopovers in the Philippine islands, around Taiwan to Kaohsiung, on to Hong Kong, arriving 14 December and writing me immediately on arrival. They had only nine days there, seeing old friends and running errands for Taiwan colleagues. They left for Taiwan Christmas Day, secured a home, spent three days in customs, and by New Year's Day 1955 were settled and ready for the seminary's second semester.

In America, my Christmas break came to an abrupt end four days later. My aunt Cathie waved me off back to Stony Brook School at the Greyhound bus terminal in downtown Philadelphia where we met up so she could hand deliver a letter from my mother who didn't seem to know the address where I was staying. Mother had very conflicted feelings about my roommate's mother, Carolyn Snell Purchase (who lived to 104) and whose home, in a "south Jersey" suburb of Philadelphia, now became my sanctuary.

"Hope you had a good trip" My aunt Cathie wrote me soon after my return to the school. Childless, her prose was stilted but I was glad to receive her gratuitous advice. "And get a lot of studying done. How's this first week back at school gone: been busy I'm sure." Her encouraging letters, in the beautiful handwriting she had learned at Chefoo, kept coming. Two years later she was dead at 51. She was right: exams started soon after we returned. I was never sure whether schools that had exams *before* the holiday weren't preferable to ones that had them *after*, thus spoiling the sense of freedom and release.

One of the reasons I was anxious about being up-to-date in my studies was the demand of *Res Gestae*, the school's yearbook. I had accepted the job of assistant literary editor but the Senior Editor couldn't get his act together and I was left with a lot of the work. Bob Pierce, a fellow Presbyterian mishkid, had a wonderful turn of phrase and made the task enjoyable. His synopses of each member of our class were prophetic and memorable. My own appearance was described by him as "Puppy dog", my likes were "Reading the encyclopaedia" and my dislikes were "2" (B) grades. My favourite expression was "Oh, my goodness". Some positives along with the general impression I was nerdish, if not weird. "He has travelled with the school gospel teams, and has given some stimulating messages." Sports accomplishments were noted as being managerial not athletic. In the class poll, among those voted "Best Dressed", "Quietest", "Most Popular", "Stubbornest" and "Best Personalities" my sole distinction was, with Stan Barnett (another mishkid)."Most intellectual". The entry "Daily Grind" in the yearbook provided a day-by-day description of significant events. Again, we had Bob Pierce with his keen eye and sense of humour. On 3 March it was recorded that "AlistaIre [sic] Donald 'Dictionary Samuel Sonnet' MacLeod reaches immortality in English class by out memorizing P.C."

On a memorable Saturday morning, 14 May, I went down to check my mailbox in the basement of Johnston Hall. There was a letter, dated the Tuesday that week from Wallace McDonald, Director of Freshman Scholarships, Harvard University. "It is a pleasure to send you the enclosed Certificate of Admission to Harvard College, which is the formal notice of the vote of the Committee on Admission to admit you as a member of the Class of 1959." The Committee had voted me a scholarship of $1050 for the year. A further amount of $300 for a job at the College was also provided. "You will be pleased to know that you have been selected for admission and a scholarship from a group of candidates which is the largest ever to apply to us. The scholarship competition has been particularly tight; there were over twenty-one hundred applicants for the three hundred scholarships available for Freshmen, Your nomination for an award indicates our belief that you are exceptionally well qualified, personally and intellectually, to profit from Harvard."

The letter, so different from the condescension I had received from McGill, made a huge impression on me. But how was I to respond? The deadline as to whether I would accept or reject this offer – which covered all my tuition and boarding expenses for the year if I accepted the job – was little more than a fortnight away. At Stony Brook, and particularly with Frank Gaebelein, there was no question as to what my answer should be. This was a major coup for the school and represented everything that they could have hoped for, a student of theirs who had gotten a full scholarship to America's most prestigious university. What is more, I gained a new respect from my classmates. I responded immediately with enthusiasm and then notified my father that I would not be going to McGill but instead would be staying in America. I received a letter from Harold Ockenga, the pastor of the church where I was still a member, saying that Park St. Church on the Boston Common had many students from Harvard and that my faith would be supported and enhanced by my time there as an undergraduate. I sent it on to Dad but he was not impressed, even though Ockenga was one of the leading evangelical leaders of his time.

"You will write courteous letters to the two Colleges you reject," Dad replied on 20 May. Both offers from Wheaton College and Harvard should be turned down. Dr. Gaebelein's entreaties to my father in a letter I never saw were unable to dissuade him. "I thought he was on my side" he said somewhat petulantly in his letter to me. He was adamant: "I am still persuaded that McGill, which is the top Canadian university, will give you a better course of study for your four years than Harvard will. And from the point of view of Christian influences, I am still persuaded that you will find more to help you at McGill than if you went to Harvard. Academically and religiously McGill is superior to Harvard in my opinion." But he held out an olive branch: "Be assured that your mother and father love you deeply and want the very best for you educationally and in every other way. Whether you choose McGill or Harvard we will back you and help you financially." It was the last word of moderation I heard in a three month debate. Shortly after I received a list of one hundred questions he wanted answered, including inquiries about my personal hygiene and other intimate details of my life, and concluding with the question #100: "Do you still love us?" I was completely devastated.

Conflict, particularly with my father, was the last thing I needed at the time. Separated from my parents and out on my own with few arrangements made for me, I became deeply troubled. My grades plummeted for the first time. It had already been announced that I was valedictorian, first in my class. I actually graduated third, to the annoyance I am sure of the person who actually was first. And I was uncertain about the summer. I had asked a pastor in Philadelphia with whom we'd had a long relationship, if he could find a summer apartment for me and my roommate Herbert Chew. He found one and I agreed to rent it. But Herbert backed out at the last moment and I had to tell him that the deal was off.

Perhaps it was just as well: rumours, never substantiated to me, swirled that he preyed on young men. Others were not as fortunate. Another classmate, known as the brawn of the class as I was the brain, was left as a mishkid in the charge of his pastor who subsequently made unwelcome sexual advances on him. He dropped out of Wheaton and bummed around Europe. Years later I accidentally reconnected with him. Shortly after, he was diagnosed with ALS. I spent a lot of time with him, vainly trying to encourage him back into a faith he so desperately now needed. He never found the way home. I was asked to conduct a religious funeral for his family when he died, another secular memorial followed for his friends and colleagues.

Final exams crowded in on me as I prepared my Valedictory speech with Dr. Gaebelein. I had researched past speeches particularly the inaugural service for the school back in 1922, quoting Francis Landey Paton's[52] opening remarks which had been based on an alliteration of the three R's. I changed the "R" to "S" and added a fourth. To please Dr. Gaebelein I overstepped the line between truth and fiction in what I said about the school and specifically my own experience. The first, "Studies"

---

52   Francis Landey Patton (1843-1932). Bermuda native who was a controversial defender of confessional orthodoxy. President both of Princeton University (1888-1902) and Princeton Seminary (1902-1913), he studied at the University of Toronto and Knox College (graduated 1865), and was ordained in the PC(USA).

lauded Stony Brook's academic excellence, looking straight at Gaebelein as I spoke. I then ventured into uncharted waters with my second "S", "Sports", way out of my comfort zone. The third "S" was "Social Affairs". I had wanted to make it "Sex" which Gaebelein diplomatically censored. Perhaps my new reading material had provided me with fresh insights. The final "S" stood for Spiritual Affairs and I ended, in true homiletical style, with a story from the Old Testament about Elisha the prophet. The whole effort, which was mercifully short, reflected where I was at the time: uptight, struggling and looking for some spiritual solace in my discomfort and fear of the future. There was no humour, the only thing that makes graduation speeches palatable.

Graduation Day, 11 June 1955

My uncle Wesley, as a former teacher at Stony Brook, was at the graduation ceremony with his wife, my mother's sister Priscilla. They drove me back to Philadelphia later that day. They had agreed to put me up in the former maid's quarters in their apartment in Overbrook for the summer. I would have much preferred to stay with my aunt Cathie and uncle Paul. On 12 May Paul had written me from Garfield Memorial Hospital in Washington that "Aunt Cathie is in Hospital and had an operation Tuesday exactly like aunt Priscilla's ... Please send a card or letter to the Hospital – Remember us both in your prayers Donald." I was stunned and deeply unsettled. First my parents had left and now the future of someone who, of all my family and friends, best understood what it meant to be a China mishkid was uncertain.

Chapter 35:

Paternal Pressure Prevails, 1955

The day after I arrived in Philadelphia, my parents called me on the telephone, an incredible achievement for my tight-fisted father, ostensibly to congratulate me on the previous day's accomplishments but actually to put further pressure on me to back down and accede to Dad's wishes. "Last night" he wrote the next day, "I tried to tell you that I did not think that you have made the best choice of a college. If it were only a choice between Harvard or Wheaton (or hundreds of other institutions I could name), I would say, choose Harvard for the best training of your mind to the glory of God, but I have persistently maintained that McGill was first choice, and I thought it was decided before we left America that if McGill accepted your application it would be McGill. I should like to know what strong reasons regarding Harvard as superior to McGill there were (if any) that made you change, and overthrow my very good reasons for regarding McGill as superior to Harvard in plan of study and Christian influences and other advantages."

So this was it, the showdown. Though often absent (or detached) from my life growing up, my father had a strong image of what he wanted his only son to be, Canadian and Christian. Nothing would shift those desires. All his life he had been disciplined, strong-willed, and consistent even in the presence of adversity and danger. As his son, I could be equally assertive. I was determined to go to Harvard, he was equally determined I would not. My future depended on my raising enough cash that summer to cover my out of pocket expenses. Everything else had been guaranteed by Harvard. Everyone congratulated me on my accomplishment but I was miserable as I felt the ground slipping out from under me.

My father disclosed his two objections to Harvard: it was "pagan" and it promoted the great books curriculum. "Have you really looked into Harvard's program of general education begun in 1948?" he asked me in a letter at the time. "I have heard it roundly criticised by professors in other Universities as giving one a smattering of knowledge of many fields of knowledge and little mastery of any field." He went on to extoll InterVarsity Christian Fellowship at McGill, placing great emphasis on a property they owned near the campus, and contrasting it to having a pastor in a neighbouring town, his description of Park St Church. He had also been in communication with Stacey Woods, who brought IVCF to America from Canada and was now General Secretary of the International Fellowship of Evangelical Students. He had made a visit to Taiwan recently as had Joe Bayly, Editor of InterVarsity's *His* magazine. As Stacey's subsequent biographer a half century later,[53] I am sure that Dad's memories of their visit were selective and only boosted his own preconceptions and prejudices. I wish that he had done as much research about McGill as he did Harvard. Had he done so, he would have realized that the first year at McGill was really the final year of High School as, at that time, before Quebec had CEGEPs to bridge the divide between high school and university, students started their university education at sixteen.

He also cited financial concerns, though with the scholarship given by Harvard my going there would not have required any of his money. He took issue with my having to do "manual work" during my first year

---

53   MacLeod, A. Donald. *C. Stacey Woods and the Evangelical Rediscovery of the University.* Downer's Grove, IL: InterVarsity Press, 2007.

and said that my parents had saved up enough money for me to be free of any need to take outside jobs. Money became a decisive factor in the next weeks. The irony was that the Board provided a modest allowance for mishkids to the age of 21 if they were still in school and, had they continued to pay that directly to me (as they did once my parents returned to the field until asked to pay it to them directly as before) I would have had complete financial independence.

I spent the next month desperately looking for work. I had assumed I could return to my previous work at the Witherspoon Building. They had needed an elevator operator but the job was taken when I inquired the Monday after I arrived in Philadelphia. I was so desperate that I even applied for a job jockeying cars in a parking lot. It was fortunate that was taken, as I did not have a driving license! A garage had an opening pumping gas but the proprietor told me I didn't look the part. Failing to find summer employment in Philadelphia and the unsettling atmosphere where I was staying, I tried New York City. Muriel Fuller immediately got me a summer position with Harper's publishing house helping organize their early computerized mailing system. I stayed at the Greenwich Village apartment of her friend, Mabel Steele Hoover, manager of the church bookstore of Morehouse-Gorham, the Protestant Episcopal publishing house. Mrs. Hoover was the step mother of Mary Hoover, the third (and final) wife of Conrad Aiken, the American poet with whom she maintained a cordial relationship. Her apartment was filled with fascinating items of literary memorabilia and her library was phenomenal. As my landlady she insisted coffee should be served without either sugar or cream as that made it a food. Her world broadened my horizons just as my father was narrowing them.

One day in August I decided that, because enough money simply hadn't come in, I had no choice but to give in to my father. I sat down at Mrs. Hoover's phone, with her permission while she was out, and called Stanford Reid who was doing a summer *locum* in Bermuda. I announced my decision and inquired of him, as Warden of Men's Residences, if there was still room for me at Douglas Hall. Very graciously he replied positively and found a place for me long after all deadlines. Because my father had now released funds for me I could quit my job early in New York City and was thus able to help Cathie and Paul move into their new apartment in Drexel Hill. My time in Greenwich Village had rescued my summer from disaster. In September Cathie and Paul drove me up to Montreal, stopping at Canajoharie en route where Paul's brother was President of Beechnut. We crossed the border; they checked into the Sheraton Mount Royal Hotel, and then drove on to 3851 University St., my address for the next four years, and settled me into my new digs.

With aunt Cathie at McGill University's Douglas Hall of Residence, 18 September 1955

I now had a third nationality thrust upon me. Born in America, raised in China, I was to have my college education in Canada. I faced a whole new set of cultural challenges. Adaptability was an asset I had learned over seventeen years. My mother wanted me to build on her New England heritage and claim her American identity. My father early wanted to settle in Canada and had wished that on me as his heir. It was our family's shared Christian experience that went beyond national boundaries and ensured an international identity. The Scriptures, worship, even hymns in the universal language of music, spoke of an identity transcending national boundaries.

In Christ there is no East or West,
   In Him no South or North;
But one great fellowship of love
   Throughout the whole wide earth.[54]

---

54   "In Christ there is no East or West" a 1928 hymn by "John Oxenham" a pseudonym for William Arthur Dunkerley (1852-1941). His collection of verse titled
Bees in Amber (1913) was a favourite of our family.

EPILOGUE

O ne Saturday morning while I was at Stony Brook School I sat with
a mishkid in the front lounge of Hageman Hall. His parents were
about to arrive by train at the station at the bottom of Chapman Parkway.
This terrified fifteen year-old had not seen his parents since their previous furlough. They were returning from Africa and had been warned by
a more compliant younger brother, also at the school, that their older
son was not what they had prayed for. Surly, angry, fearful, depressed, he
was experiencing a complete emotional meltdown. He raised his voice
as he reflected bitterly as to why he had been abandoned, what they
would now think of what he had become during their absence, and, by
inference, how little he valued the religion that had sent them to Africa.
As he spoke I found myself reflecting on my past with gratitude that I
had been spared such psychic disruption.

When teaching missions history at seminary there was no subject
that excited more engagement on the part of students than that of missionary children. My father's great missionary hero, David Livingstone,
was our starting point. The oldest of his five children, Robert Moffat
Livingstone, named after his maternal grandfather, another missionary hero, left South Africa at the age of eighteen and fled to Civil War
America, joining the Union Army as a paid substitute. He enlisted under
the pseudonym Rupert Vincent because, as he explained to his father,

"I have changed my name for I am convinced that to bear your name here would lead to further dishonours to it."[55] Father was unrelenting: "My heart is rather sore for that bad boy has gotten into the American army and will be made manure of for those bloody fields,"[56] a prediction which proved tragically true.

The missionary as hero, typified by David Livingstone and Robert Moffat, presented difficulties for their children. Achieving the image of heroic self-sacrifice – so common in evangelical churches during this period – was difficult when the realities of the petty squabbles and jurisdictional fights surfaced on the field. Missionary martyrdoms, whether it was the Boxers or the Aucas, inspired an image of service and self-sacrifice. It was hard for mishkids, who sometimes felt neglected or ignored, to live up to that image because the disconnects were apparent. Letters home always had a reference to the kids and how they were doing, but woe betide any mishkid who strayed from the path of truth and virtue. Sending and supporting churches took notice.

With the collapse of Christendom in the West the pressures on mishkids reentering their parents' homeland could be intense. With a declining confidence in the rubric of a "Christless eternity" into which, missionary publicity affirmed, millions were passing, was the expense, the effort, the sacrifice, really worth it? Was the image of heathen darkness sustainable anymore? Universalism took a heavy toll on the missionary effort. Was that whole missionary effort merely putting grass skirts on naked native women, as Michener said in his novel *Hawaii*? Pearl Buck famously affirmed that "I feel no need for any other faith than my faith in the kindness of human beings." When a China mishkid affirmed that credo her parents' faith no longer held together. The cult of niceness would never have sent Absalom and Caroline Sydenstricker to China to share, through adversity and danger their faith in Jesus Christ as Saviour and Lord.

---

55   Jeal, Tim. *Livingstone*. New Haven, CT: Yale University Press, 1973. 282

56   Jeal, Tim. *Livingstone*. New Haven, CT: Yale University Press, 1973. 281.

The contrast between my father's experience of missionary life and mine therefore could not be more different. He was brought up in a faith mission, one passionately committed to "the evangelization of the world in this generation" as the watchword of the Student Volunteer Movement affirmed. On graduation from seminary, my father opted for a denominational mission soon to experience theological turmoil. My world was schizoid: those who were "sound" and those who were not. Our family often felt much more comfortable and compatible with the China Inland Mission than our own American Presbyterian Mission. But the Presbyterians looked after us well and paid a generous and predictable salary. Their medical and pastoral care, particularly of mishkids such as me, was exemplary. It was a confusing reality for a China mishkid. And that reality was simply that some of the so-called more "liberal" (or "Boardy") missionaries were much better company: more compassionate, less judgmental, and more creative and cultured.

Indeed, being a China mishkid meant that I acquired, as an only child, a whole family of honourary siblings, aunts and uncles that I would not otherwise have experienced. My parents had cultivated an extensive supporting network of contemporaries, people from their Wheaton experience, followed by seminarians from my father's Princeton class that bonded closely throughout their long lives. Being a mishkid meant that people prayed for you, were committed to you, and supported you. Much of this I lost when I changed countries, something that my father had never factored in. His insistence I went to McGill ultimately resulted in a change in my own national identity. My father was, essentially, a man without a country as are many mishkids. He only changed his citizenship out of necessity after his wartime incarceration.

The transition from secondary to post-secondary education, usually at ages 17 or 18, is determinative for a safe adjustment of mishkids to productive adult life. This requires mentoring, guiding and instructing either by parents or their substitutes. Driving a car, having a bank account, making decisions, being able to cope on your own: these are essential to the future well-being of a mishkid. The integration of the fragments of an interrupted childhood into a cohesive unity is something mishkids need. Mishkid marriages can lack the stability and strength of rootedness in a specific culture. It can be hard for a spouse to understand the complexity of their partner's past which has shaped them into the person he or she has married.

The China mishkid experience has enriched the rest of my life. Being introduced from birth to a civilization much older and richer than one's own, gave me a unique vantage point growing up. Familiarity with a second language provided verbal skills that were very broadening. There was a depth, a catholicity of outlook. that brought unique privileges and responsibilities growing up. The depth of faith and trust in a sovereign God Who through all the changing political and economic circumstances of revolutionary China, could be totally relied on and Who in adversity, trial and even death itself, was a very present Help in trouble made a profound impact on many (though admittedly not all) of us China Mishkids. We had seen God put to the test and God had never let us down.

At a 2008 reunion dinner of alumni/ae of the Shanghai American School I was called over *to* a table where six women were seated. They inquired as to why I, unlike each of them, still affirmed the faith that sent our parents out across the Pacific. I replied that through all the times of suffering loss and separation, and with all their limitations and failings, my parents' faith had stood the test of time. And I pointed to a vibrant Christian community in China today that is a living testimony to the truth of the gospel that our parents taught and lived. That was the ultimate gift I had been given as a China mishkid.

APPENDIX:
Farewell to China

Leaving NCTS, September 1949

11 Hengshan St., Shanghai
9th September 1949

The Faculty,
North China Theological Seminary,
Mei Yuan,
Wusih, Kiangsu

Dear Brethren,

The time has come when I must make a decision soon with regards to whether or not I should return to the Seminary this autumn. I am praying much for Divine guidance and I shall also be glad to have the counsel of my brethren. For this reason I am writing this letter.

When I came down here seven weeks ago I heard that the families of some Shanghai residents had returned here from Hong Kong, and had been allowed to join their husbands and fathers. So I wrote Mrs. MacLeod it would be the better course for me to stay here and for them to return to Shanghai. Mrs. MacLeod received my suggestion and replied by radiogram that she was ready to come if it was feasible,

Since then the course of events has been downward and the general picture has become darker. There is no transportation available between Hong Kong and this part of China, nor is there any likelihood that there will be any in the next weeks. Donald must, of course, enter some school in September. And now there will be no school here for the Shanghai School is closing its doors on account of the heavy taxation , and yesterday I learned that the China Inland Mission has received a telegram from their school in Kuling advising them of the difficulties there and telling them that no new students should be sent there this autumn. It has become abundantly plain now that Mrs. MacLeod and Donald cannot return for the present.

On the other hand, there is reasonable expectation that a ship will come to Shanghai from the United States about the middle of September to evacuate Americans. To find out the facts I went down to the offices of the American Presidents' Lines and had a talk with Mr. Wyse, the general manager. He told me that the "General Gordon" is expected to sail from Shanghai of September 17. It is coming at the request of the State Department which is negotiating with the Chinese and Communist governments for permission and promise of safety, to repatriate America nationals who wish to return to the U.S.A. These negotiations are not completed, but the company is confident that it will be arranged and is booking applicants for passage. They fully expect that the ship will be filled with some 900 or 1000 passengers.

The ship will sail by way of Hong Kong and Manila. I inquired about passage to Hong Kong as I am not intending to return to U.S.A. Mr. Wyse says that that was not the purpose of the voyage which was to take through passengers all the way home. But, after I had explained that my family was in Hong Kong, he said that there might be a place in steerage. He advised me to enter my name and begin the long process of obtaining permission from the authorities to leave Shanghai.

So I am faced with the alternatives of preparing to leave for abroad next month or passing up this chance and returning to Wusih if I can get permission to do so. It is a very hard decision to make for I should like no work better than teaching at the Seminary but I also love my family in Hong Kong who cannot now return here.

Should I decide to return to the Seminary I would have to get permission to travel to Wusih and live there. I have not yet heard of any foreigner being given a permit to go inland; but I know of several who have been refused this summer. Those foreigners who have left Shanghai for interior destinations travelled on return passes to their homes of residence. But I suppose it would be possible to get permission. But there seems to be doubt as to whether North China Theological Seminary will be able to open on account of financial stringency. And if it does begin classes in September would be able to carry on long enough to make my return and all this might involve with jeopardy to liberty, worthwhile. I would not consider it worthwhile for instance, to be imprisoned for 2 or 3 years for the sake of teaching 2 or 3 months this autumn! I have had sufficient experience of this sort of thing.

The other alternative would be to stay in Shanghai and leave on the first available ship for Hong Kong, which might be sailing the middle of September. This alternative has the advantage of being with my family which is most desirable from a personal point of view, and especially so in the present dark and ugly world situation. If I appraise the current "cold war" between Russia and the West aright, I think that the coming twelve months will be most critical and may make clear to us whether there is to be a shooting war or increasingly assured prospects of a truce.

As I have said, I have no interest in returning to the United States now. I wish to stay on this side of the Pacific Ocean and continue to work for the Seminary. If I were in Hong Kong for a time I should not be idle. I have a great deal of literary work projected. This summer I am writing a commentary on the Sermon on the Mount in connection with

the course in Christian Ethics which the Faculty asked me to teach. I should continue this and other work. The new curriculum and the new subjects which I may be asked to teach in coming years would keep me busy with study and preparation for a long time to come. I should be ready when the opportunity came to teach several classes, and courses at the Seminary.

Or there might be a chance to accept the invitation I received some months ago to join the staff of the Canadian Presbyterian Seminary at Taipeh, North Taiwan. I am told that "Kuo-yu" is taught in all the schools in Taiwan and that the standard pronunciation is coming into use more and more. In Taiwan I should feel that I was still in China helping the Chinese Church. And this link between NCTS and the Canadian Presbyterians might be very valuable to both in years to come.

There is also the possibility that I might teach in the Theological Seminary in Manila, the Philippine Islands. I am told that English is used there in the classroom so I would not have to use another language.

I have written so fully about the alternatives and possibilities as they seem to me in order that you may have the facts before you and help me in reaching a decision in this important matter. I would greatly appreciate any advice you send me.

With Christian greetings and brotherly love,
毛克禮

Donald MacLeod is research professor at Tyndale Theological Seminary, Toronto. He has been President (and a founder) of the Renewal Fellowship Within The Presbyterian Church in Canada and is also a past president of the Evangelical Fellowship of Canada. Awarded the Donald Grant Creighton Award for his 2004 biography of W. Stanford Reid, he is President of the Canadian Society of Presbyterian History since 2010, he has been a frequent contributor to academic papers and conferences. He holds two honourary degrees from Gordon Conwell and Westminster Theological Seminaries. He is married to Judith and they have two adult sons and five grandchildren. Since they moved back to Canada from Boston twenty-one years ago the MacLeods have made their home in Brighton, Ontario.